AF474000

ANATOMY OF PACKAGING STRUCTURES

sendpoints

ANATOMY OF PACKAGING STRUCTURES

Second printing of the first edition, December 2022

sendpoints

PUBLISHED BY Sendpoints Publishing Co., Ltd.
ADDRESS: Unit 23, L1/F Mirror Tower, 61 Mody Road, Tsim Sha Tsui, Kowloon, Hong Kong, China
PUBLISHER: Lin Gengli
CHIEF EDITOR: Lin Shijian
LEAD EDITOR: Dean Ho
EXECUTIVE EDITOR: Qiaomei Xian
DESIGN DIRECTOR: Lin Shijian
EXECUTIVE ART EDITOR: Dean Ho
PROOFREADING: Weiji Li

SALES DIRECTOR: Philip Tsang
TEL: +852 6296 2246
EMAIL: sales@sppub.com
WEBSITE: www.sppub.com

ISBN 978-988-79284-8-5

Printed and bound in China.

Facebook

Instagram

Twitter

CONTENTS

BASIC PACKAGING STRUCTURES

Paper packaging structure is a special kind of plastic arts, which links the paper material with every part of a commodity by the techniques such as folding and gluing. Good packaging structure design with strong functionality is crucial to a brand image and the user experience it offers.

Therefore, when designing a paper packaging structure, one must consider the following factors.

1. Protectiveness

Packages are firstly made to protect the goods it contains from breaking and sometimes they are used to protect the users from the possible harms of certain special products inside the packages.

2. Portability

One of the major attractions of the goods in a supermarket is their portability made possible by the packaging design, which is especially so in the case of goods that are not convenient to carry around because of their heavy weight or unusual forms.

3. Creativity

A distinctive packaging structure that stands out from all others is undoubtedly more appealing to the wandering eyes of the customers. The unique design can usually better represent a brand's public image and even spice up people's lives.

CARTON STRUCTURES

Cartons are economical and versatile containers in strong demand. Carton boxes come in various forms. It is mainly made by folding or gluing different paper materials.

FOLDING CARTONS

1. Tube Folding Cartons

This type of carton was firstly defined as a box that has a cover smaller than all other panels of the box. Now, it is mainly defined by its assembling feature: both the bottom and the top panels are fixed by folding flaps.

Basic Structure of Tube Folding Carton

1, 2, 3, 4 - Main Panel
5 - Top Closure Panel
6 - Dust Flap
7 - Glue Flap
8 - Bottom Closure Panel
9 - Tuck Flap

Tube Folding Carton Template (a)

Tube Folding Carton Template (b)

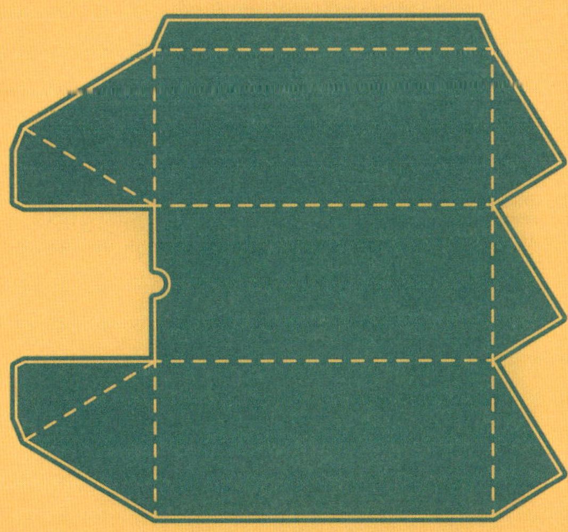

Tube Folding Carton Template (c)

2. Tray Folding Cartons

The cover panel is the largest panel of a tray carton. A tray folding carton template centers around the bottom panel, rounded with four panels folded in right angle or oblique angle. Hence, unlike a tube folding carton, the bottom of a tray folding carton doesn't have to be sealed by assembling the cover flaps.

Basic Structure of Tray Folding Carton

1, 4 - Inner Panel
2 - Left Side Panel
3 - Right Side Panel
5 - Rear Panel
6 - Front Panel
7 - Cover Panel
8 - Bottom Panel
9 - Tuck Flap
10, 11, 12, 13 - Closure Panel

Tray Folding Carton Template (a)

Tray Folding Carton Template (b)

Tray Folding Carton Template (c)

3. Tube-Tray Folding Cartons

Tube-tray folding cartons are often made of one single piece of paper. The structure gets into form by the rotating of the side panels, with the bottom panel being formed naturally without flaps.

Typical Tube Style Tray Folding Carton

K-shaped Tube-Tray Folding Carton Template

Star-shaped Tube-Tray Folding Carton Template

4. Non-Tube and Non-Tray Folding Cartons

It is formed by the relative movement of major panels around a certain cut line, instead of following the principles of tube or tray folding structure. This type of carton is always partitioned into two or more sections.

Typical Non-Tube and Non-Tray Folding Carton

GLUED CARTONS

Glued cartons, also called assembled cartons, are often made by gluing veneer material with base cardboard. Once assembled, glued cartons cannot be shipped flat. The paper used to make these cartons is usually about 1-1.3 mm in thickness.

There are three types of glued cartons that are commonly used nowadays.

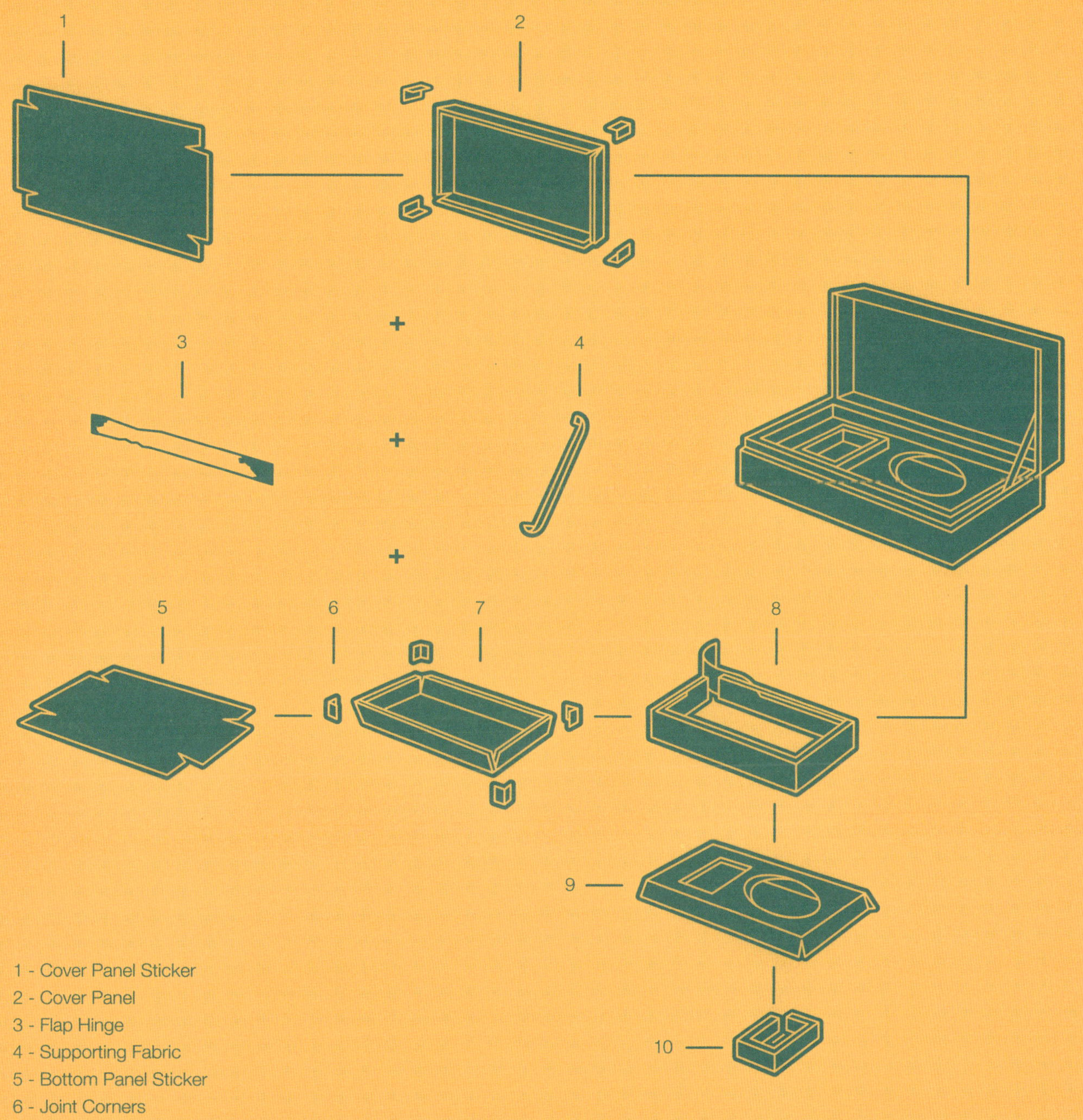

1 - Cover Panel Sticker
2 - Cover Panel
3 - Flap Hinge
4 - Supporting Fabric
5 - Bottom Panel Sticker
6 - Joint Corners
7 - Bottom Panel
8 - Inner Frame
9 - Partition Panel
10 - Partition Panel Frame

Structural Components of Glued Carton

1. Tube Glued Cartons

Structurally, the side panels and the bottom panel are formed separately and then fixed together by a sticker which usually is also decorative.

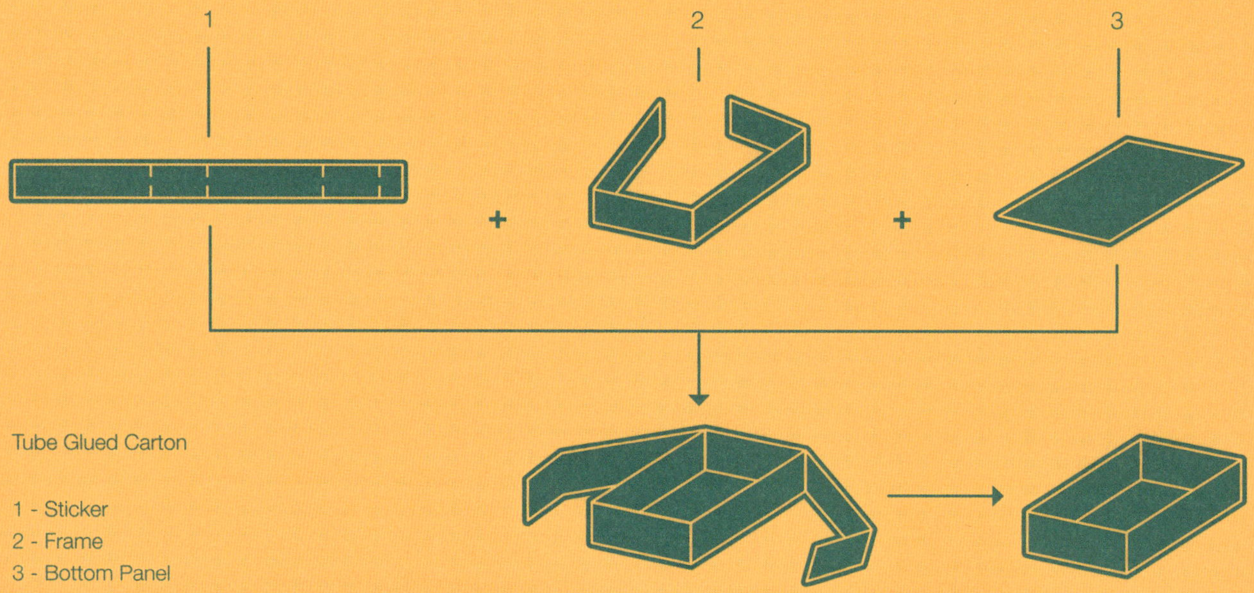

Tube Glued Carton

1 - Sticker
2 - Frame
3 - Bottom Panel

2. Tray Glued Cartons

This type of carton is often formed by a single piece of paper including side panels and bottom panel.

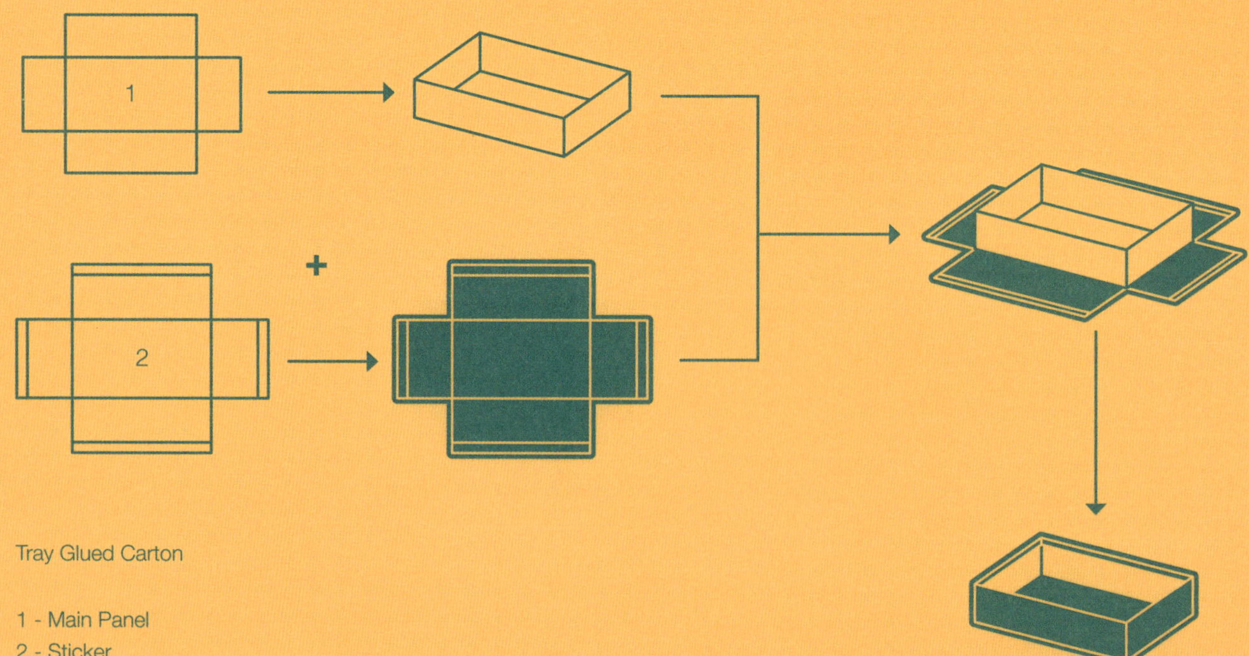

Tray Glued Carton

1 - Main Panel
2 - Sticker

3. Tube-Tray Glued Cartons

In a double-framed structure, the side panels and the bottom panel are formed in the way as a tray carton while the inner frame a tube carton. Likewise, in a structure composed of a main carton and a cover, one component is formed in the way as a tray carton while the other a tube carton.

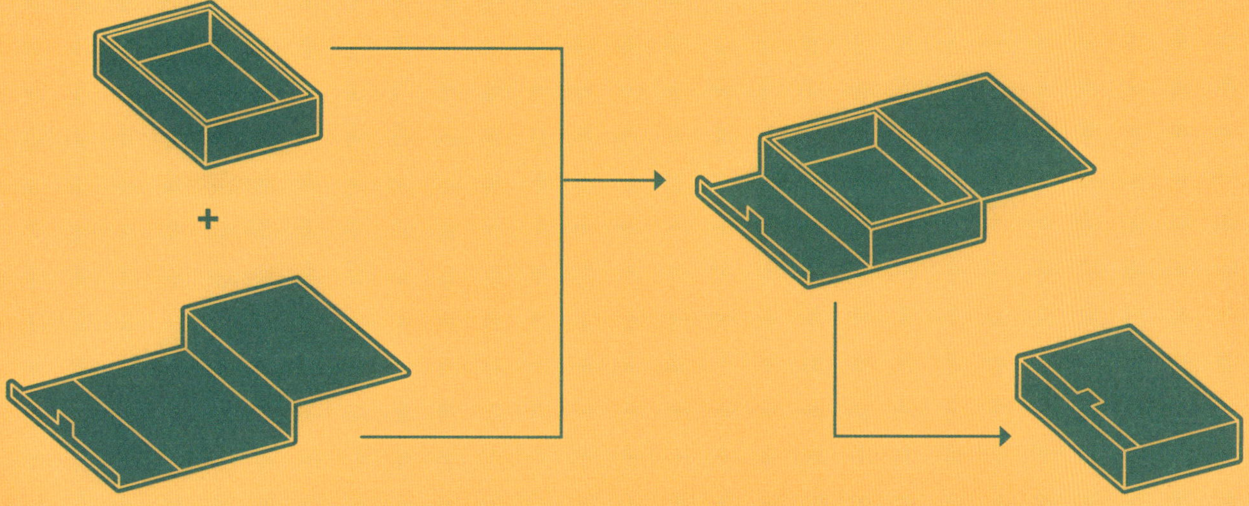

Tube-Tray Glued Carton

The above mentioned basic structures of folding cartons and glued cartons are the ones that are commonly used nowadays. With the advancement of new techniques in the packaging industry, there are even more fresh ideas from packaging designers to develop new packaging structures and styles. The ever-growing demand for goods packaging in the consumer market also help push forward the development of new package design.

TEMPLATES

3
2
1
1
2
3

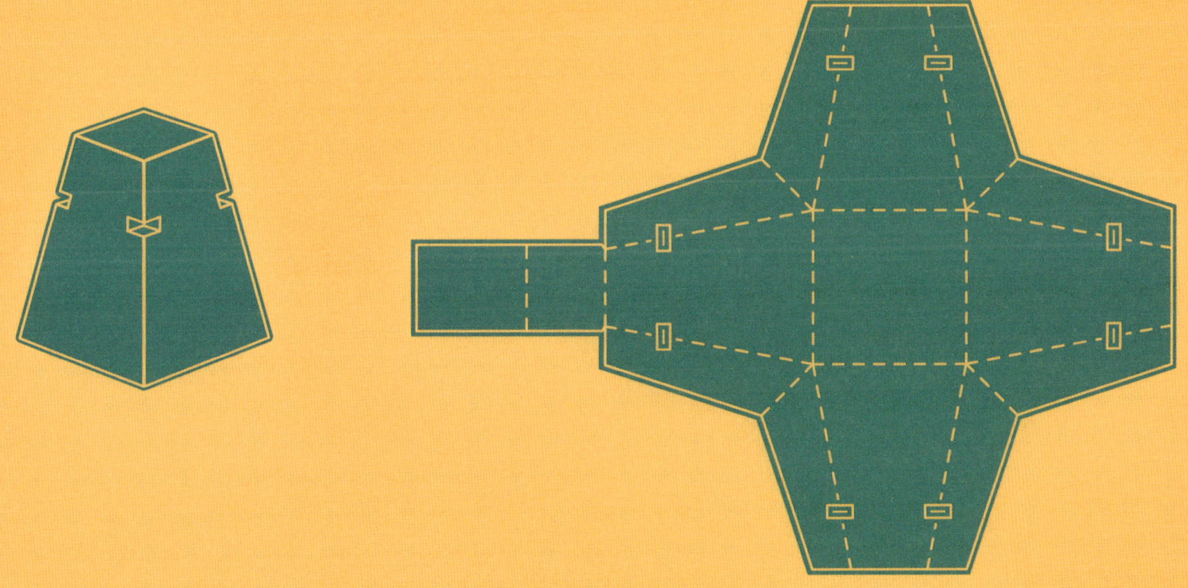

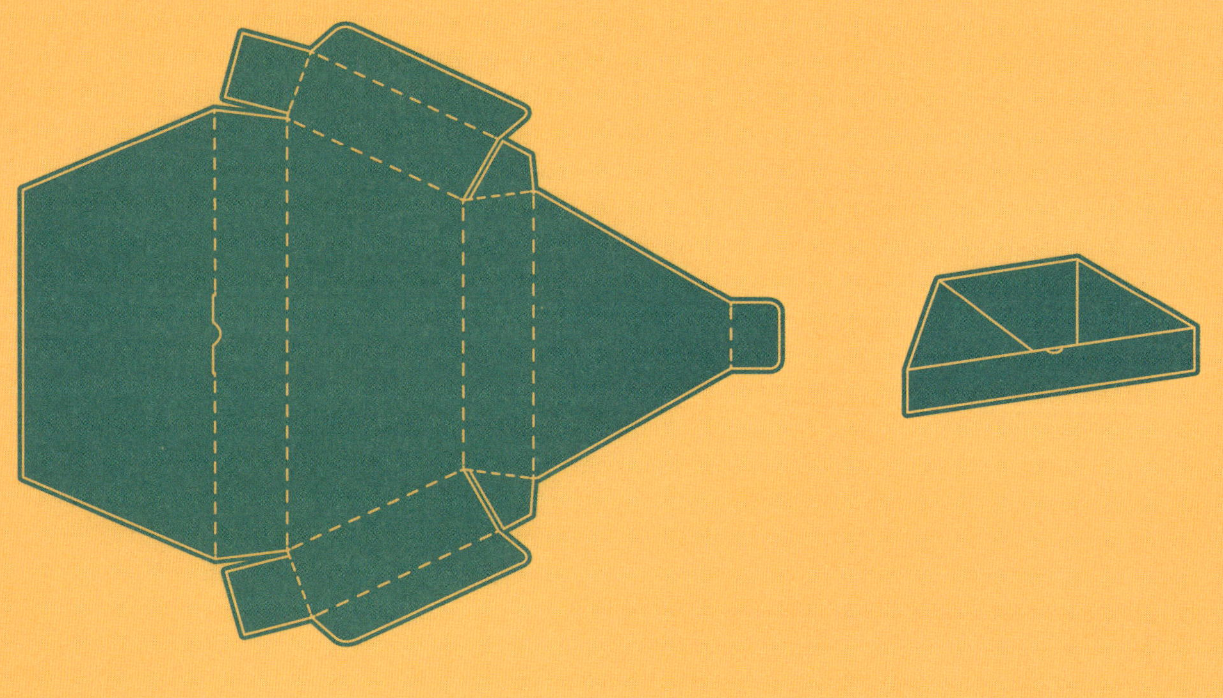

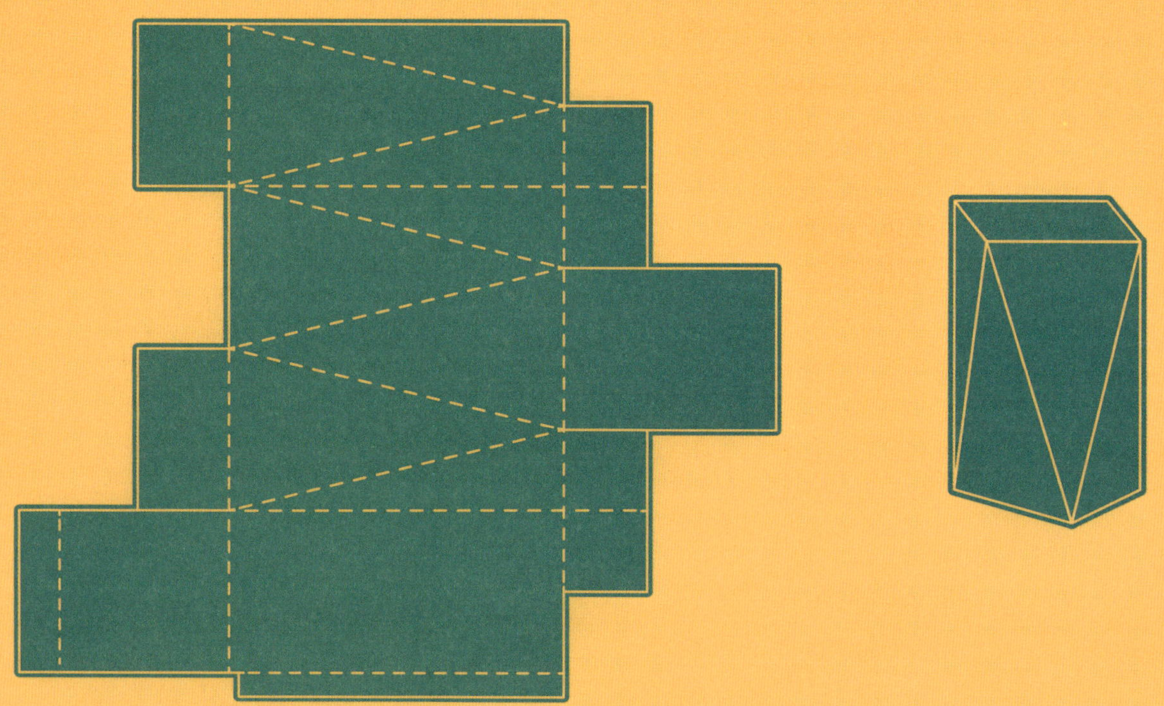

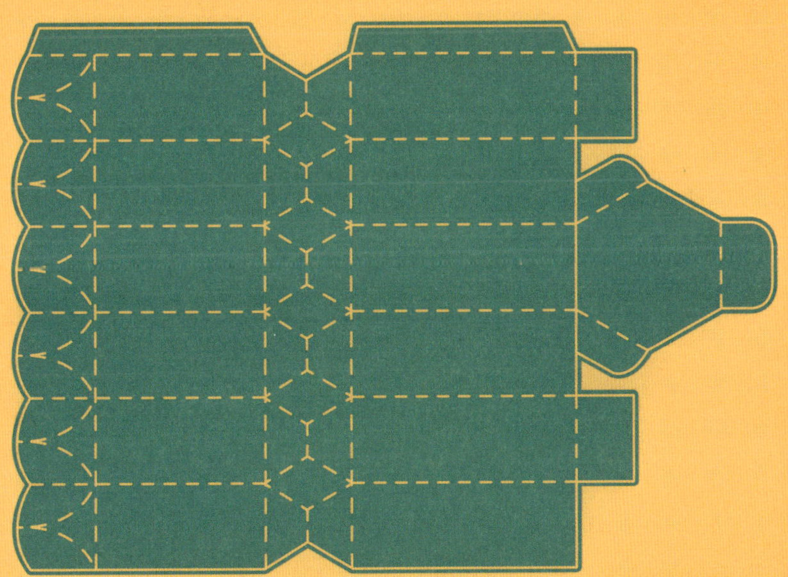

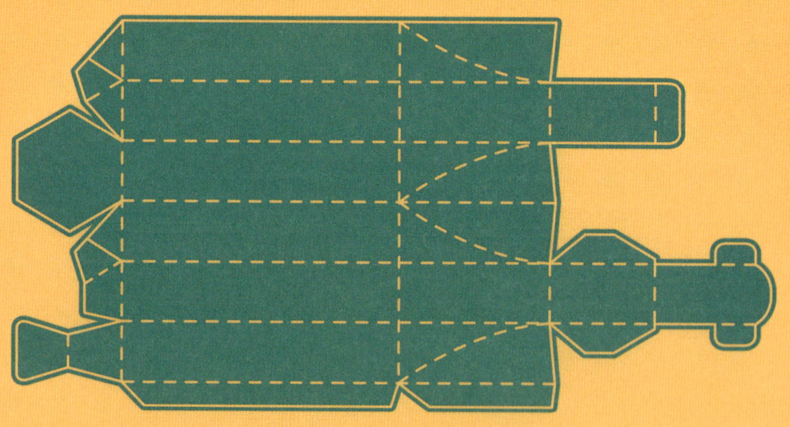

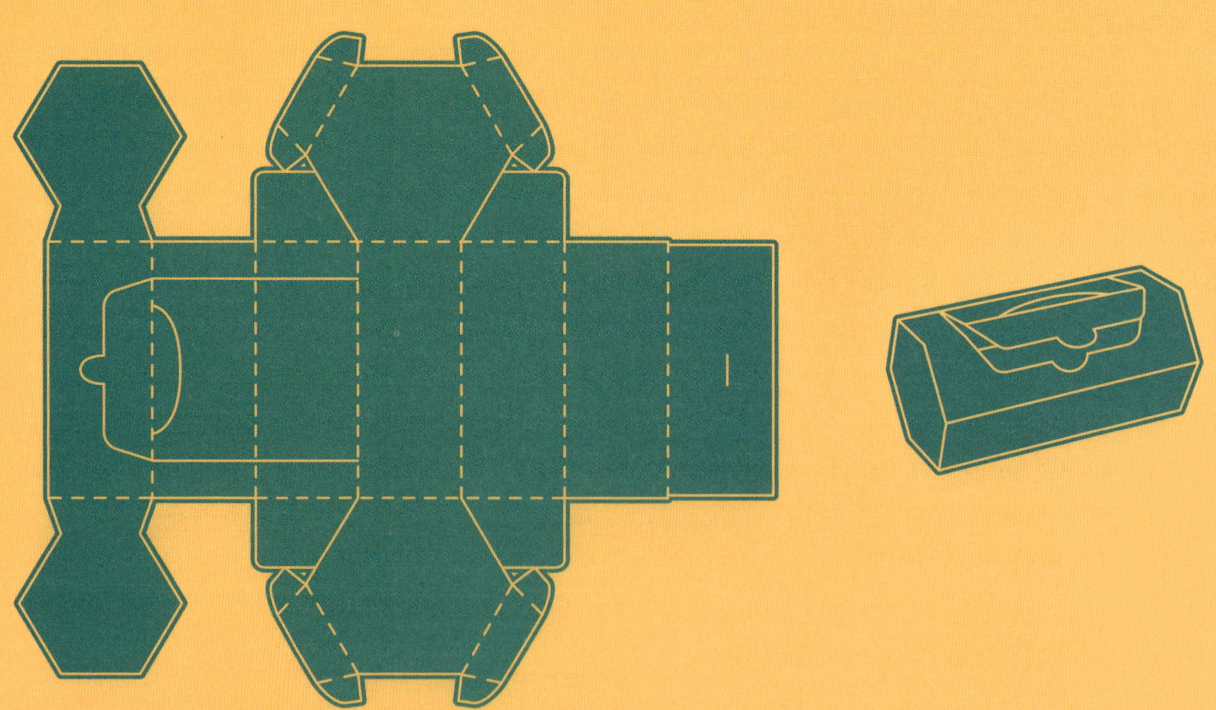

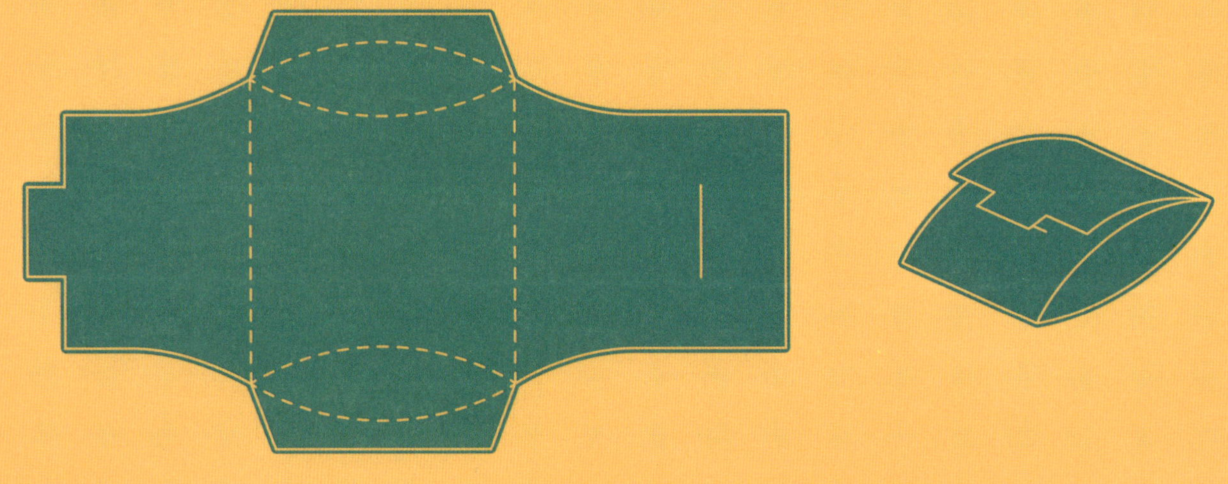

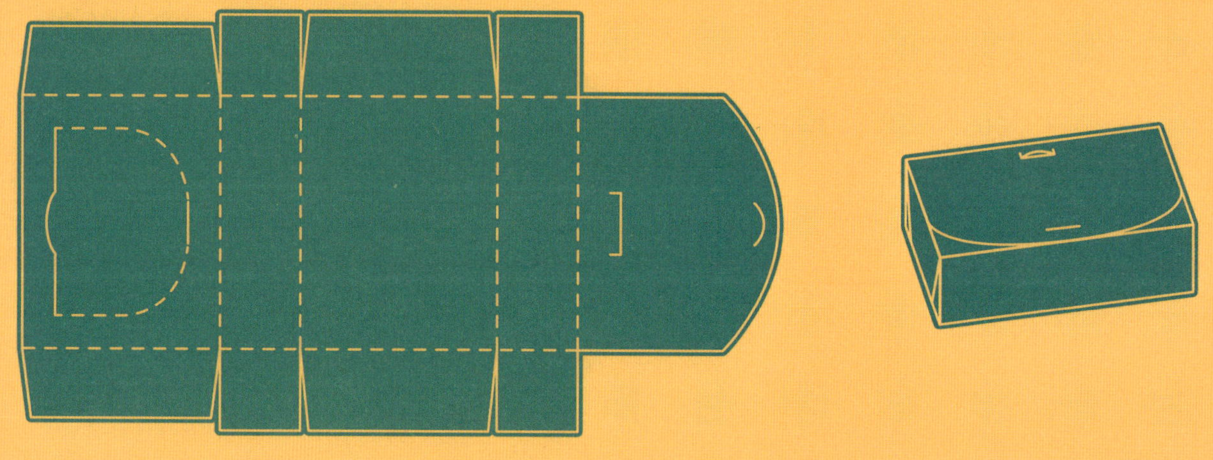

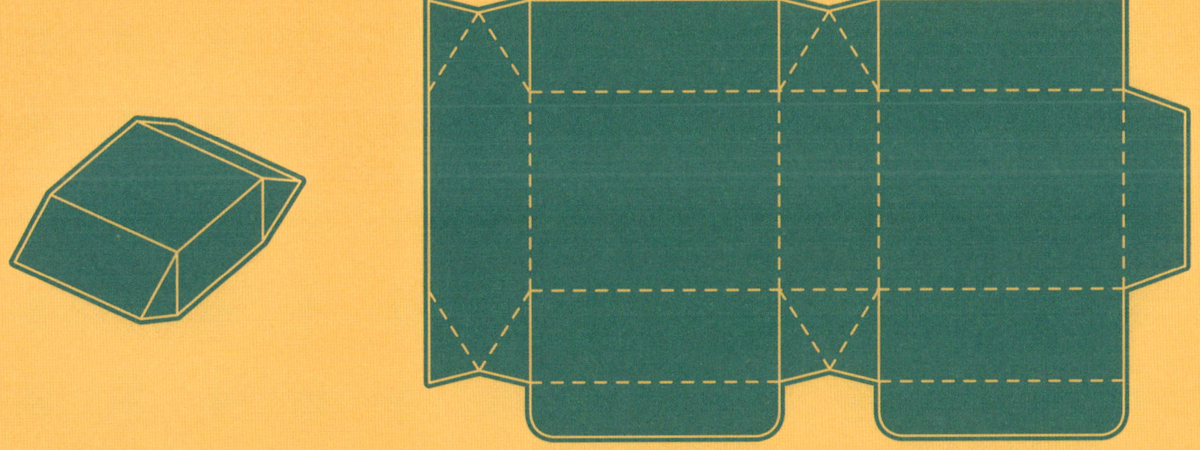

PACKAGING PROJECTS

EVRIPOS TEA

Design Tina Touli

This project aims to redesign a package that houses four varieties of tea. The cylindrical shape of a mug works beautifully in this design. Each type of tea has a specific illustration that forms a complete flower or leaf when four tea bags are placed together.

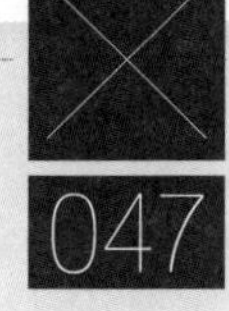

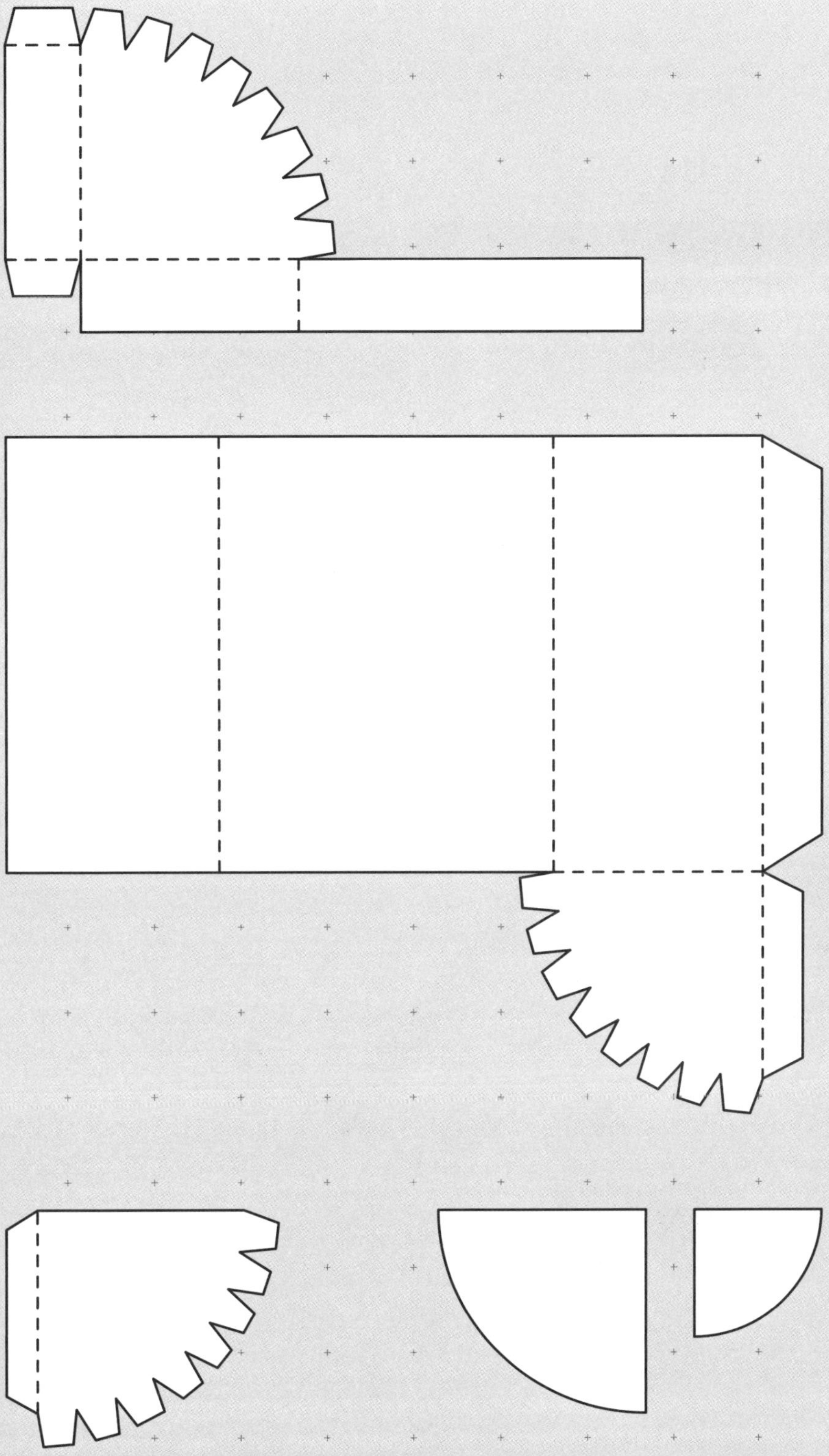

PIANO COLOUR PENCILS / CRAYONS

Design **Tina Touli**

This project is part of the "Eye Music" packaging series. It examines the relationship between visual communication and music. When the packages of crayons are placed into the gaps between those of colour pencils, a keyboard comes into form. The frequency of each music note can relate to the wavelength of a specific colour. Each packaging contains only seven colours of pencils or crayons that correspond to the seven music notes.

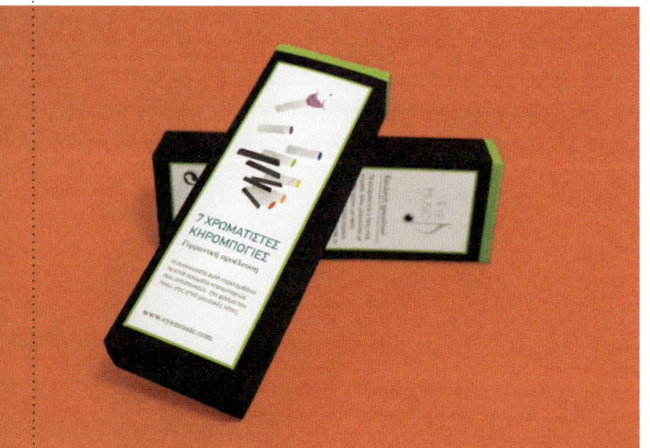

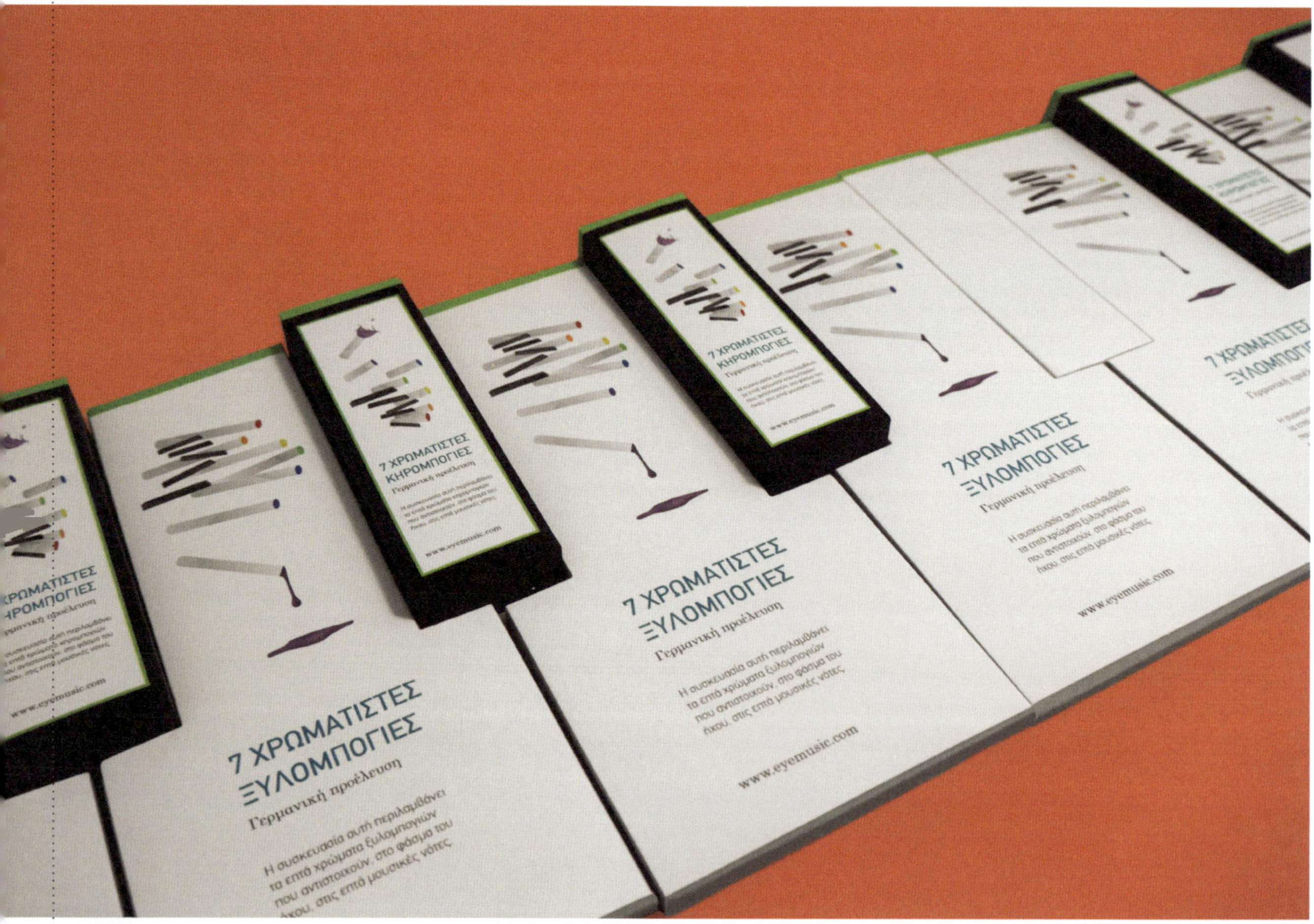

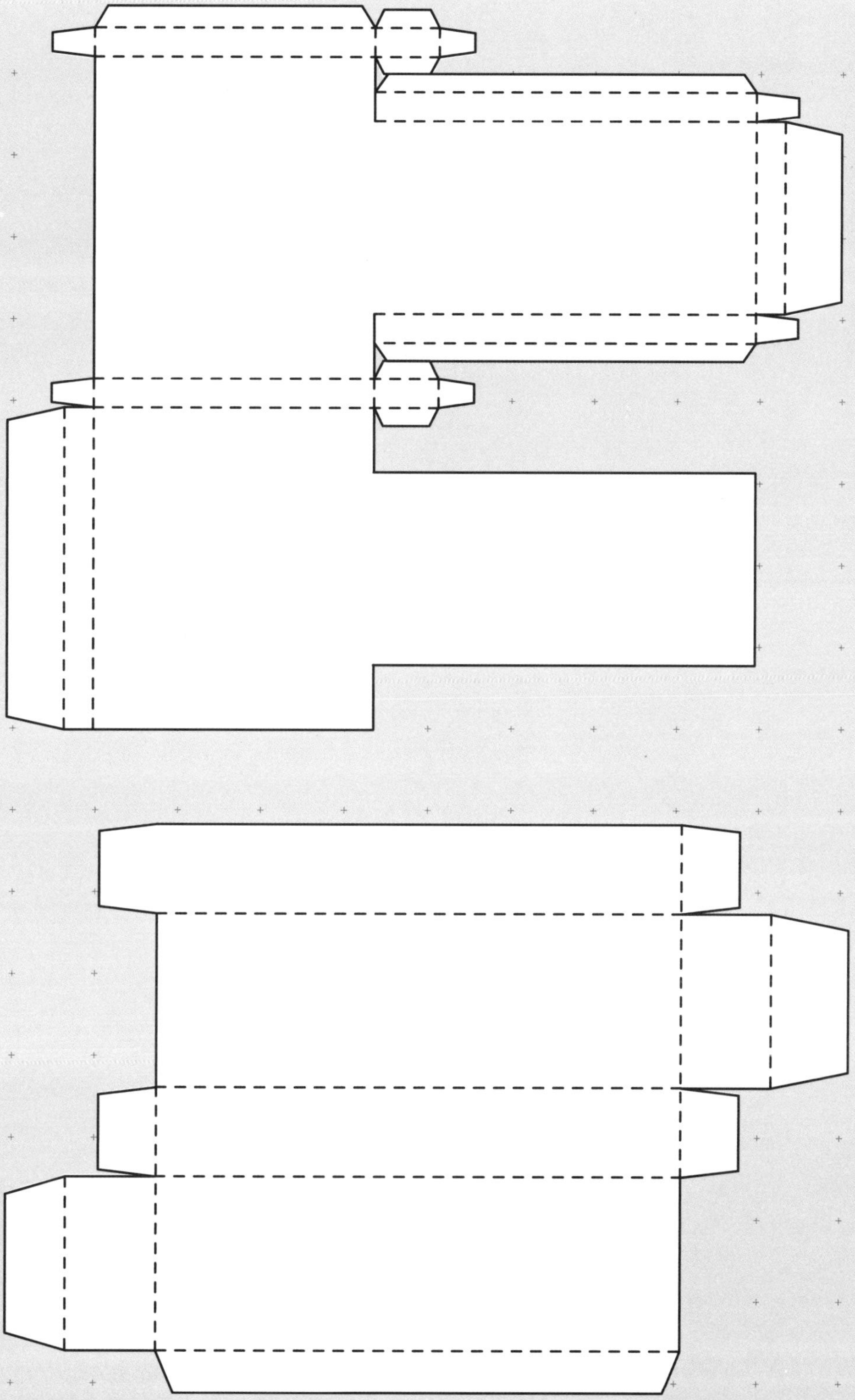

BRAZILIAN DELIGHTS

Embaré, which means "tasty tree" in the native language in Brazil, is one of the major companies in the food industry in Brazil. Brazilian Delights includes caramels of six typical Brazilian fruit flavors: açai, mango, pitanga, cupuaçu, graviola and papaya. The packaging design showcases strong Brazilian nature and the origin of the flavors. The images portray the indigenous legends retold over several generations about the fruits used in the product.
In presenting the tropical flavors with interesting stories, the origin of Brazilian culture has been reserved.

Design **Gustavo Greco, Tidé, Leonardo Freitas, Lorena Marinho, Flávia Siqueira, Cláudio Carneiro, Laura Scofield, Alexandre Fonseca, Marden Diniz**

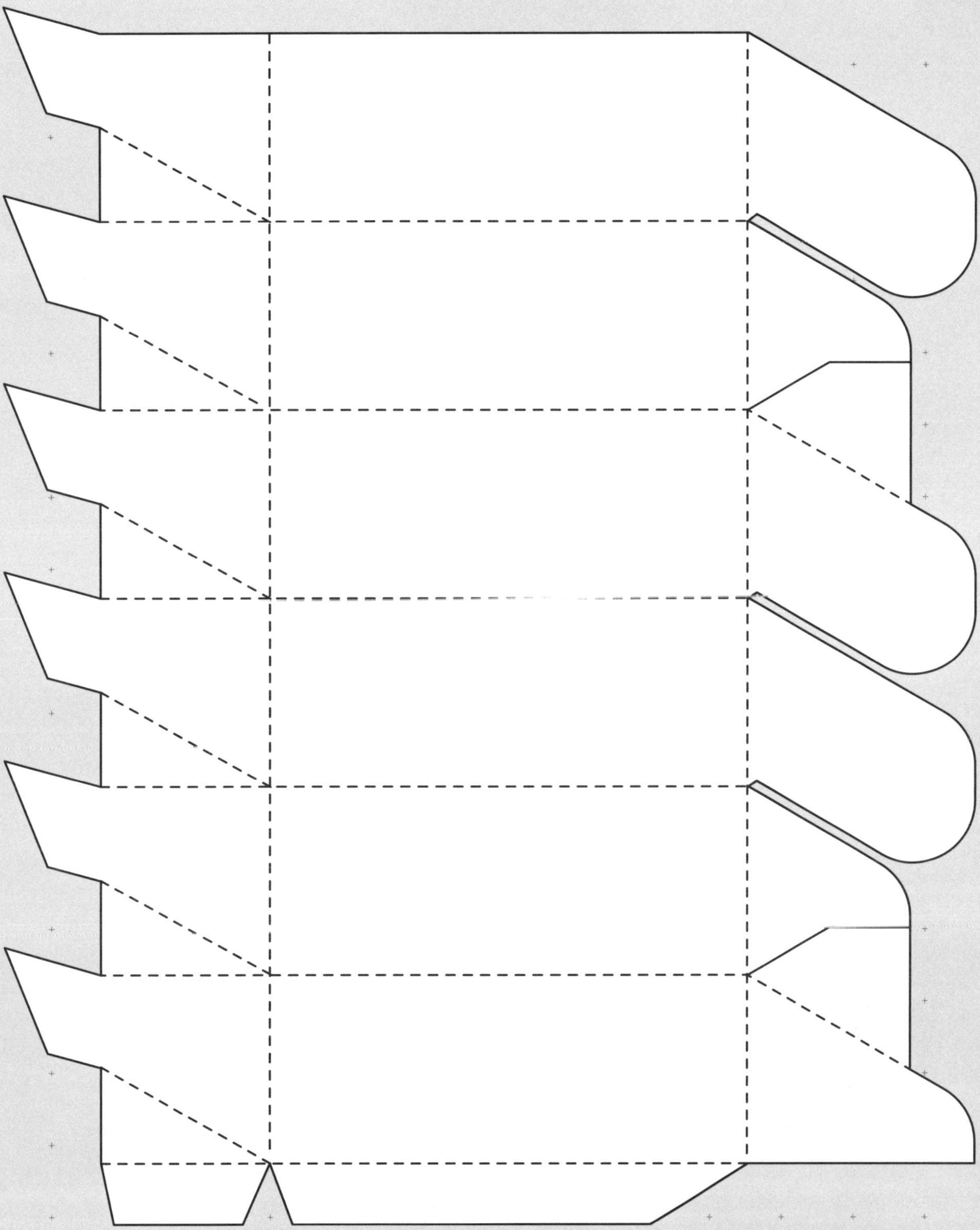

CATARSIS

Design Mau Silva

CATARSIS is a Mexican broad line of relaxation products made with natural flowers. The objective of this project was to create a series of packages that would reflect the brand concept and allow the simple design to generate a unique experience. A design like this could be appealing to both the female and male customers.

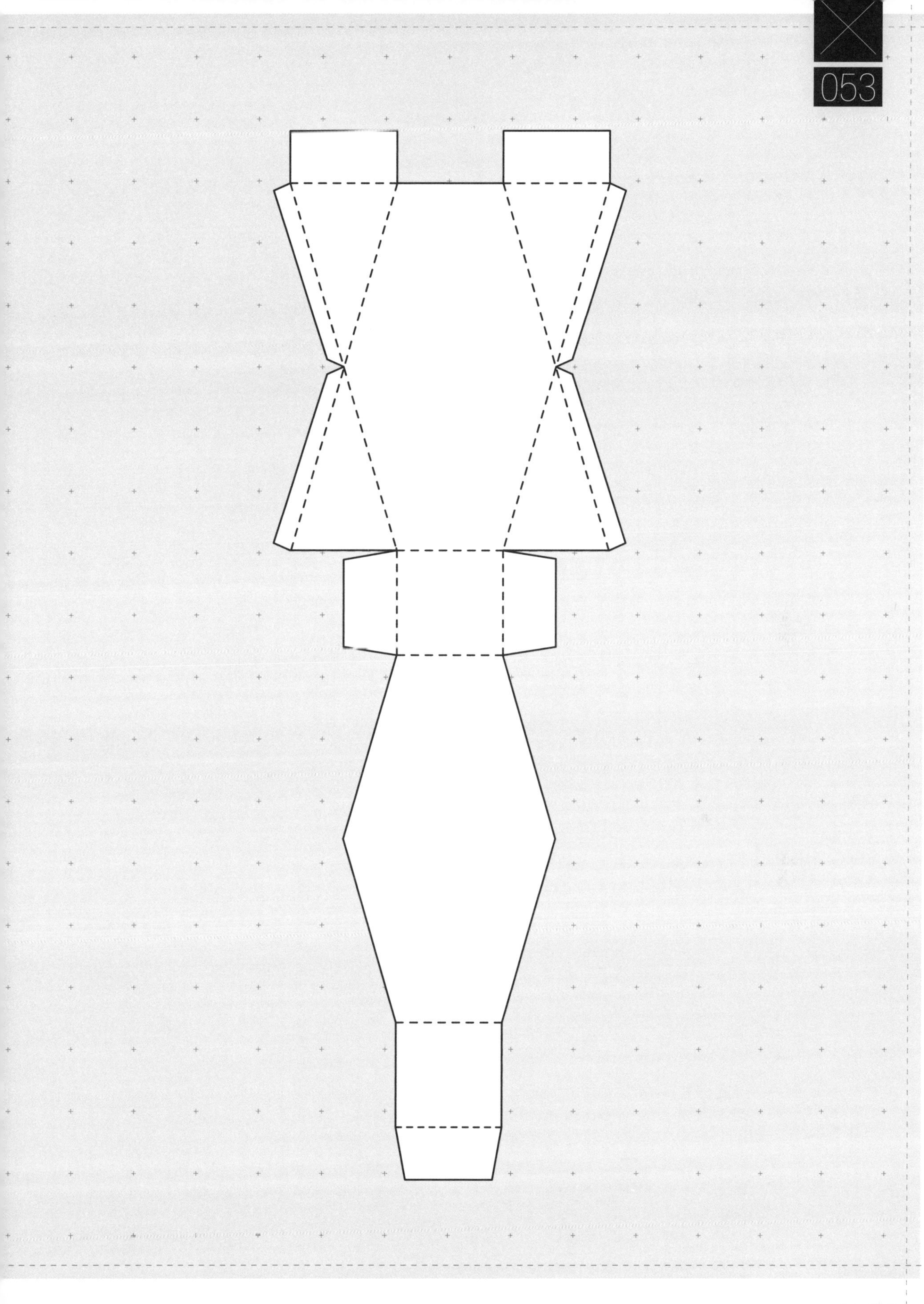

CHRISTMAS CARD PACK

Design **Loli Stavroula, Christoforidou Caterine**

As a new and innovative design office specialised in packages and wrappings, the studio decided to prepare something more than just a greeting card to their customers for Christmas. At last a fragrance with the essence of jasmine was sent out as a New Year greeting. The fragrance was placed in a separate box whose shape reminds people of an angel and the topped paper petals resemble a jasmine. The "Curious Metallic Ice Silver" paper induces the necessary sparkle of the holiday, while the rhinestones add a glamorous touch.

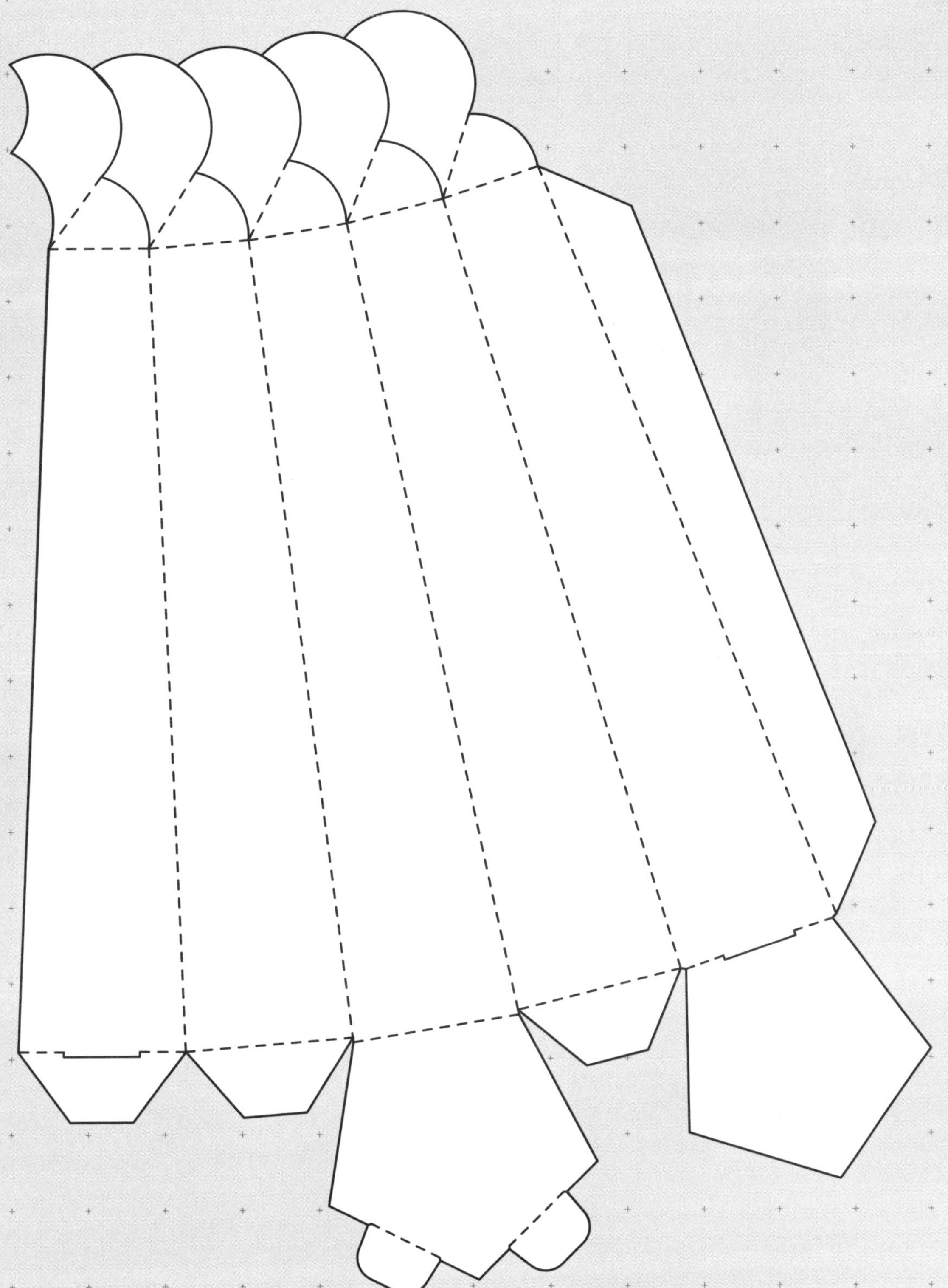

FØLE

Design **Saana Hellsten**

FØLE, which means "sense" in Norwegian, is a fictional luxurious and organic skin care product line. The ergonomic shape of the bottle originates from stone tools. The braille on the bottle and box make it accessible to the visually impaired. The tactile materials and the process of opening the carton enrich the user experience.

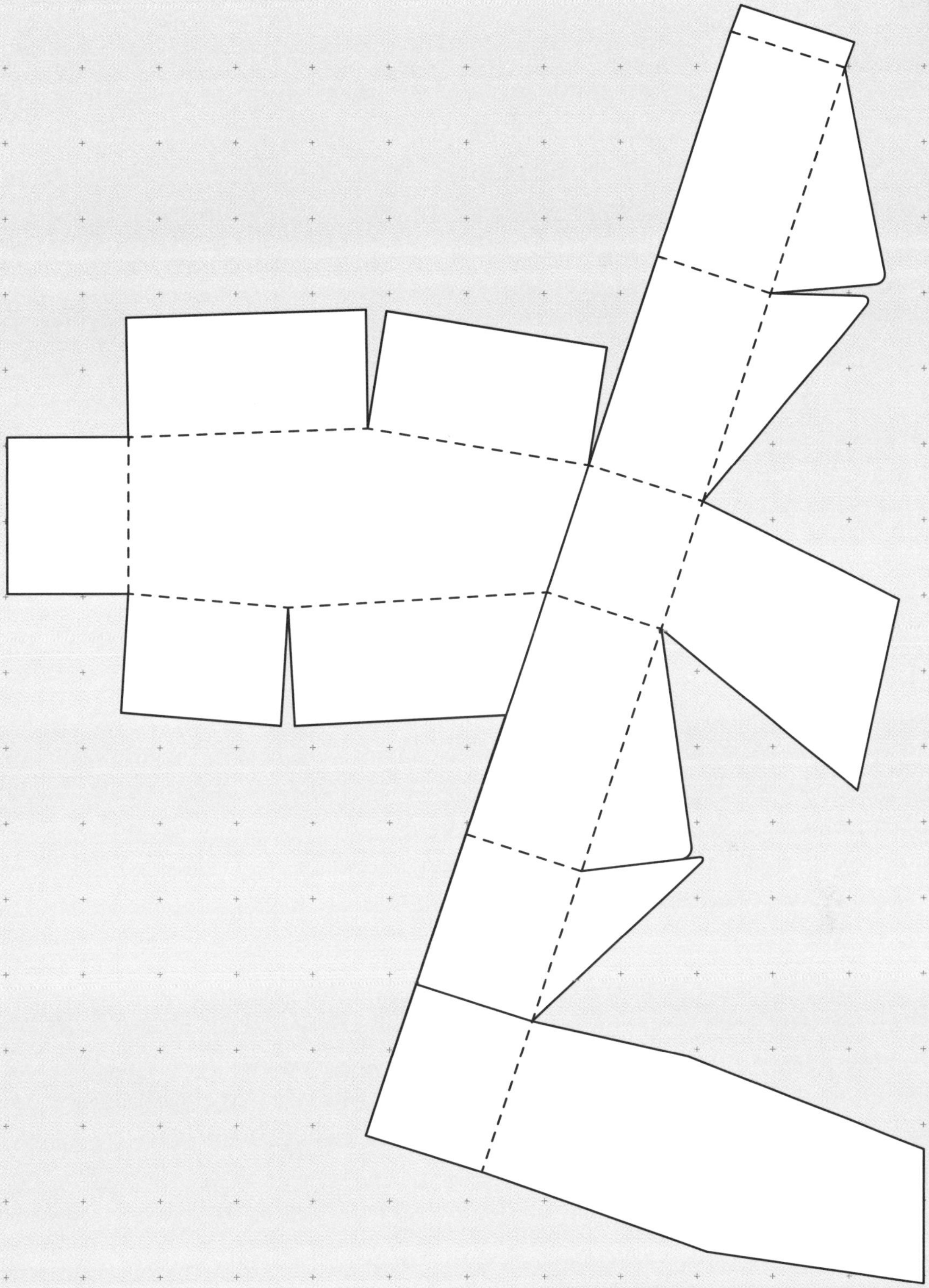

GOJI SERUM

Design Loli Stavroula, Christoforidou Caterine

Goji Serum is an innovative skin care product in Greece. The aim was to design a package that would look like a jewel and could be handily placed in handbags. The gold lettering on superfine paper with a special pattern of goji berry, and the unconventional triangular prism packaging are suggesting that it is the gold that glitters.

GOLDEN SPIKE

Design Mau Silva

The objective of this project was to develop a package capable of protecting the chocolates inside and at the same time easy to pack and store without losing the visual appeal. The shape of the packaging is an inverted spike, taking inspiration from the brand name Golden Spike. The design also allows for space saving as the package could be placed on top of each other.

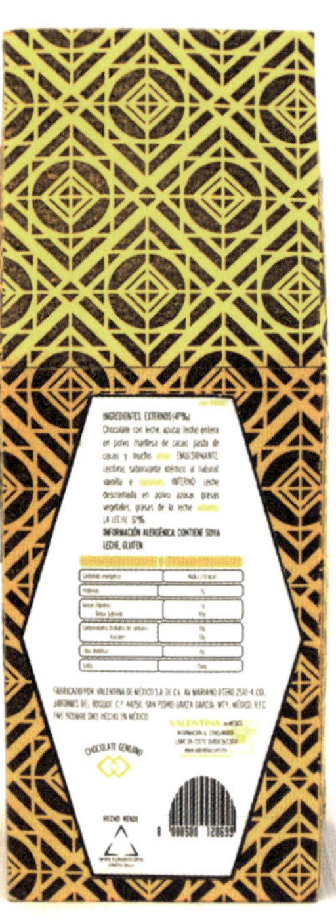

061

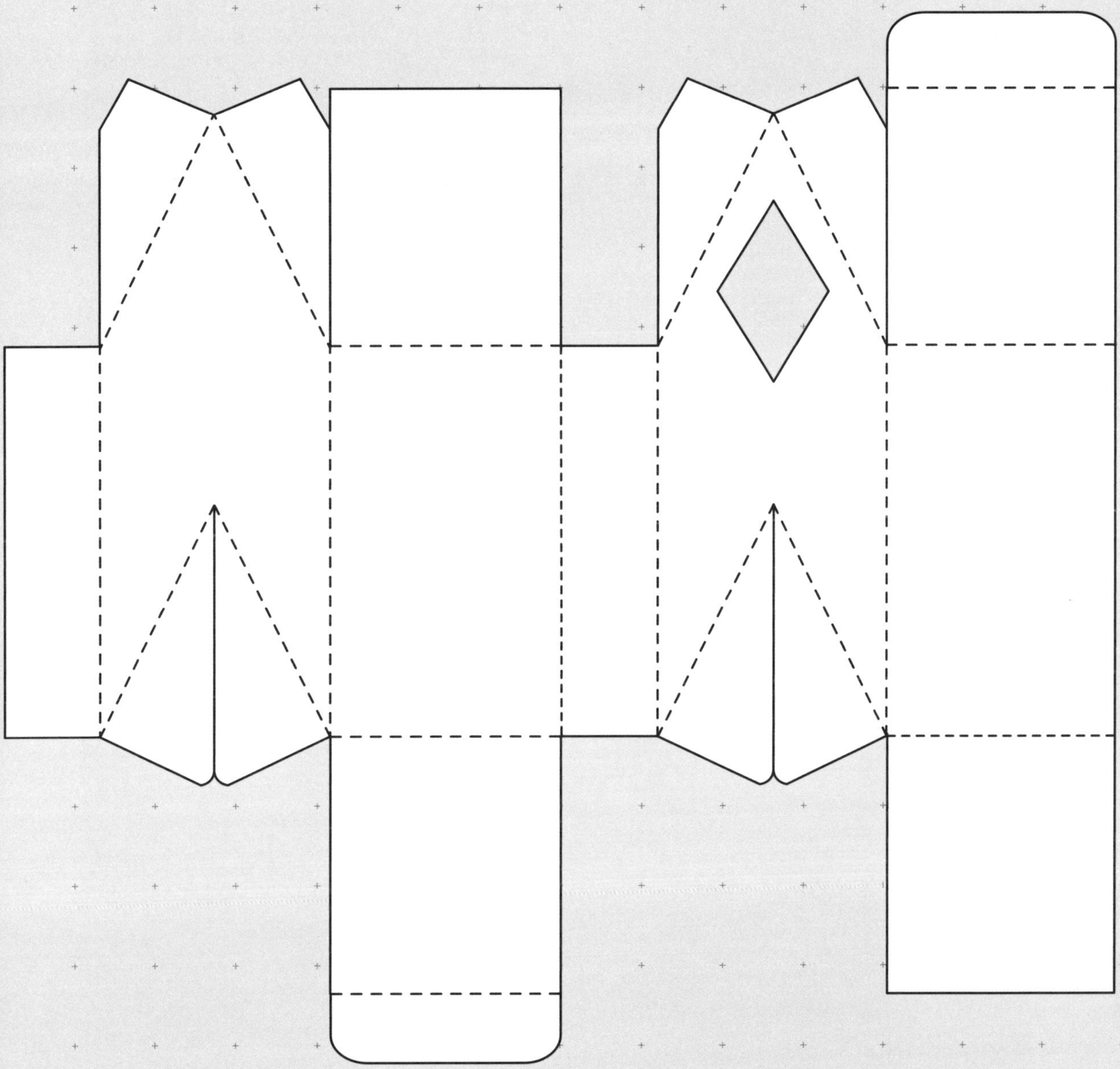

THE BREAD BOARD BAKERY CAFÉ

Design Dan Stark

This unique package was created to make ordinary, everyday bakery goods something special. Opening each section of the lid, one gets the feeling of unwrapping a present, revealing the delicious content within. Taking environmental protection into consideration, the designer made this package with a single piece of cardboard without any use of glue.

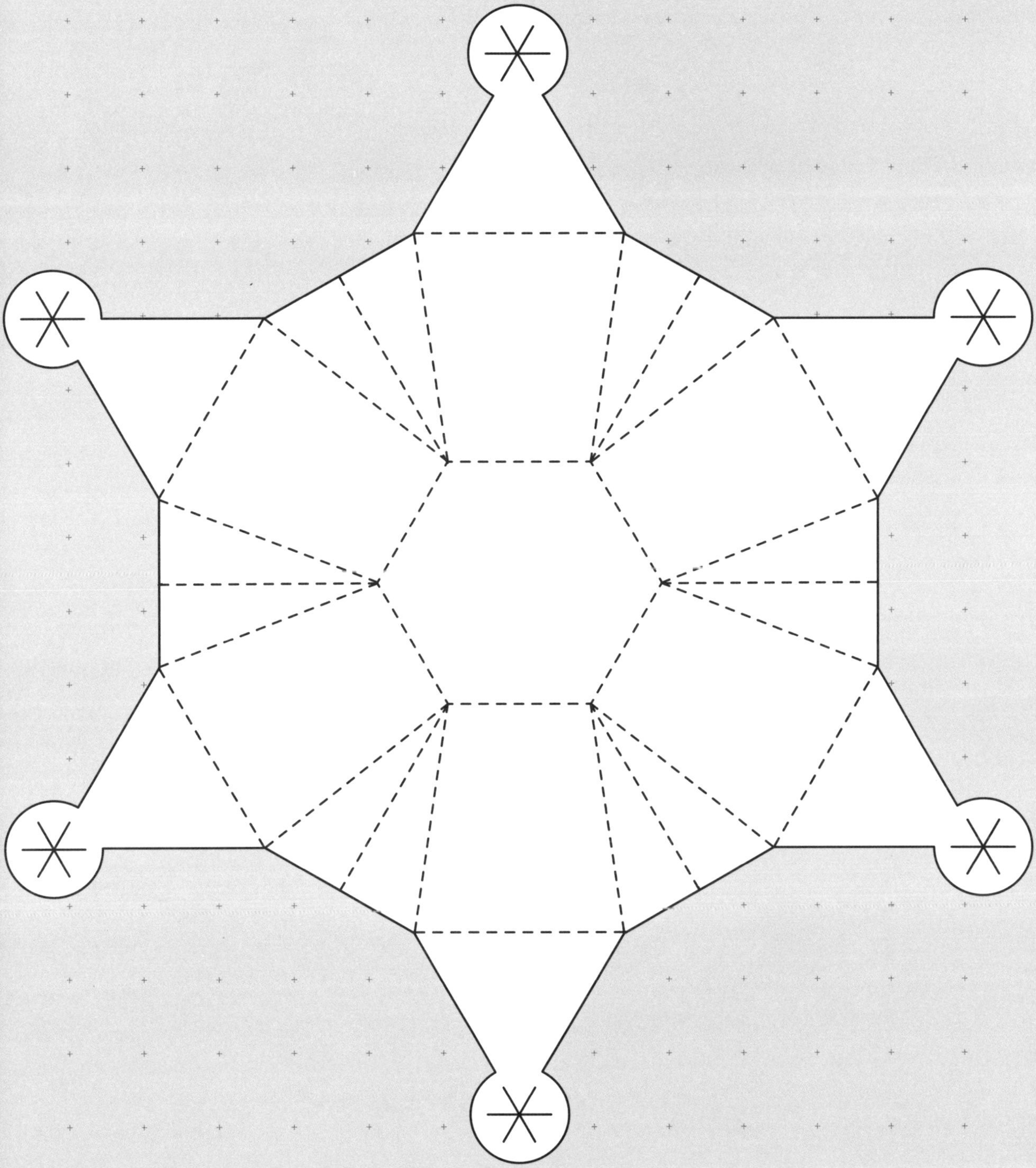

ÖRFLÖGUR MICROCHIPS

Design **Edda Gylfadottir, Gudrun Hjorleifsdottir, Helga Bjorg Jonasardottir**

Microchips are healthy, low fat potato chips. They come housed in a small box that unfolds into a bowl, perfect for sharing. Once all the chips have been eaten, the box's interior graphics reveal intriguing facts (in both English and Icelandic) about potatoes and their significance to the country, all playfully placed around a map of Iceland. The box is made of recyclable cardboard.

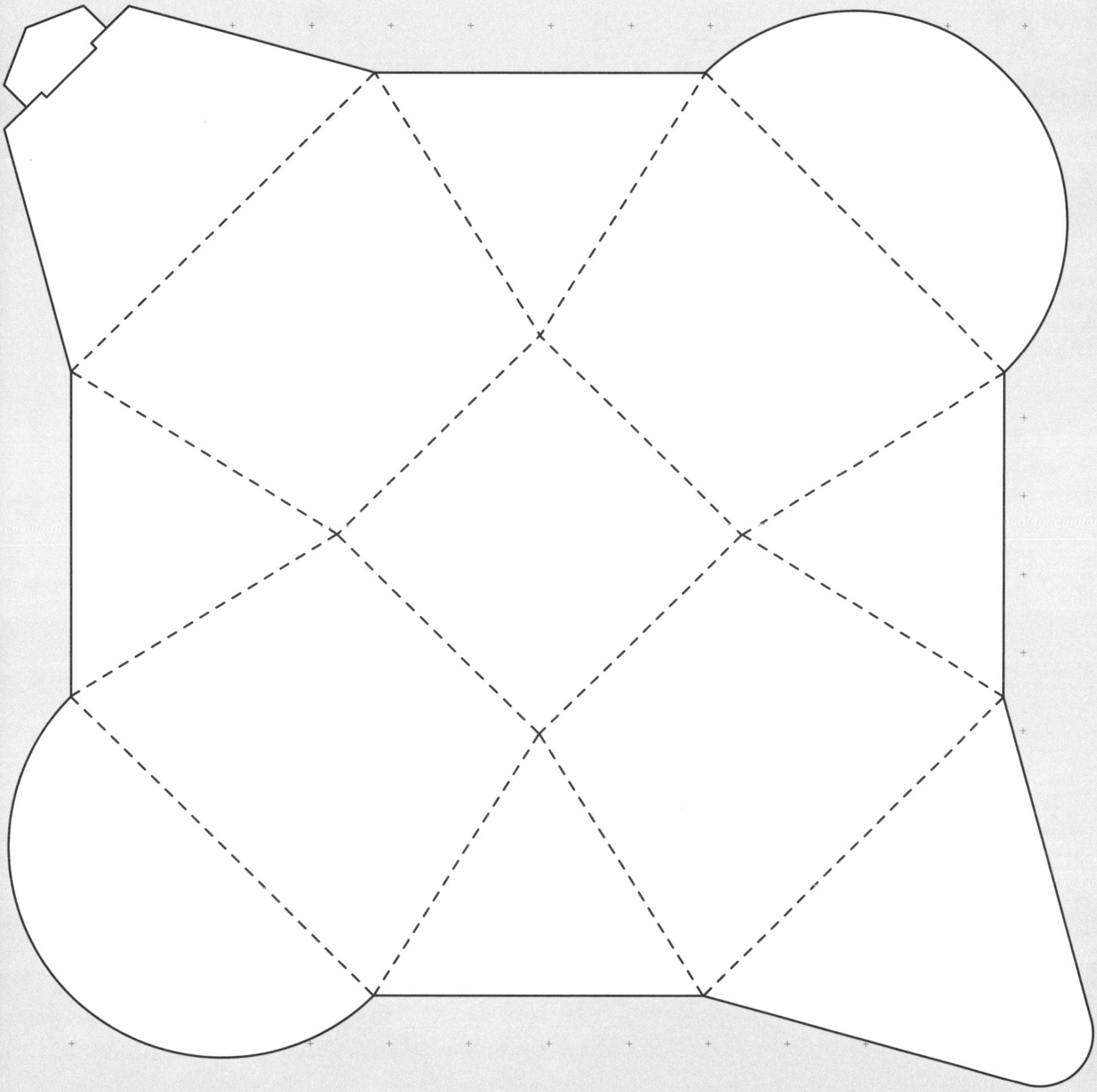

CANDIED FRUIT

Design **Camila Peralta Wieland**

The structure of this snack cardboard box was inspired by the origami folding techniques. The packaging is both easy to recycle and sufficiently attractive that one would want to keep and reuse it.

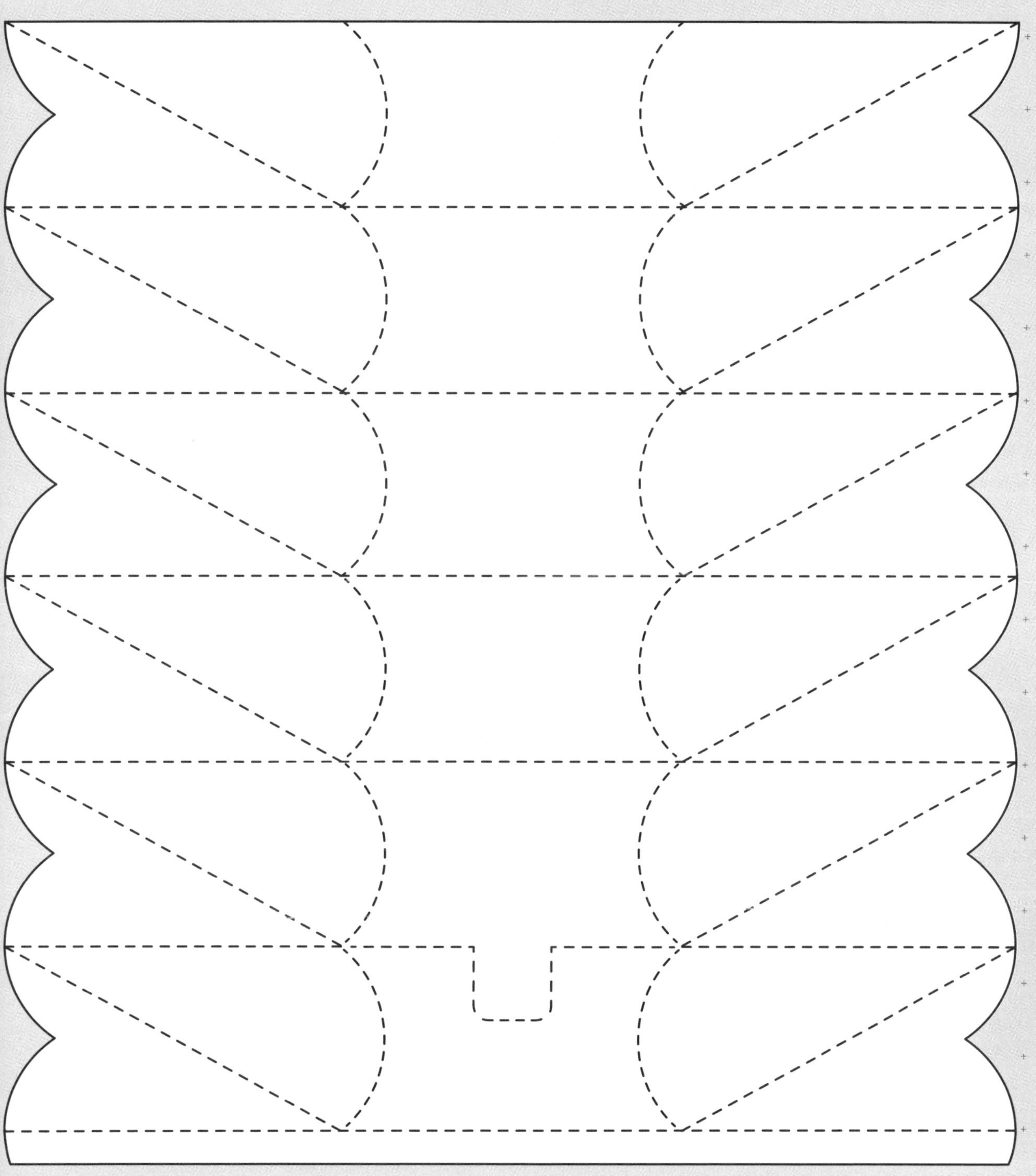

THE BODY SHOP: ELEMENTS

Design Christopher Downer

The redesign of the packaging for Elements range was motivated by the aspiration to re-establish the connection between the five core values of the brand, the product packaging and the on-shelf appearance of the products.

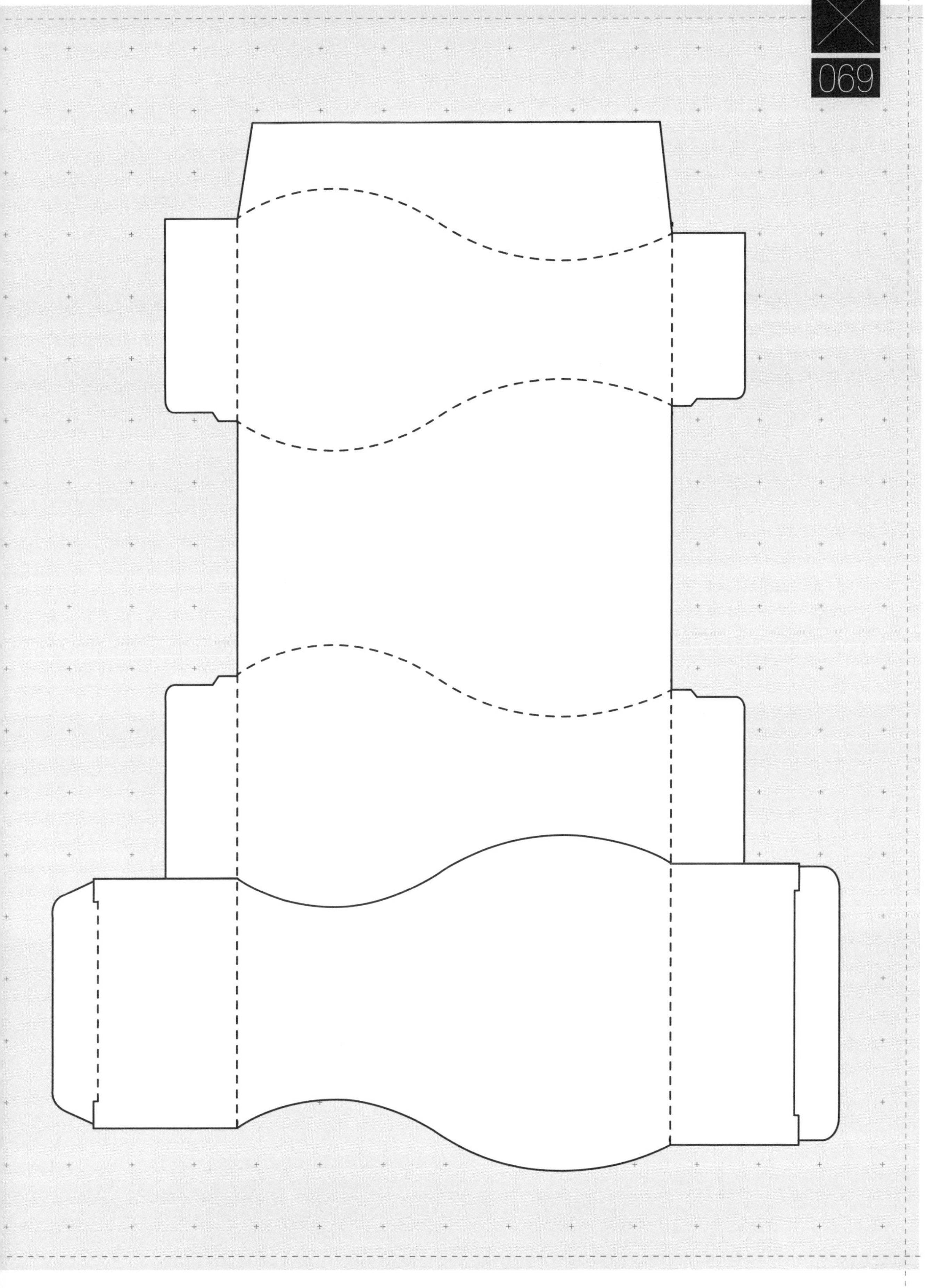

BON BONS

Design Christopher Downer

Watershed Cinemas wanted a new range of sweet packaging for a children's event they host every Saturday. The result is the Bon Bons range of sweets with moving faces packaging that keeps the children entertained. The package can be reused to store collectables.

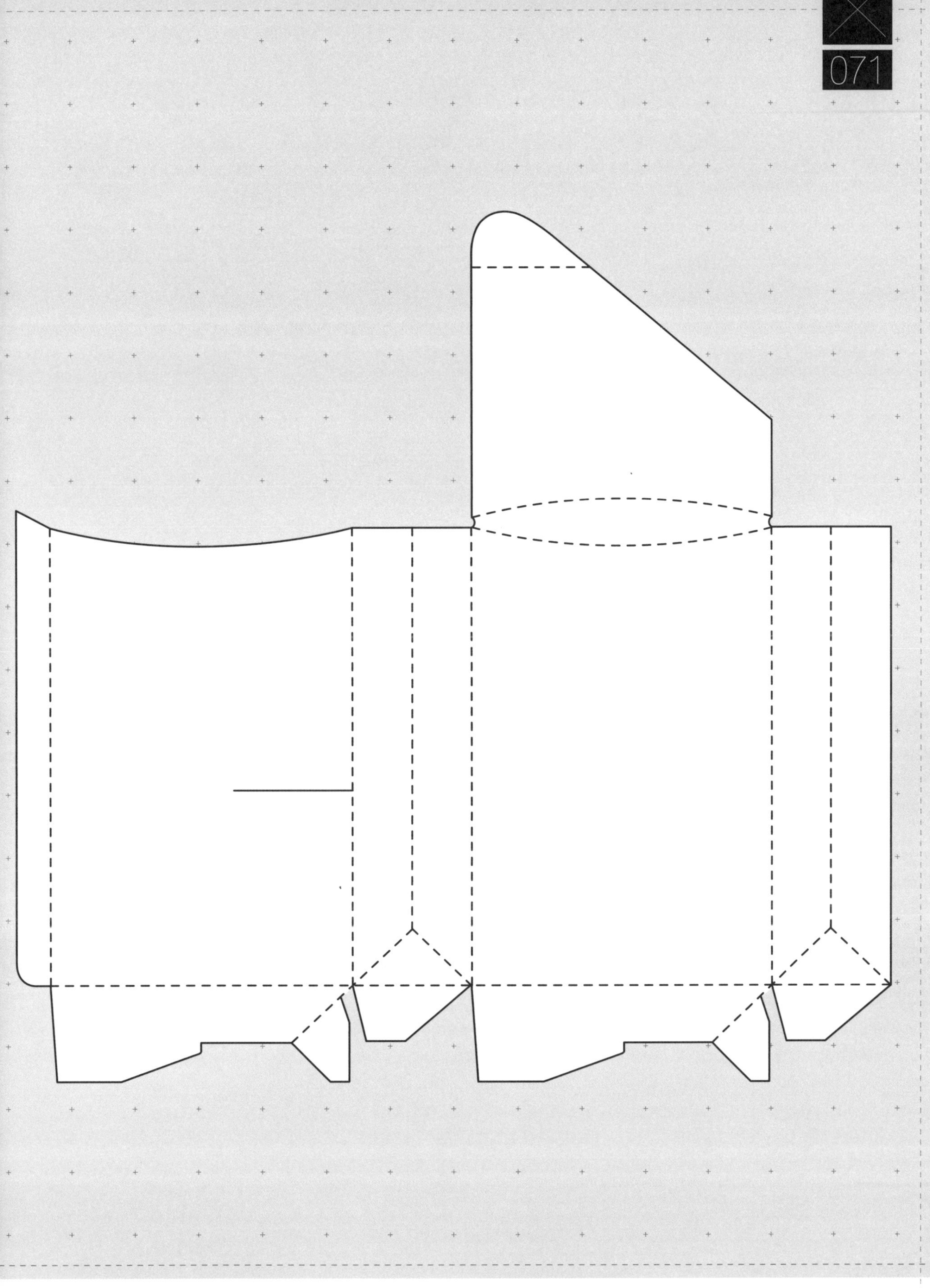

MACAROONS IN A BOX

Design Elsa Deprun

The brand Rannou Métivier strives to be simple, young and dynamic. The identity takes as a starting point the five generations which worked in this family owned confectioner. The packaging was inspired by the shapes of the poudriers of antan.

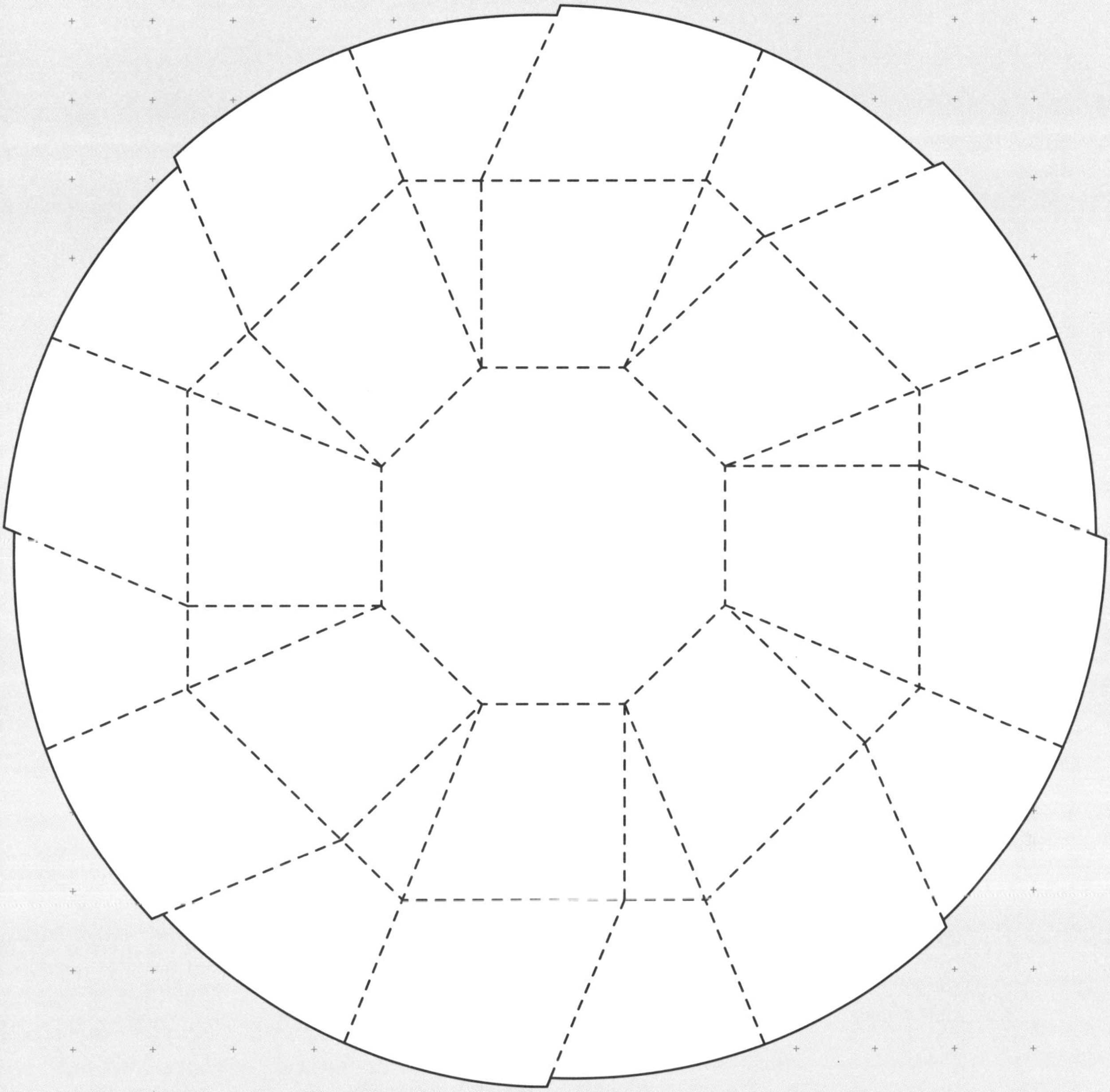

NEW LIMP EGG

Design Elsa Deprun

This is a limited edition egg packet produced exclusively for the French supermarket chain Le Bon Marché. The simple but original packaging offers a double protection for the eggs and was designed to be re-used. The inner packaging is removable, washable and can be used as egg cups.

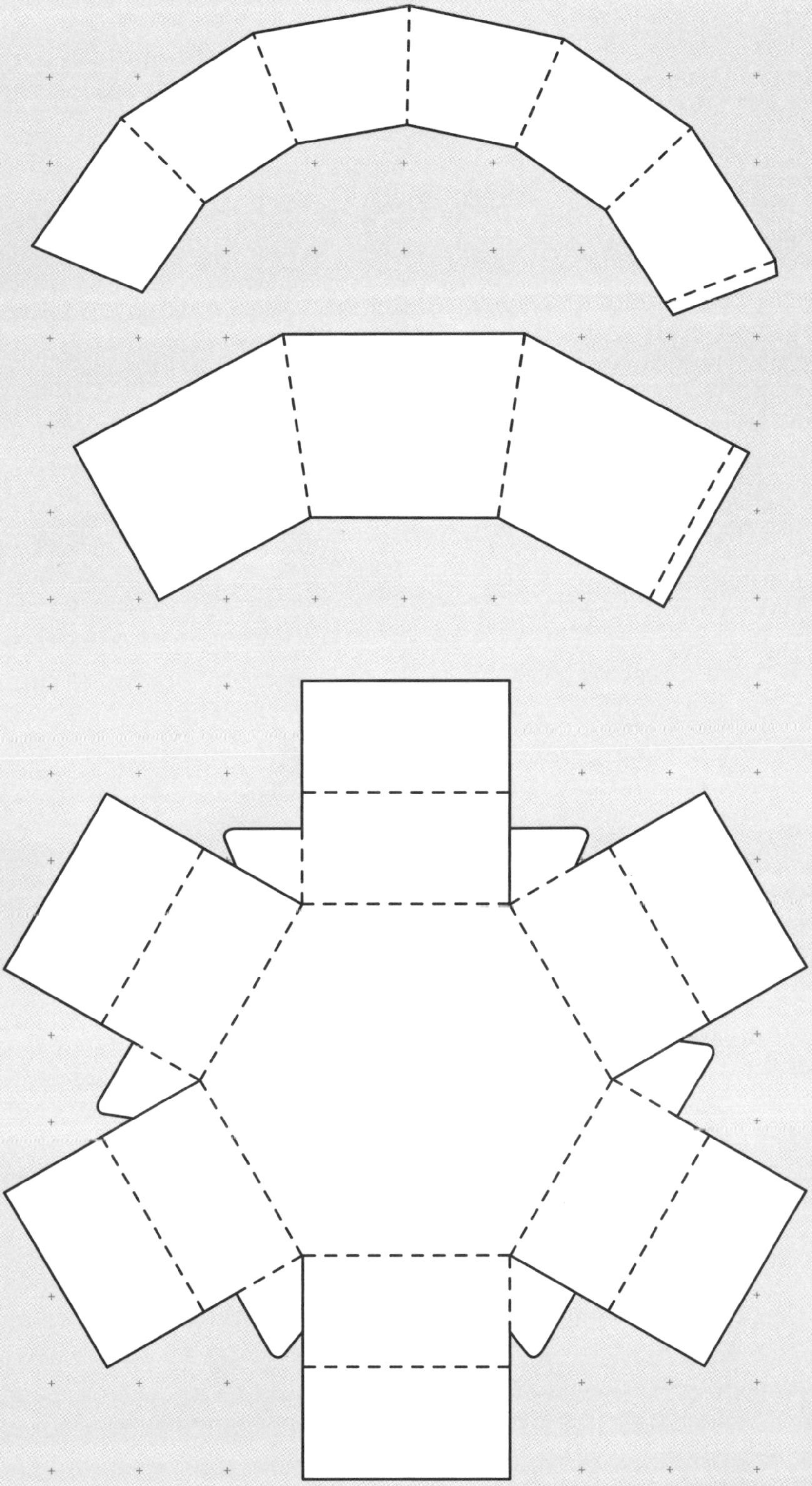

LUNCHBOXES

Design **Emma Smart**

Emma Smart wanted to make lunch a little more fun by transporting you to somewhere different, away from your desk and computer. The idea was to make the consumer interact with the lunchbox by enabling them to use the packaging while eating. The "healthy" lunchbox created the scene of a picnic completed with grass and frisbee. The "children's" lunchbox was set on a sandy beach with a colourful bucket and spade, and finally the "satisfying" lunchbox is turned into a dinner table setting, with fancy traditional china, napkins and wine glass.

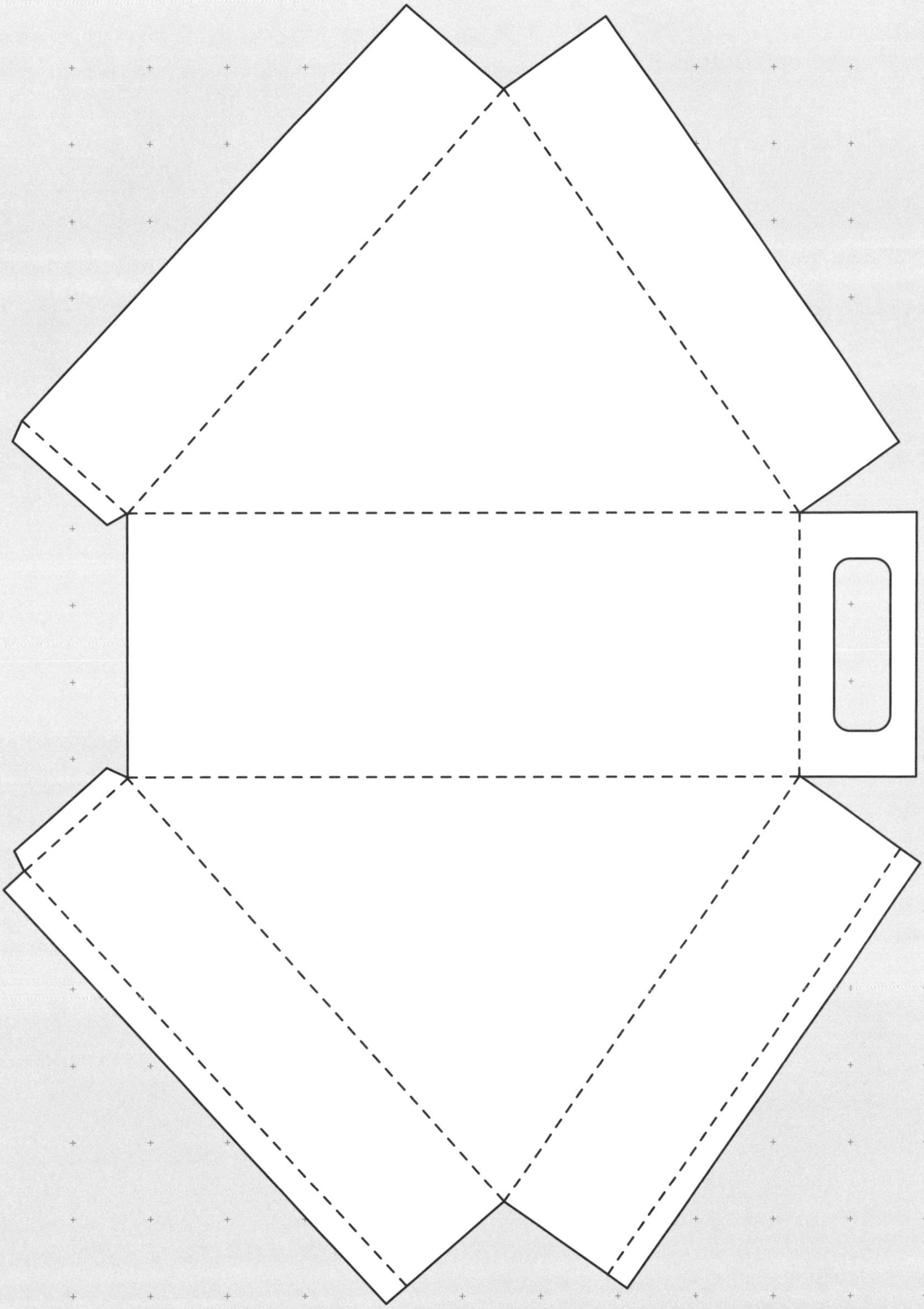

CHOCOLATE IN A BOX

Design Elsa Deprun

The design again draws on the long history of this French confectionery firm which has passed through 5 generations of the same family. The shape of the box was inspired by the form of antique powder boxes, while the gold and pink colour palette emphasizes the delicate, vintage look.

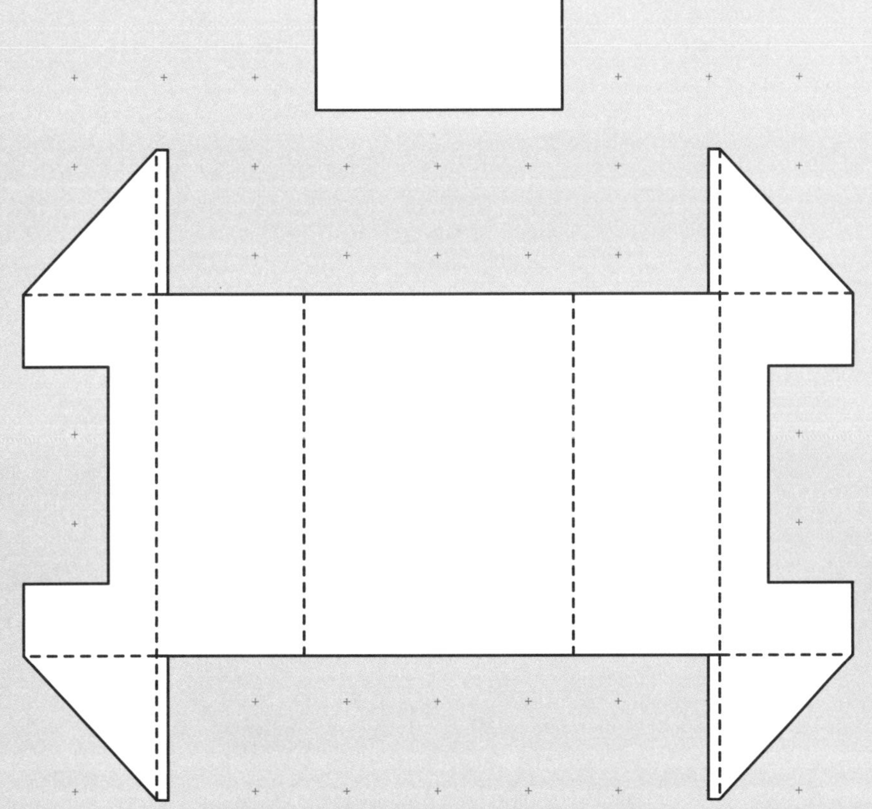

*BRODOFINO

Design **Fabio Bernardi**

The design concept is to have fun with the children's favorite pasta, stelline. The pyramid box opens at the top and the tip can be used as a sealing cap. On each side of the pyramid there is a stelline-made character with different facial expression.

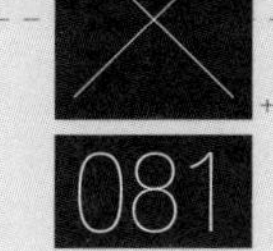
081

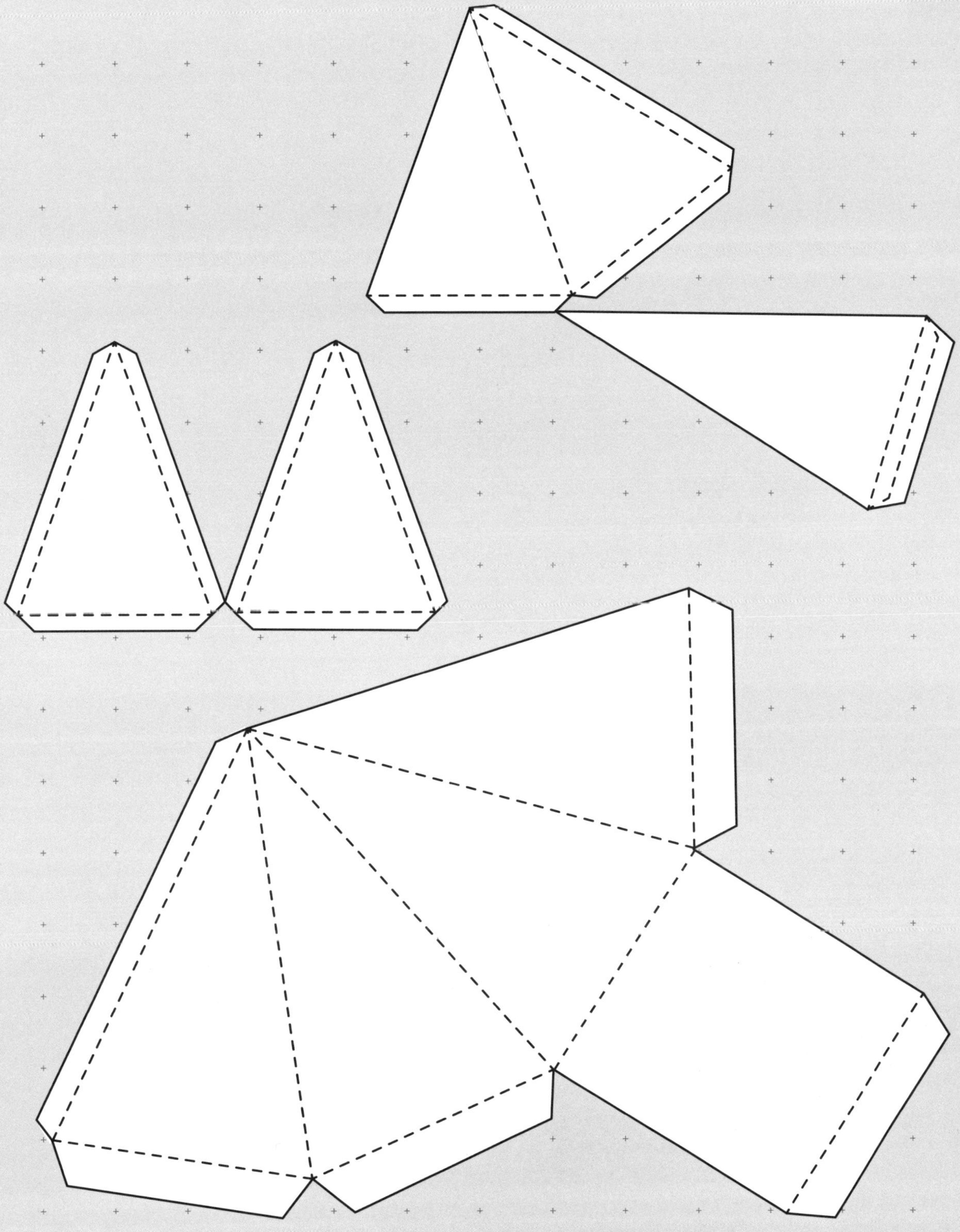

GAUTHIER CHOCOLATES

Design **Mathilde Fortier, Geneviève Soucy**

To mark the New Year celebration, Gauthier offered a special box of chocolates to their clients. The box, entirely made of cardboard, is based on organic forms in warm brown palettes. There are coasters inside the box.

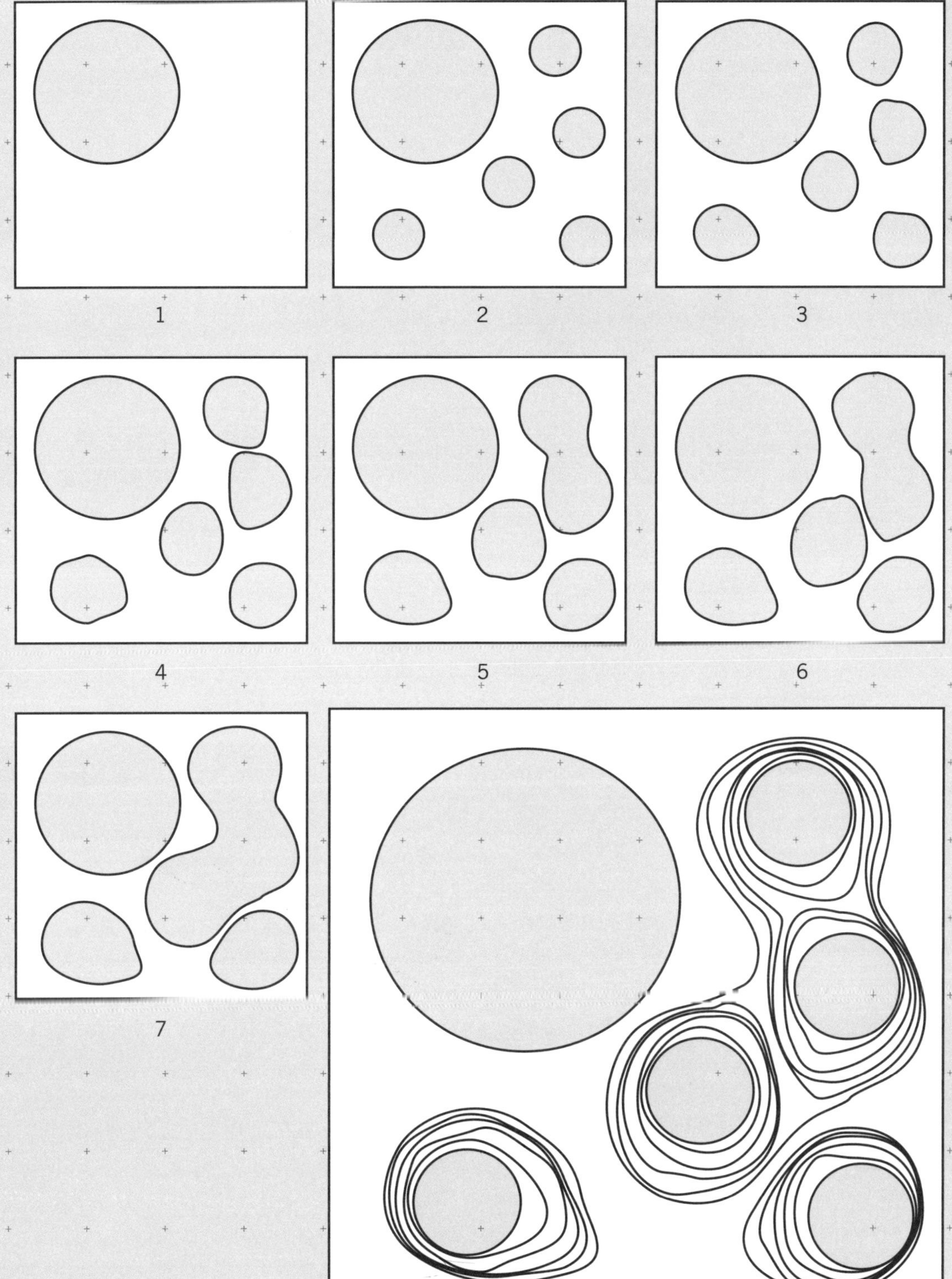
1
2
3
4
5
6
7

GAUTHIER BOTTLE

Design **Mathilde Fortier, Sébastien Legault**

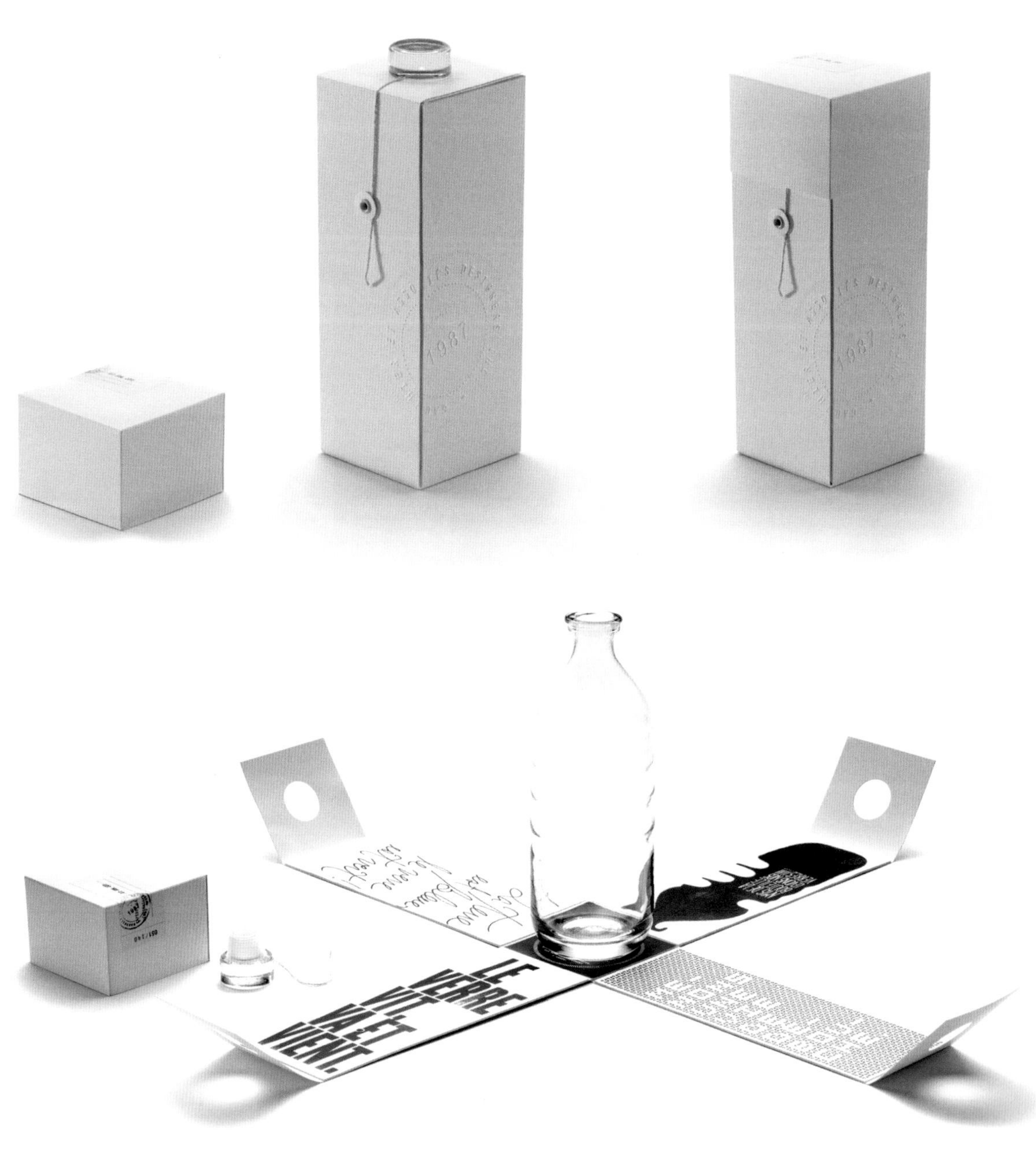

For a New Year gift, Gauthier offered its clients a glass bottle bearing the message "Let's eliminate plastic bottles and lift the glasses to celebrate the power of glass!". The box's clean and classic exterior conceals its revolutionary rallying cry. Once the bottle stopper is pulled off the box disintegrates as if in an explosion, with its panels coming apart and folding down, and the words contained inside it bursting out.

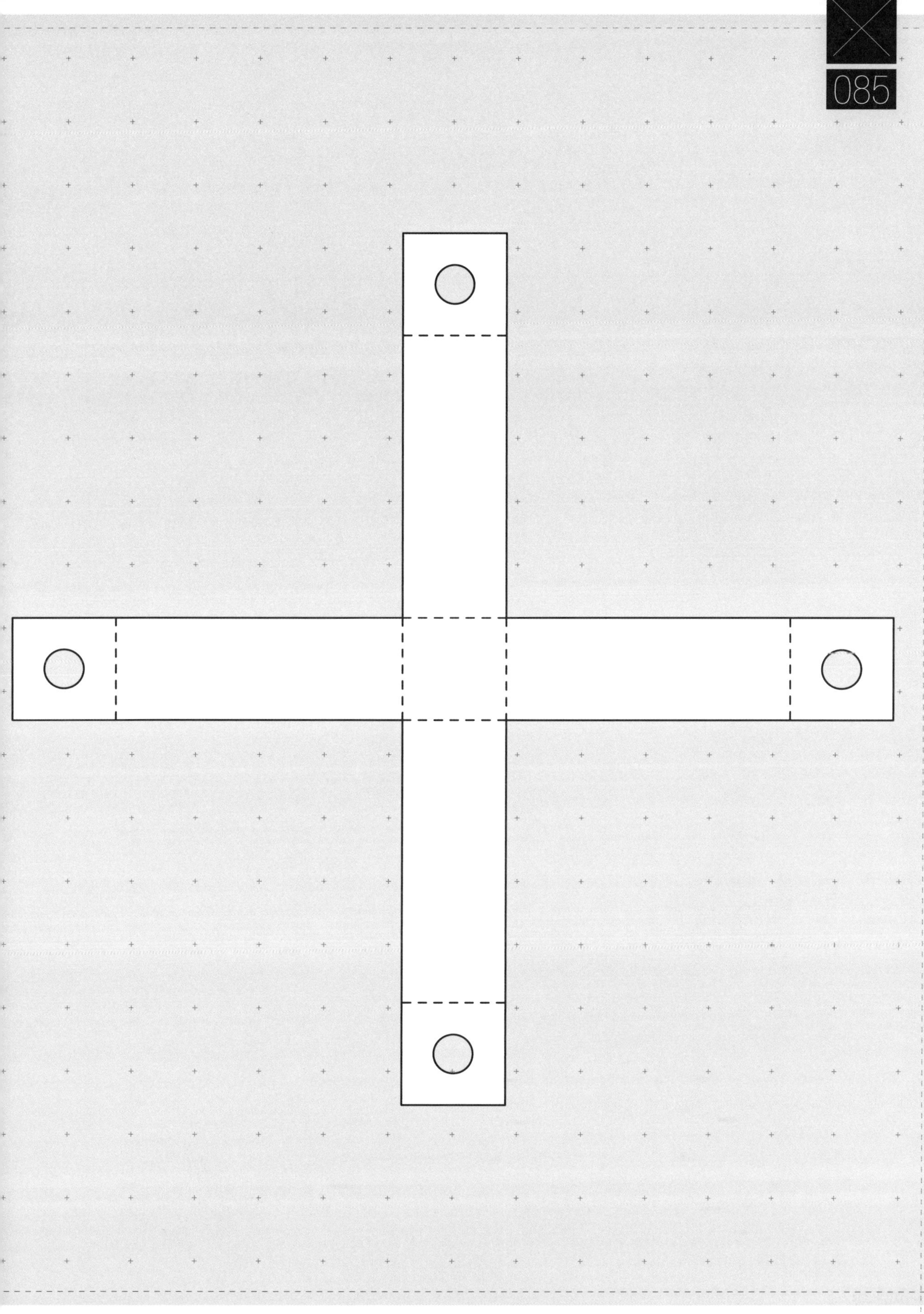

KID ROBOT, KAT VON D

Design Mei Cheng Wang

This special edition KidRobot figure and package was inspired by famous tattoo artist Kat Von D. The package emulates her gothic-elegant style, such as in her fashion and makeup lines. A black-on-black exterior is more refined yet the intricate laser cuts and patterned panels keep the tattoo influence.

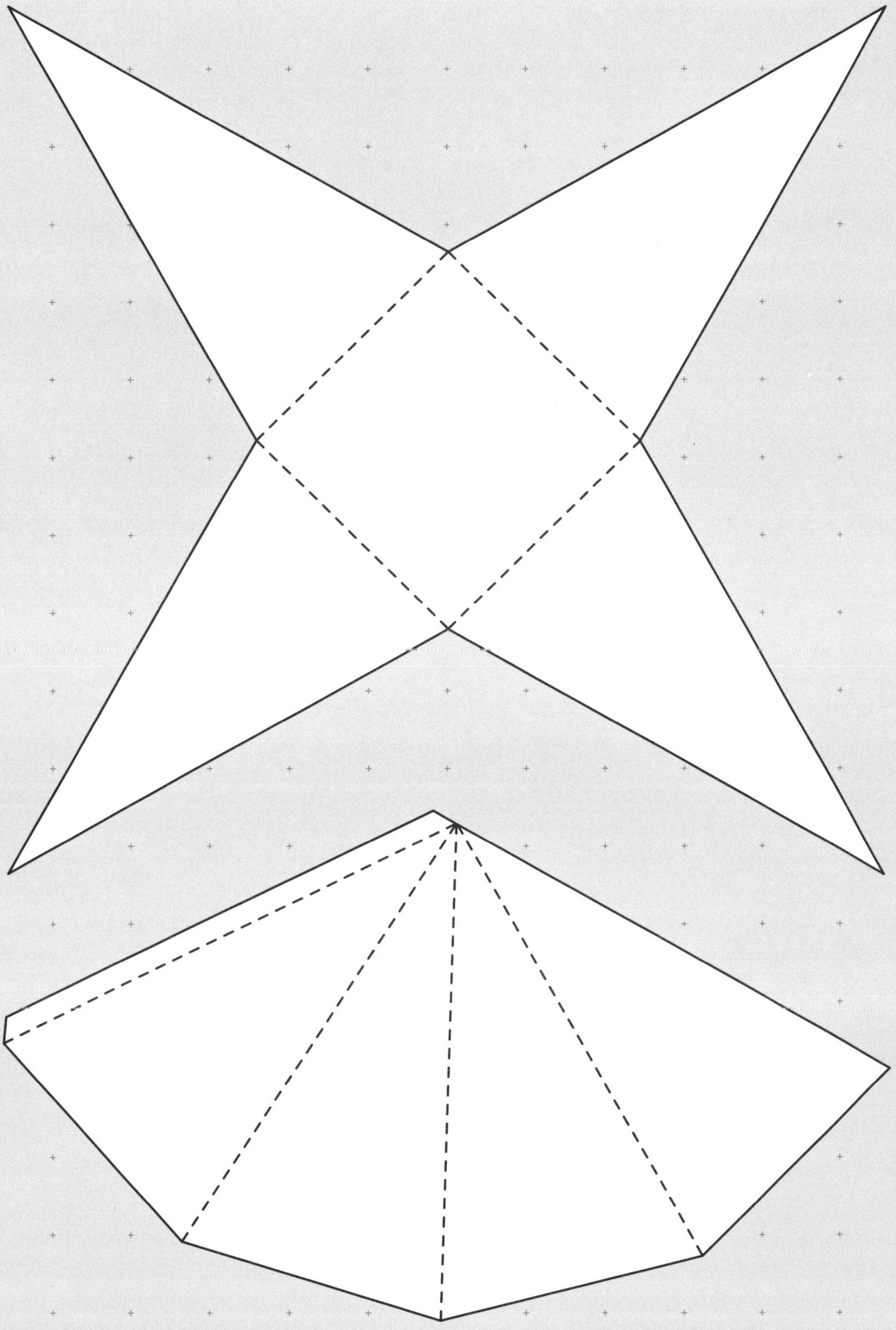

ECO-FRIENDLY CHINESE TAKE-OUT

Design JoAnn Arello

The typical styrofoam and plastic American take-out containers create a tremendous amount of non-biodegradable waste. This concept packaging was designed using eco-friendly materials to eliminate the use of plastic carrying sacks. The divider is glued to the bottom of the box allowing the boxes to be nested for transportation and storage.

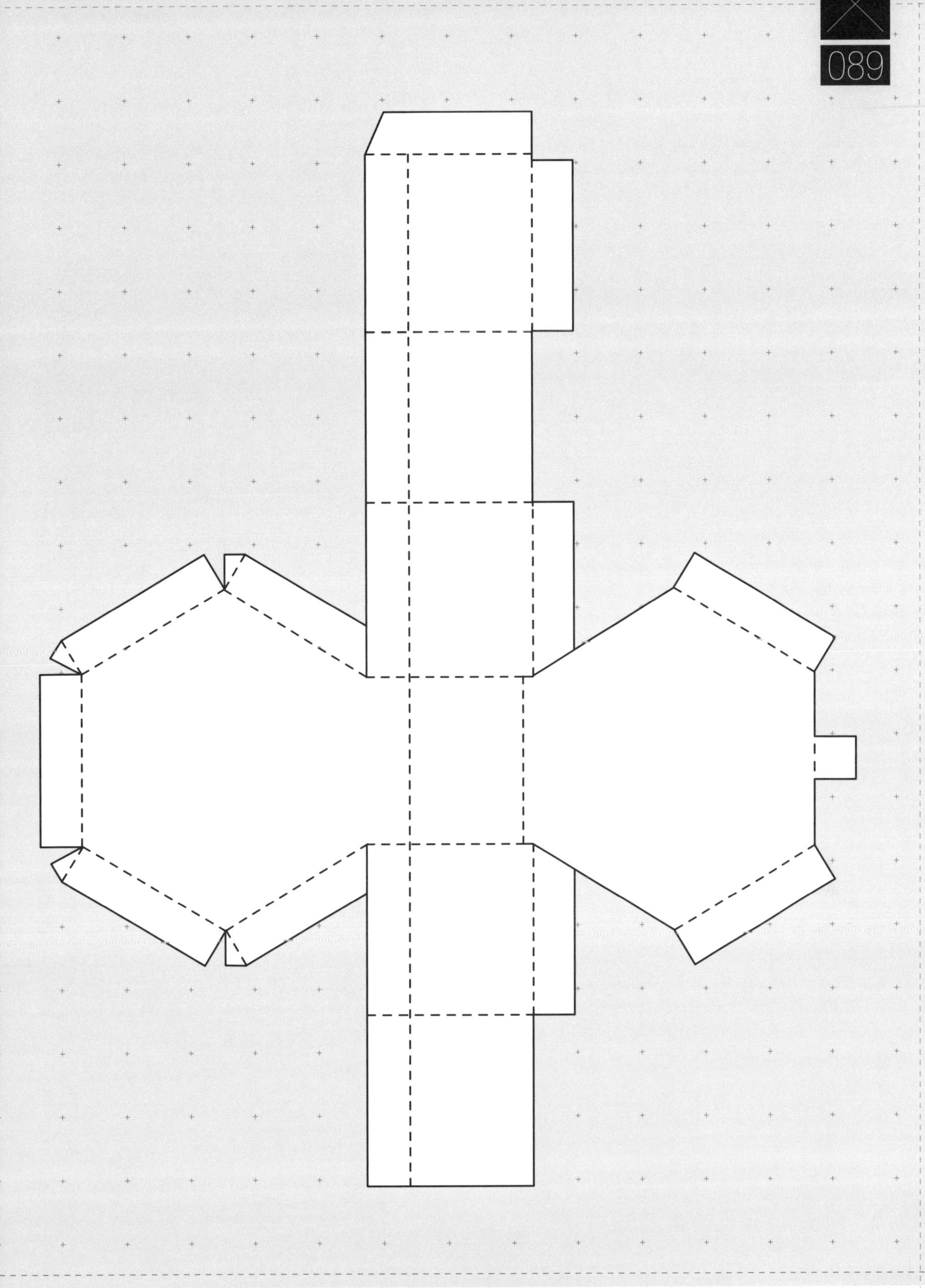

EINEM CONFECTIONERY CHOCOLATES

Design **Julia Agisheva**

This is a series of packaging for Einem Confectionery chocolates. The packets follow the form of animal totems to identify each product with an animal spirit. The packaging design is a reference to the origins of chocolate in pre-Columbian American culture, while the stylization of the imagery and the simple light sans serif typography used convey the contemporary roots of the design.

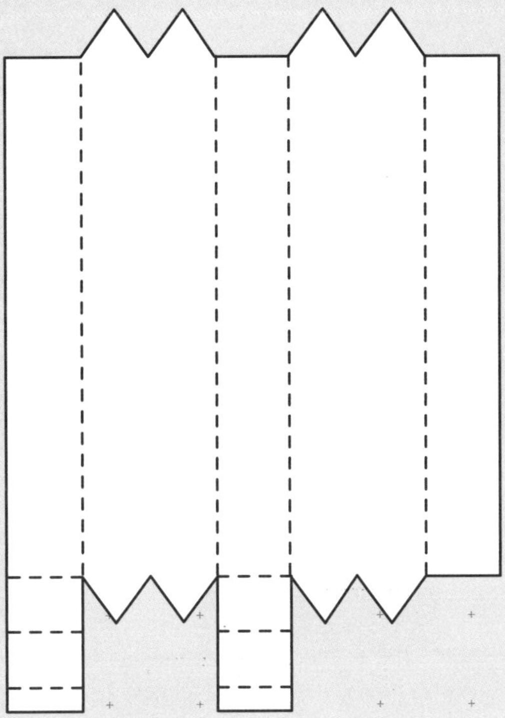

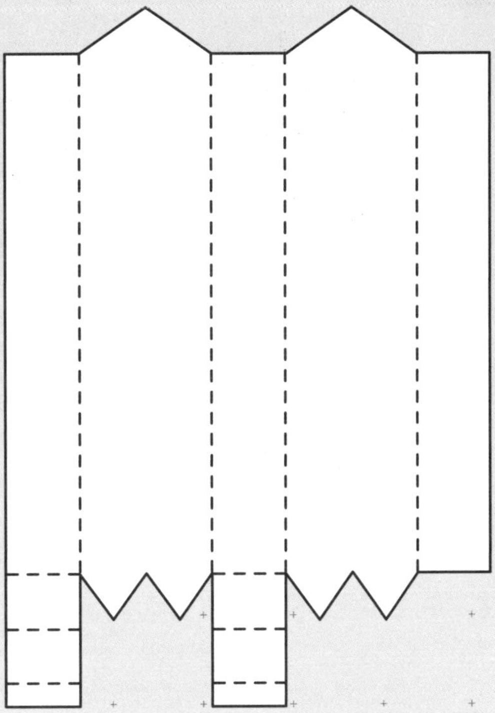

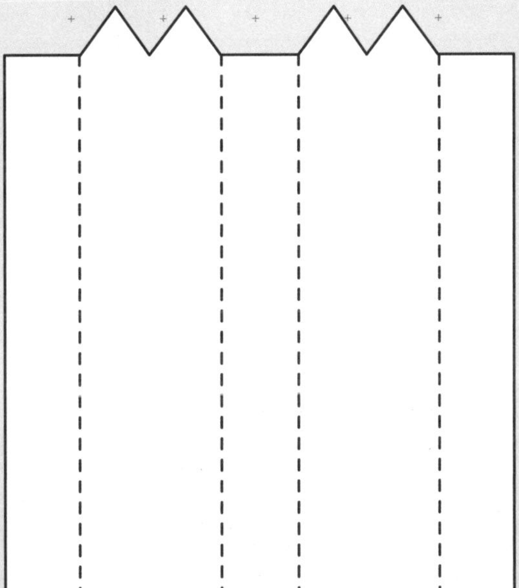

NOO-DEL

Design **Helen Maria Bäckström**

The brief for this project was to create a reusable package design. Noo-Del is a playful and simple packet that stands out on the shelves. The geisha imagery used, in which chopsticks are playfully incorporated as hairpins, implies the cultural provenance of the food contained. The packet is easy to carry and can be placed directly into the microwave to heat up the noodles before consumption.

093

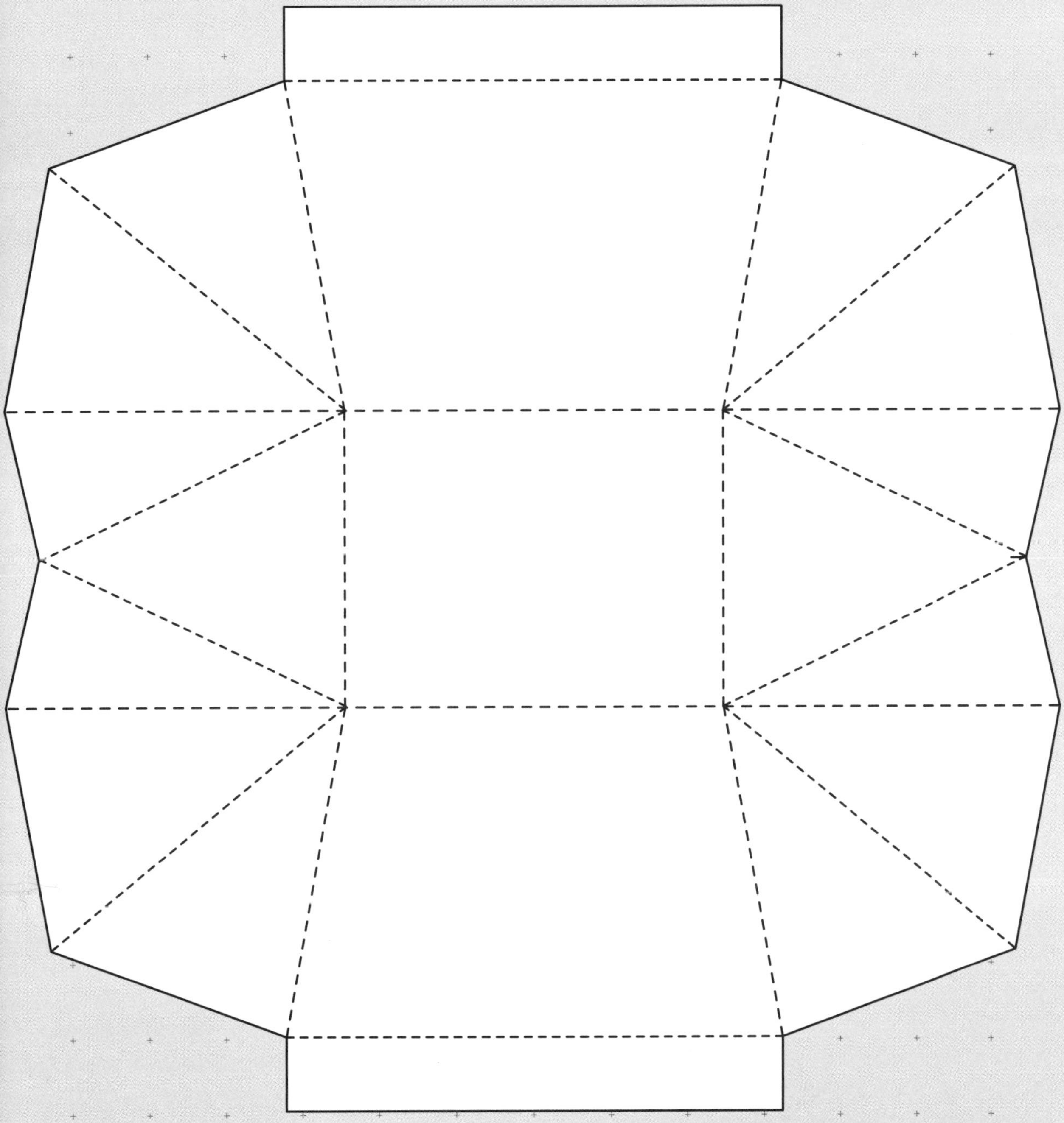

YUAN HO SOY SAUCE

Design **Su HaoMin**

The redesign of the packaging for the gift box evokes both luxury and high fashion. The corrugated paper used for the box conveys the high quality of the product, while the bottle design and the handmade packaging reflect a traditional ethos.

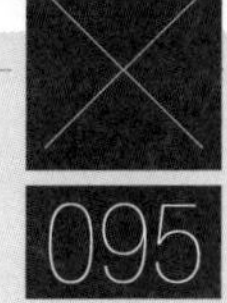

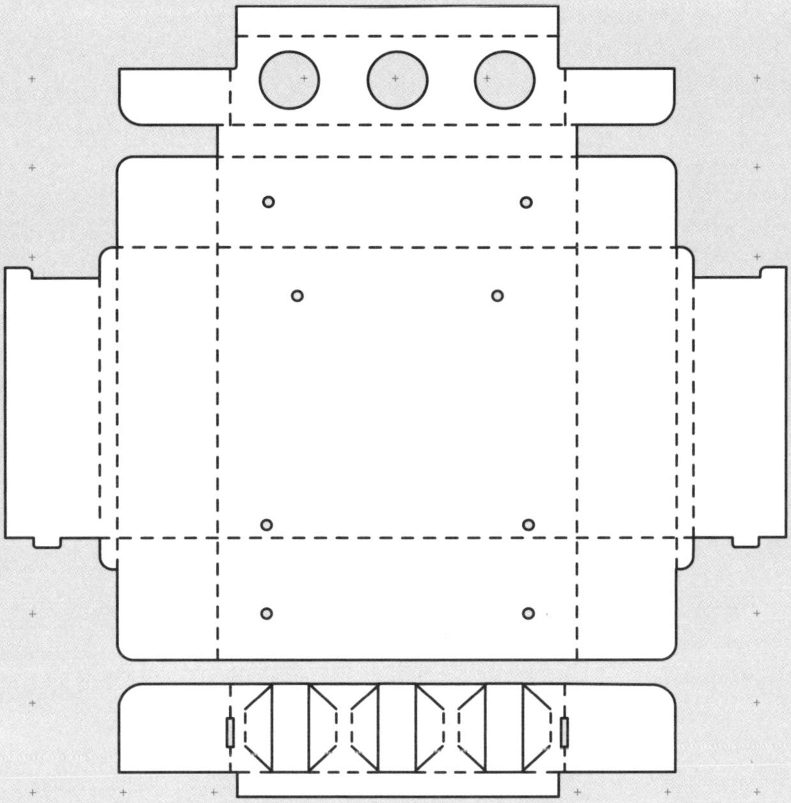

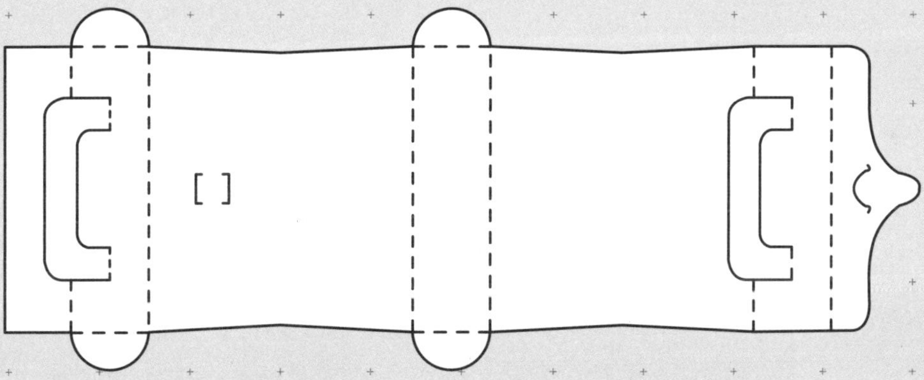

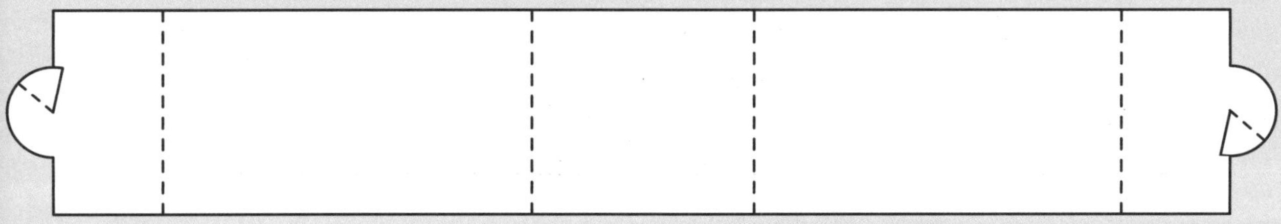

HANDMADE SOAP GIFT BOX

Design Su HaoMin

This product was part of an initiative to help farmers in Taiwan, China to use surplus fruit crops and seek new business opportunities through the production of peripheral products. The graphic design of the boxes employs plant motifs and oriental calligraphy to give them an exquisite and natural touch.

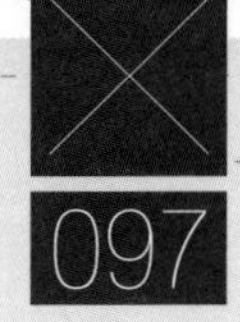

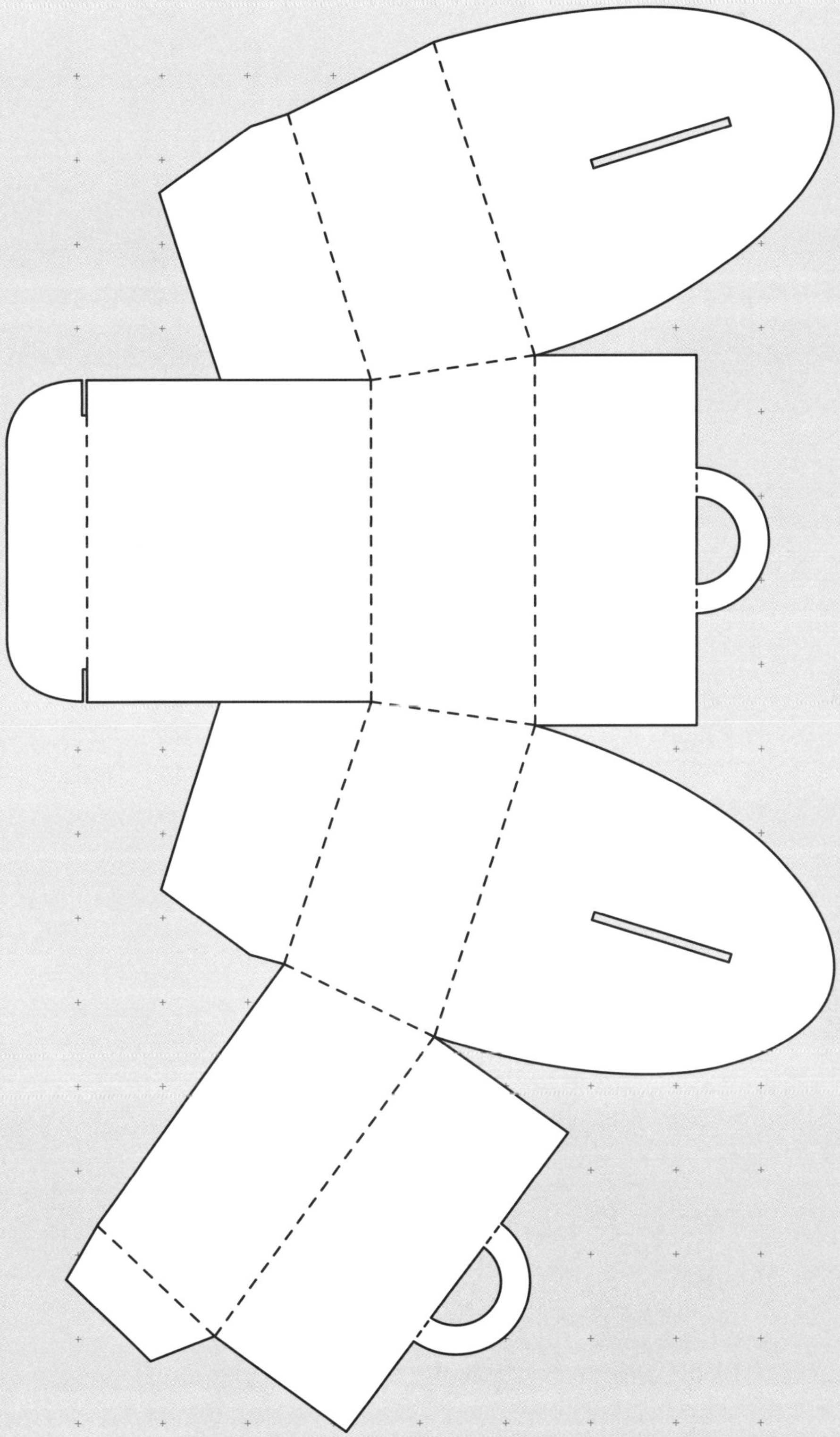

OBAMITAS

Design **Susana Castillo, Fidel Castro**

The Obamitas brand concept is about hope, fun and joy. The challenge was to create, launch and publicize the product in relevant media on the lowest budget possible. Obama's presidential campaign was the first one that used social networking media, through which it managed to connect with and cheer a large number of people. Likewise, "Obamitas" biscuits (the name means "little Obamas" in Spanish), which are promoted and sold online, are intended to bring a smile to consumers.

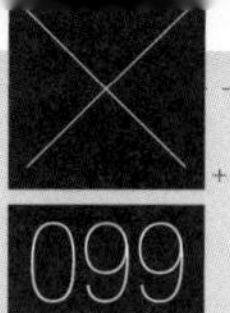

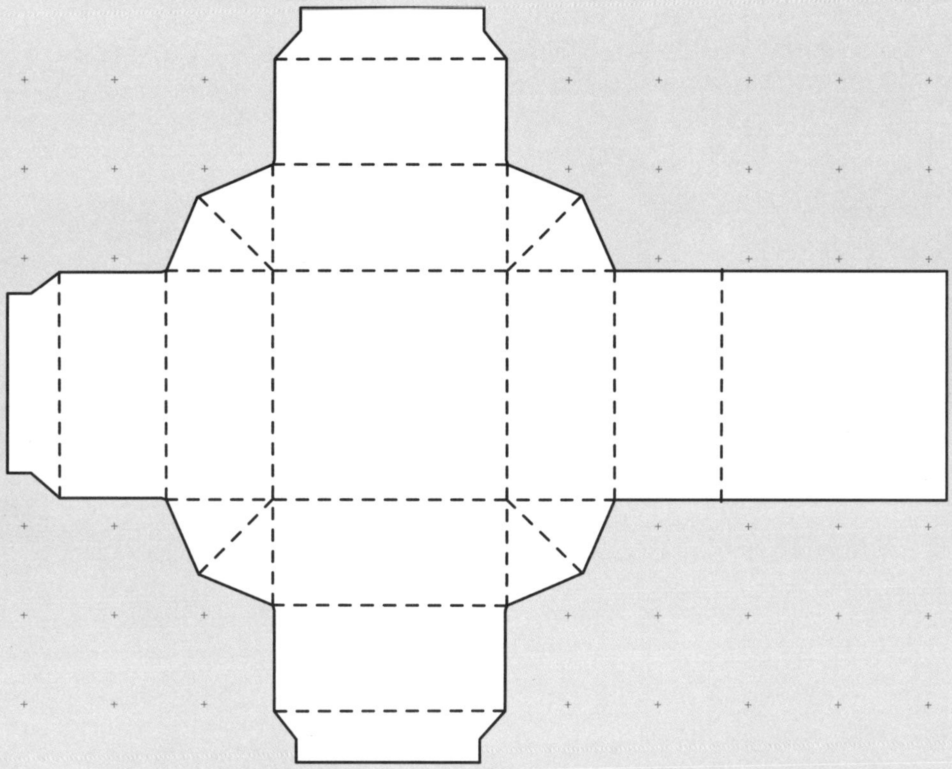

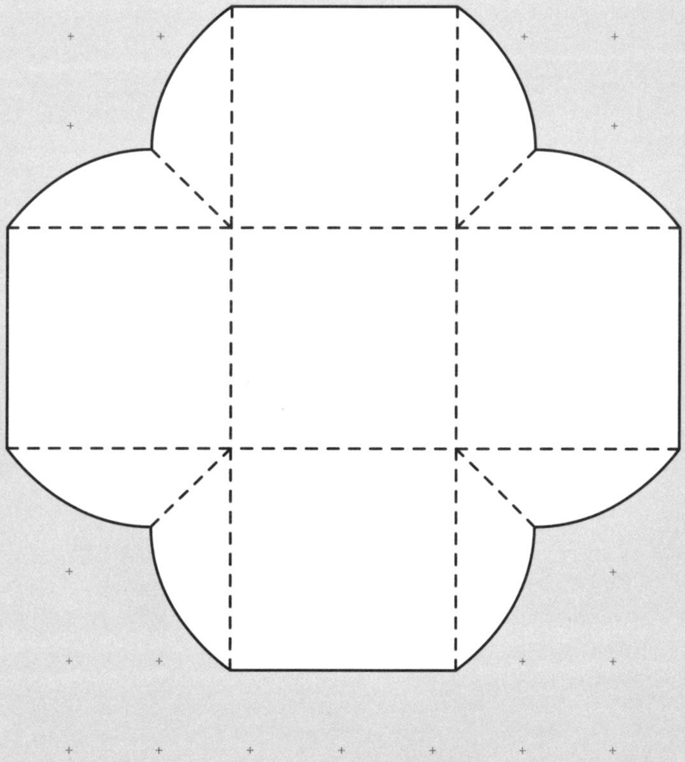

STAKK CERAMICS

Design   Phil Wareing

This project comprises an attractive yet sturdy presentation box for porcelain teacups and saucers. The flexibility of the design makes the packet adaptable for other products. The playful appearance was inspired by the functional interior construction, which holds the products firmly in place. The outer box is easily opened to reveal the contents.

Photo by Theo Alers

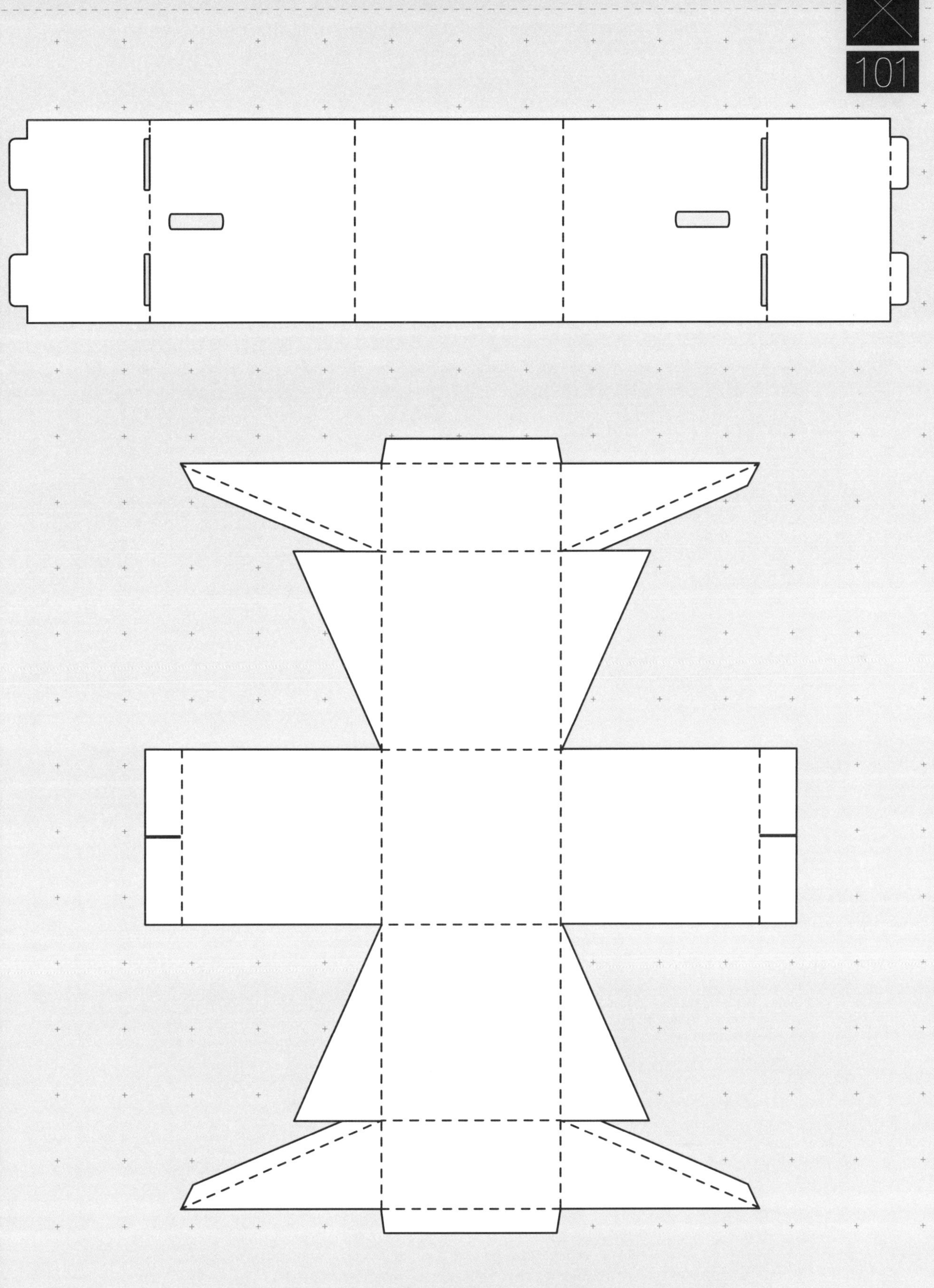

PLEASANT RIVER SOAP

Design **Taja Dockendorf, Sara Rosario**

The designer drew inspiration from vintage styles and the product itself to create this package. The hand crafted soaps are partially visible and the graphics reveal the soap's ingredients in a playful, cheeky manner. The design made easy transportation and packaging, enabling the company to expand its distribution.

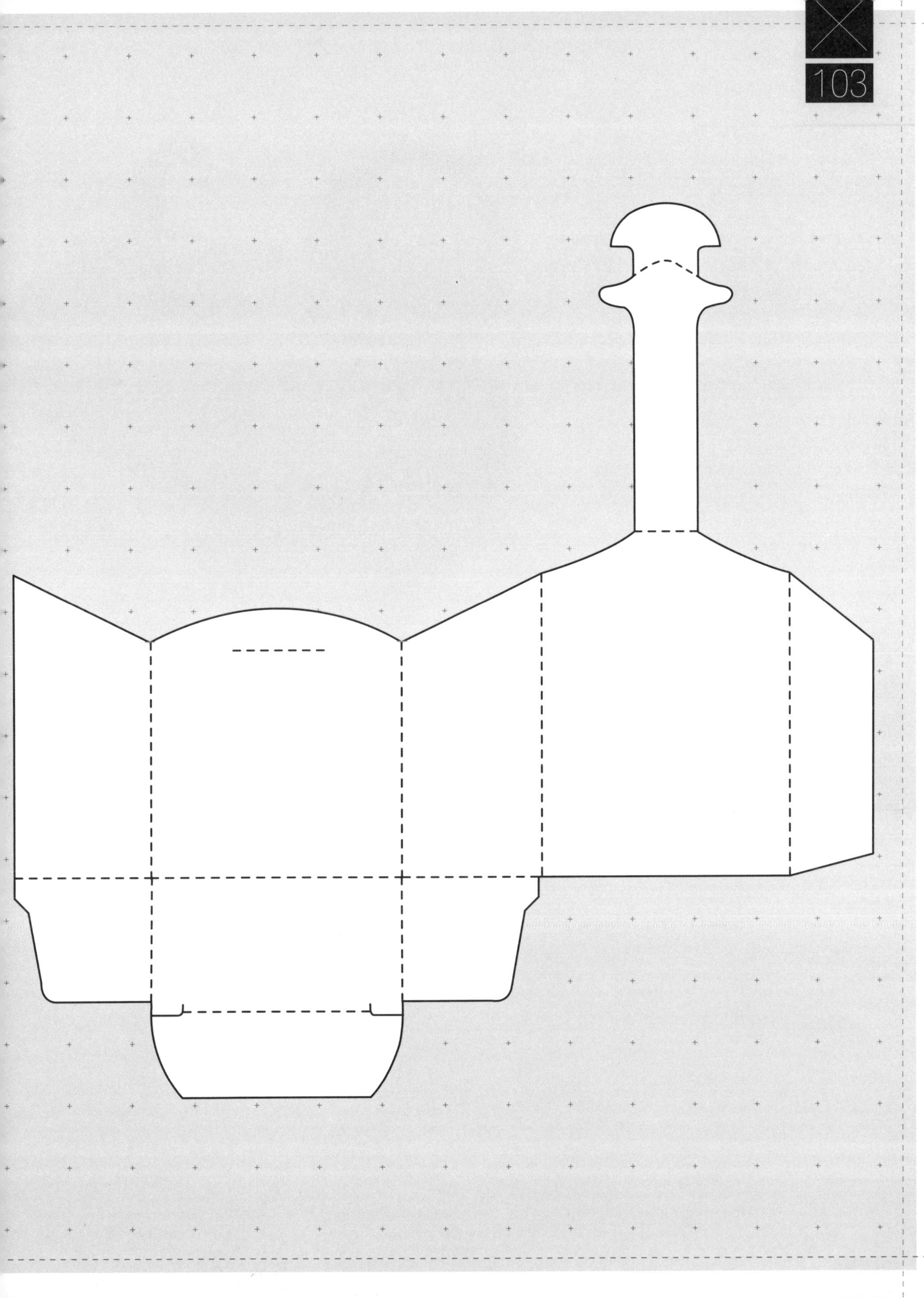

LUMBER

Design **Sandra Elizondo**

Inspired by the form of a log, this package design works with the concept of extracting its components in order to create different pieces while building an awareness for paper consumption and production. The most unique trait of these packets is their transformation into a clothes hanger, coaster, piggy bank, or storage container. The hanger/coaster pieces are engraved with the brand logo and a beautiful tree ring design which is visible once the two pieces come together to make the coaster.

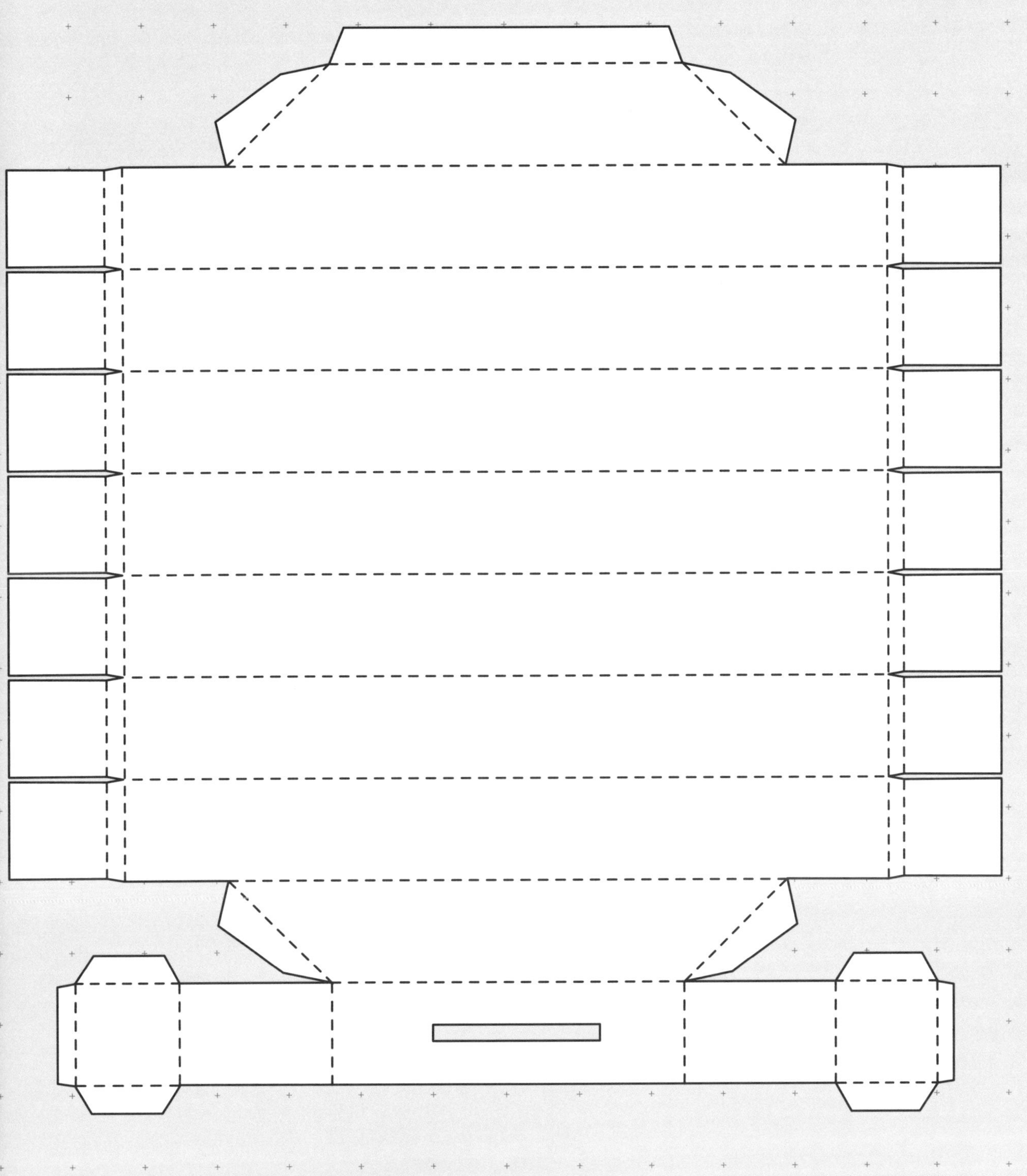

FURO SHIKI SWEETS PACKAGE

Design **Hada Tomoko**

The paper material was specially chosen to resemble a traditional Japanese food parcel wrapped with a Furoshiki (a traditional Japanese wrapping cloth). The packaging can be stored flat for easy storage. After the sweets are placed inside, the packet is fixed with a seal.

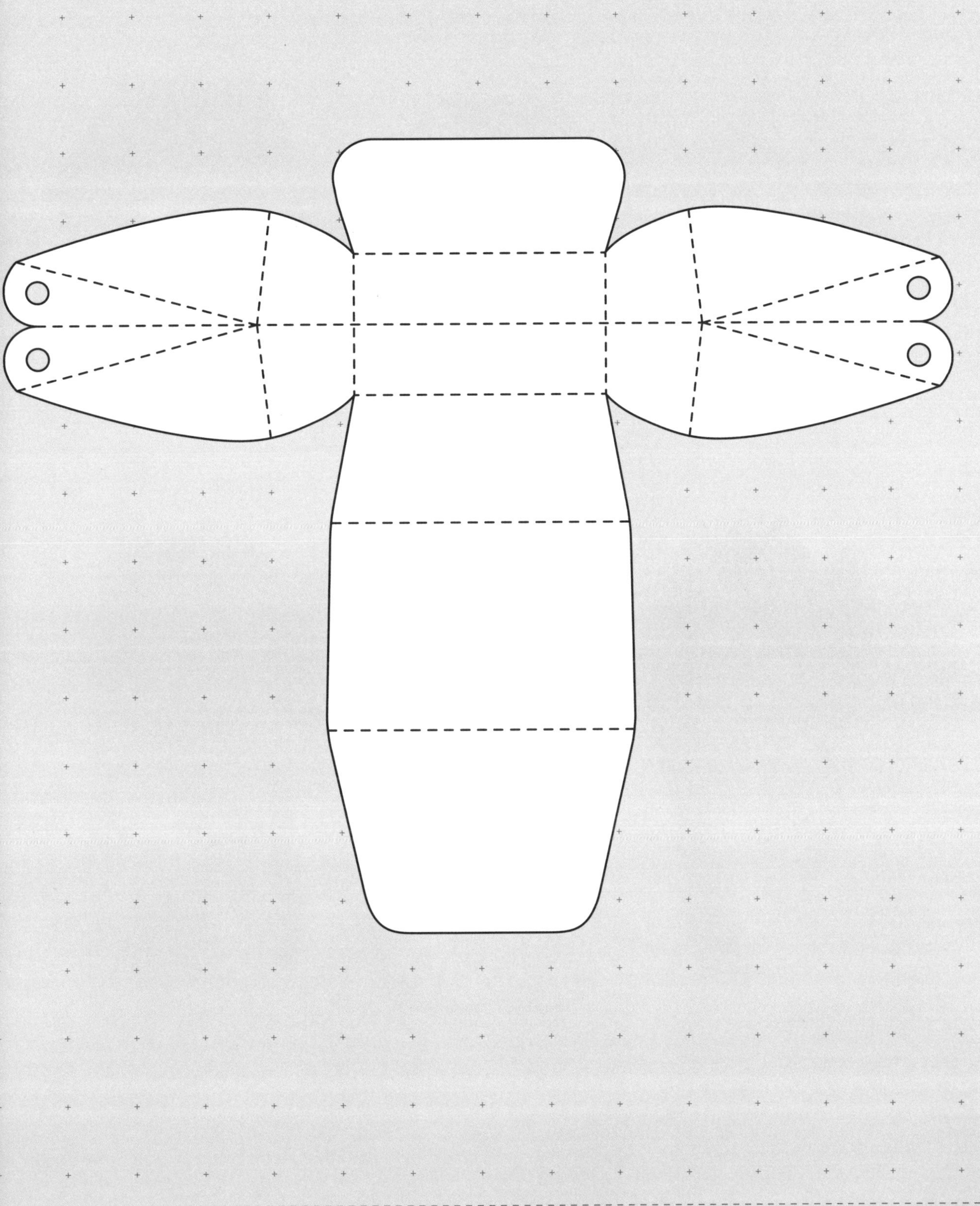

NIOBE BODY CARE

Design **Yana Carstens**

The objective of this design was to create an identity and packaging for a product in the cosmetics service industry. The hand bag shape of the package highlights the soft feminine touch of the brand.

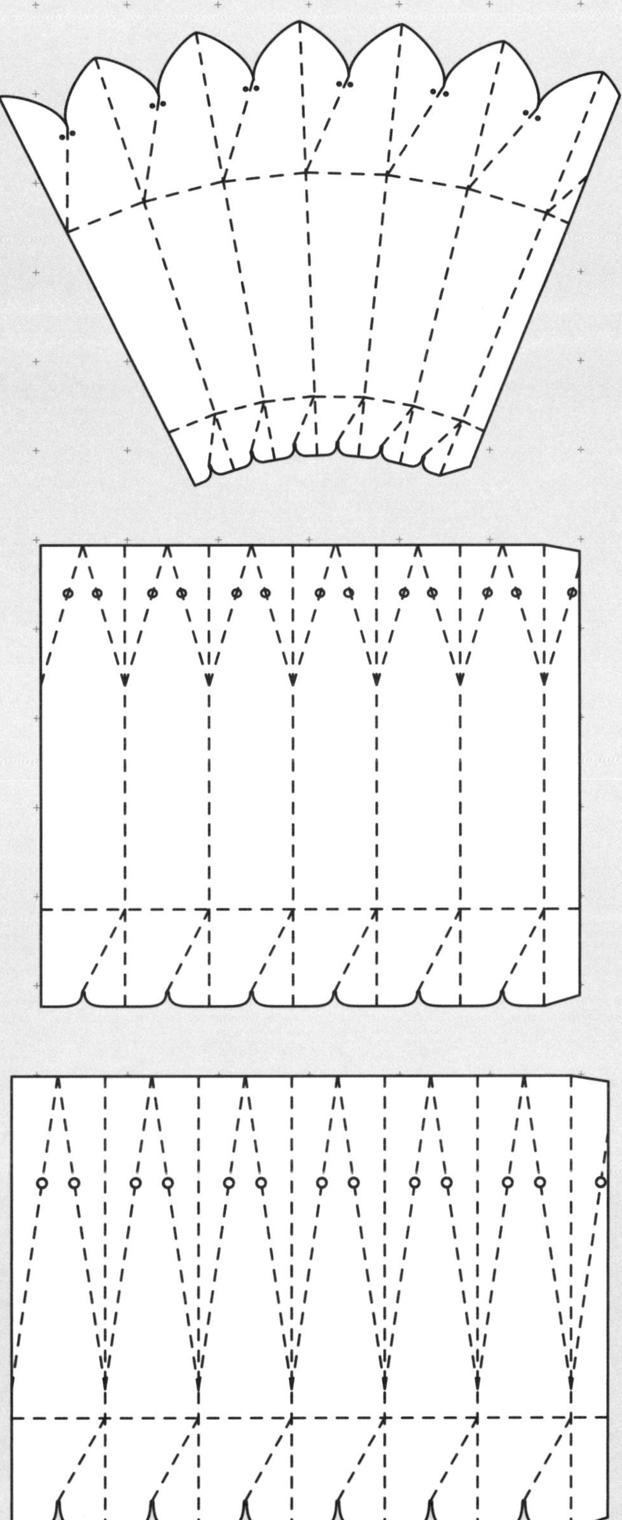

KIWI SHOP

Design Rezo Gamrekelidze

Kiwi is a brand that produces very unusual and colourful gift objects. It asks for a packaging that matches the spirit of its products and communicates the company's individual approach to each product. The packaging also meets the technical requirements for transporting papier-mâché animals including being sufficiently strong and even having holes to let the air circulate so that the products could dry out.

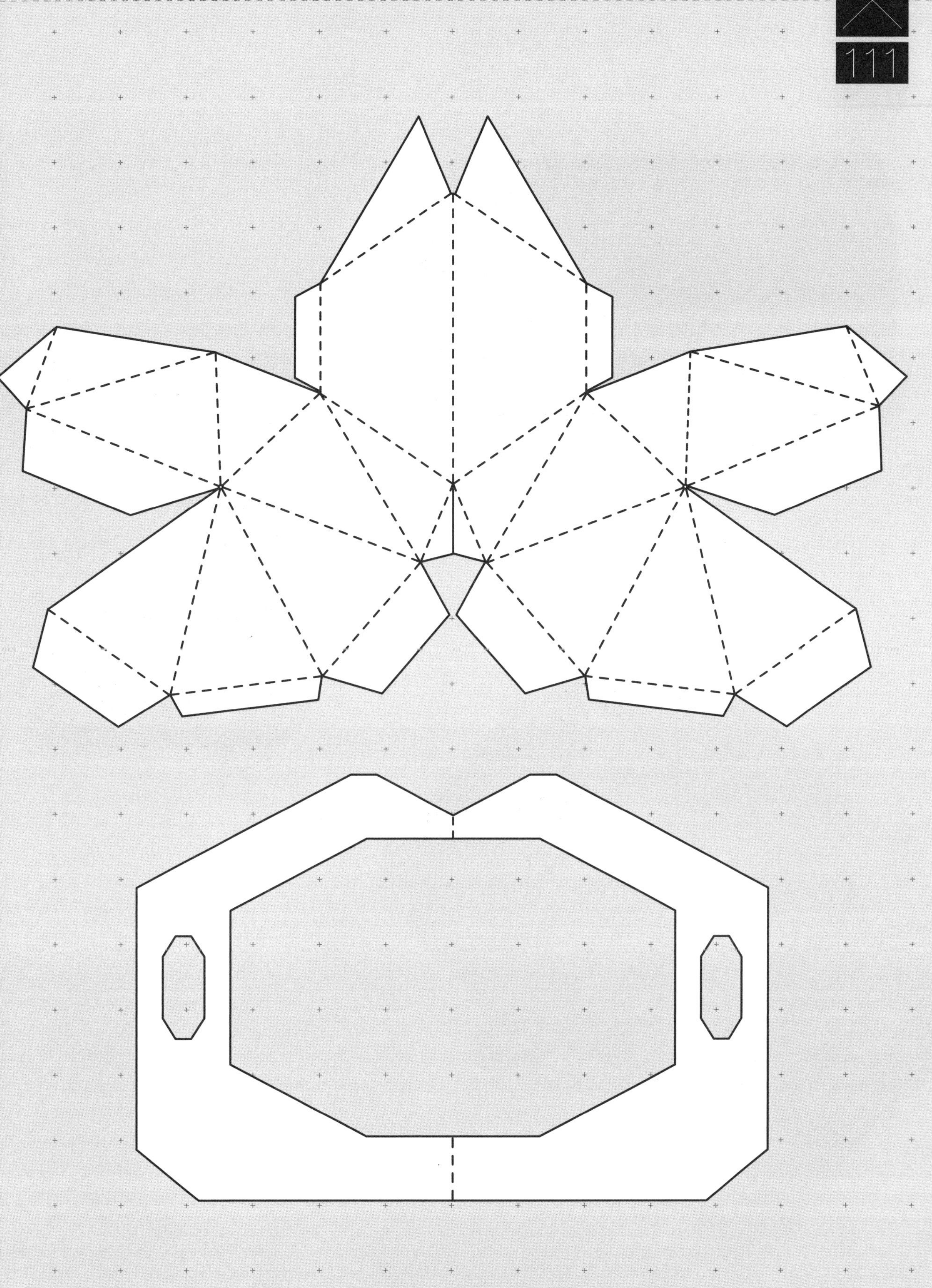

NIKE VAPOR STROBE EYEWEAR

Design **James Owen Design**

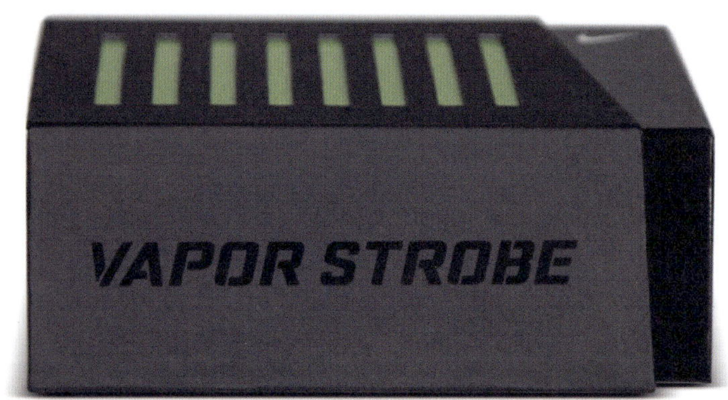

Innovative eyewear technology requires innovative package design. The core functional benefit of this packaging is communicated as soon as the user opens the box. Die-cut holes in the box top alternately hide and reveal or "strobe" the Sparq green rectangles as the lid is pulled up to uncover the eyewear case and accessories inside.

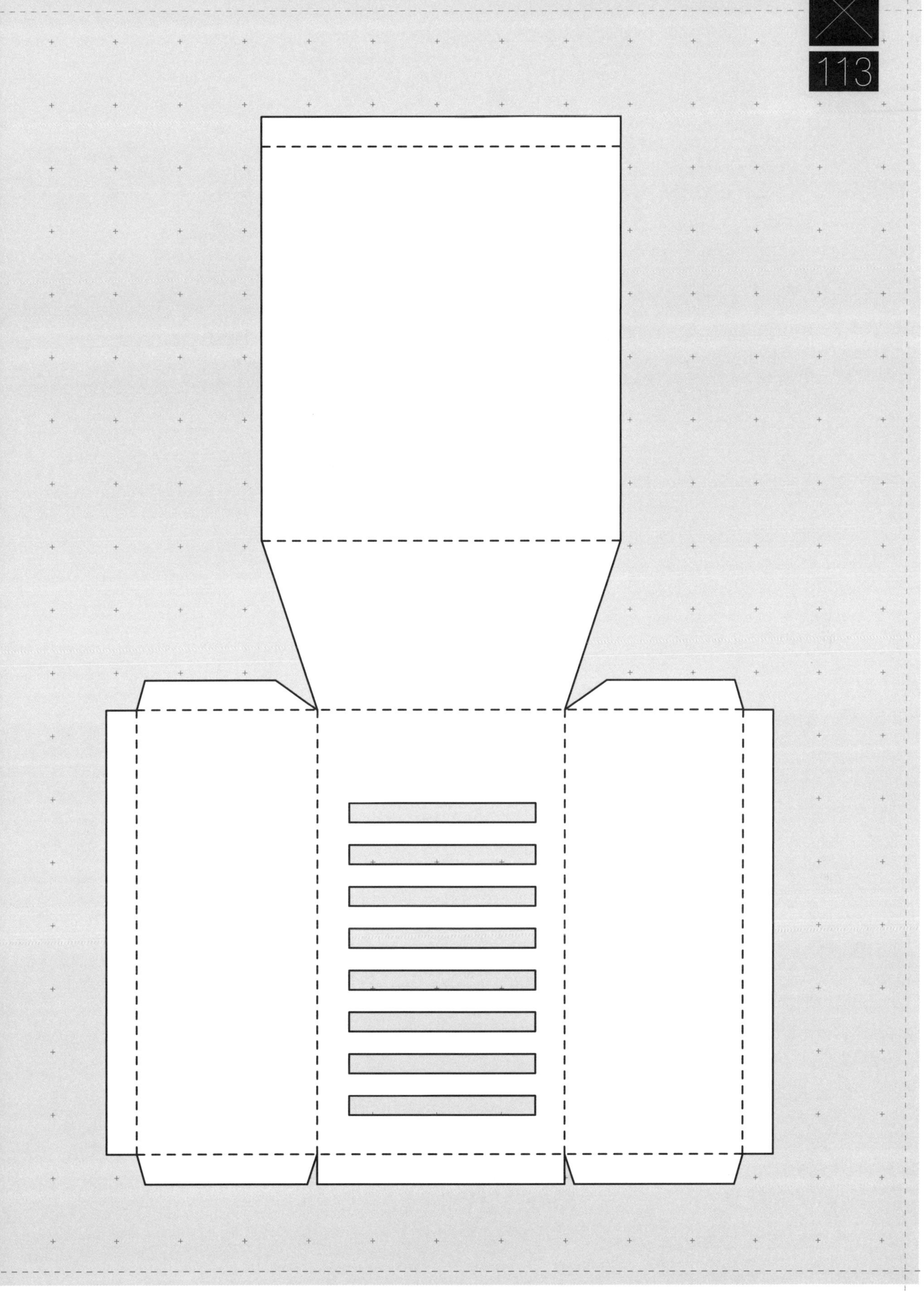

PAULIN'S HARDWARE FASTENERS

Design **Man Wai Wong**

This package design is a conceptual redesign for Paulin's hardware fasteners made from 100% recycled materials. The beauty of the container lies in the fusion of personalization, functionality and reusability. The boxes interlock to form a customized storage unit and each box can also be turned inside-out to form a solid-coloured container for use in the home. Constructed from one piece of paper without any adhesive, the package can be transported or stored flat.

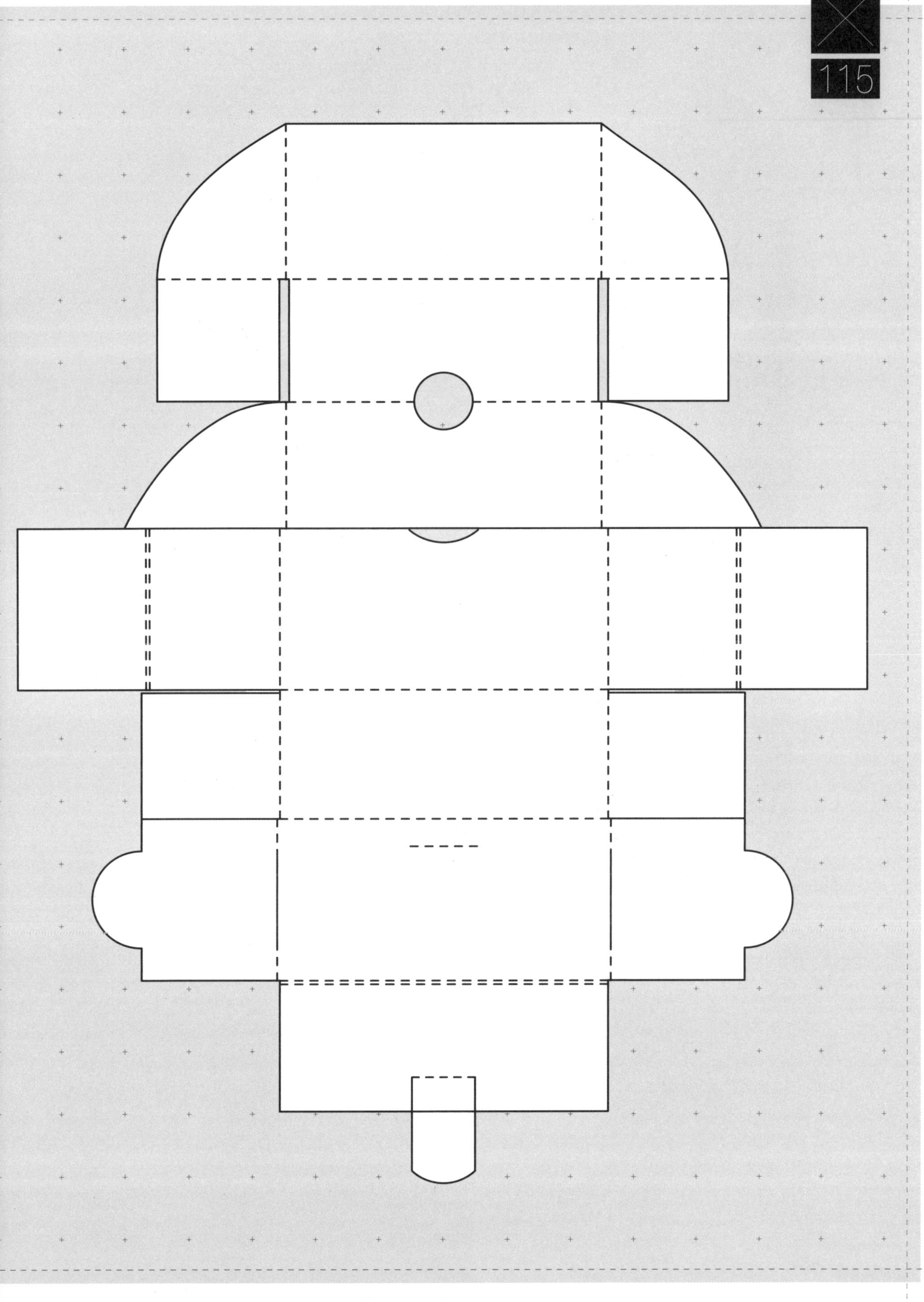

THE INTERESTING WINE

Design **Marin Balaic, Boris Matesic, Tanja Topolovec**

The basic idea was to create a package that would emphasize the bottle and not hide it inside a box. The designers also wanted to eliminate the need for a separate carrier bag by designing the packaging to perform this function. The result is a simple, elegant packaging that's very economical in terms of the materials used in its production. The package can be used to store, display and carry the wine.

PA, OLI I SUCRE

Design Sergio Ortiz Ruiz, Lluís Puig Camps

"Pa, oli i sucre" means "bread, oil and sugar" in Catalan. With ambition to reinvent the traditional Catalan snack, a new packaging was designed with a modern twist which is to allow the visibility of the product, and to let people enjoy their snack on the move without trouble. It is economical and sustainable because of its one-piece structure without the use of any adhesive.

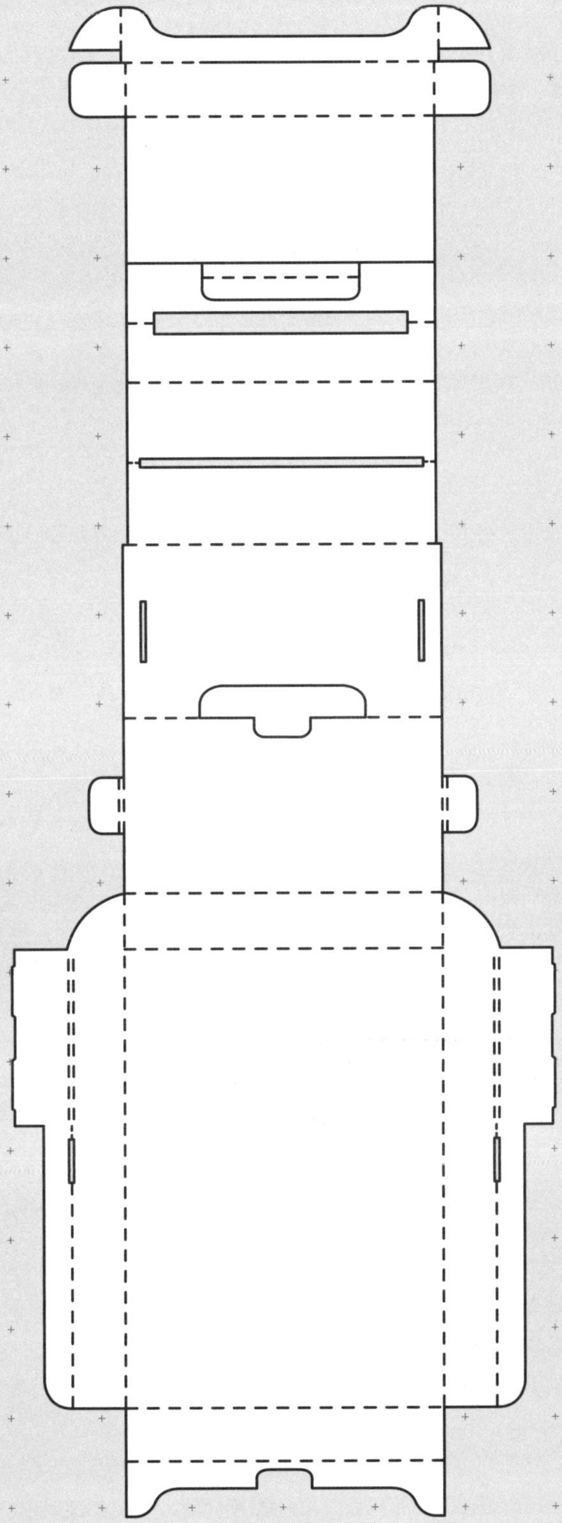

BUNCHES BY BLOMRUM

Design Helena Gyllensvärd

A sheet of paper might be the simplest packing solution for a bunch of flowers. The water resistant paper is brown on the outside with the brand image, and white inside where there is a communication between the shop and the client—in this case there are tips of how to take care of the flowers.

VINKARA WINES

Design **Yeşim Bakırküre**

As a rule, champagne and sparkling wines worldwide are produced primarily with France's most popular white and dark skinned varieties of grapes. But Vinkara decided to produce Yaşasın sparkling wine with Kalecik Karası grapes harvested at their vineyards. So its packaging also displays a perfect fusion of traditional and unconventional thinking: an elegant look with a flexible structure.

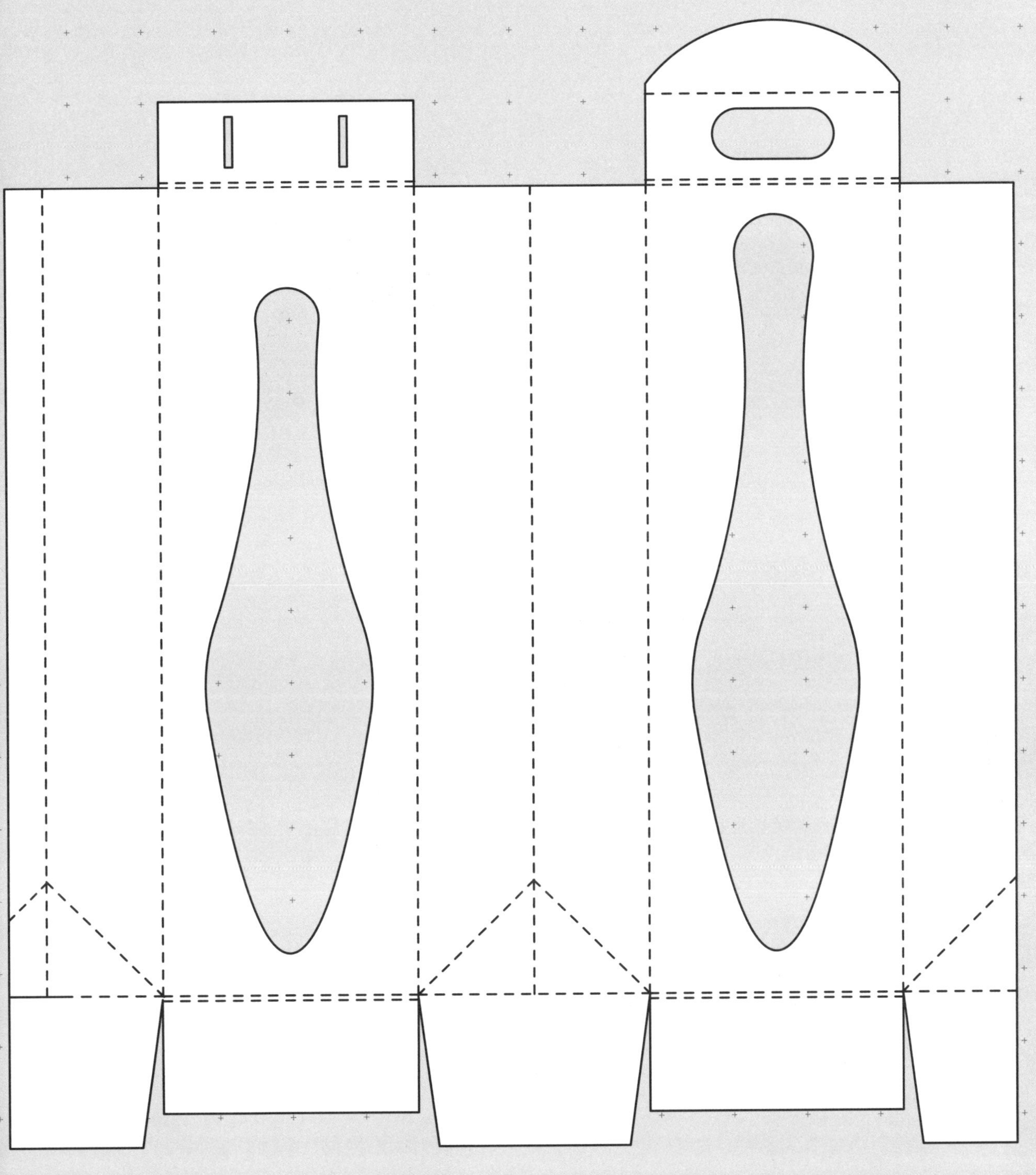

EGGS HIVE

Design **Chaiyasit Tangprakit**

Eggs Hive is an egg packaging inspired by the structure of beehive. The hexagon form greatly enhances the strength of the box, since it can bear weight better than any other structure. The package is made of kraft paper, which is raw, strong and eco-friendly, and assembled without the use of glue.

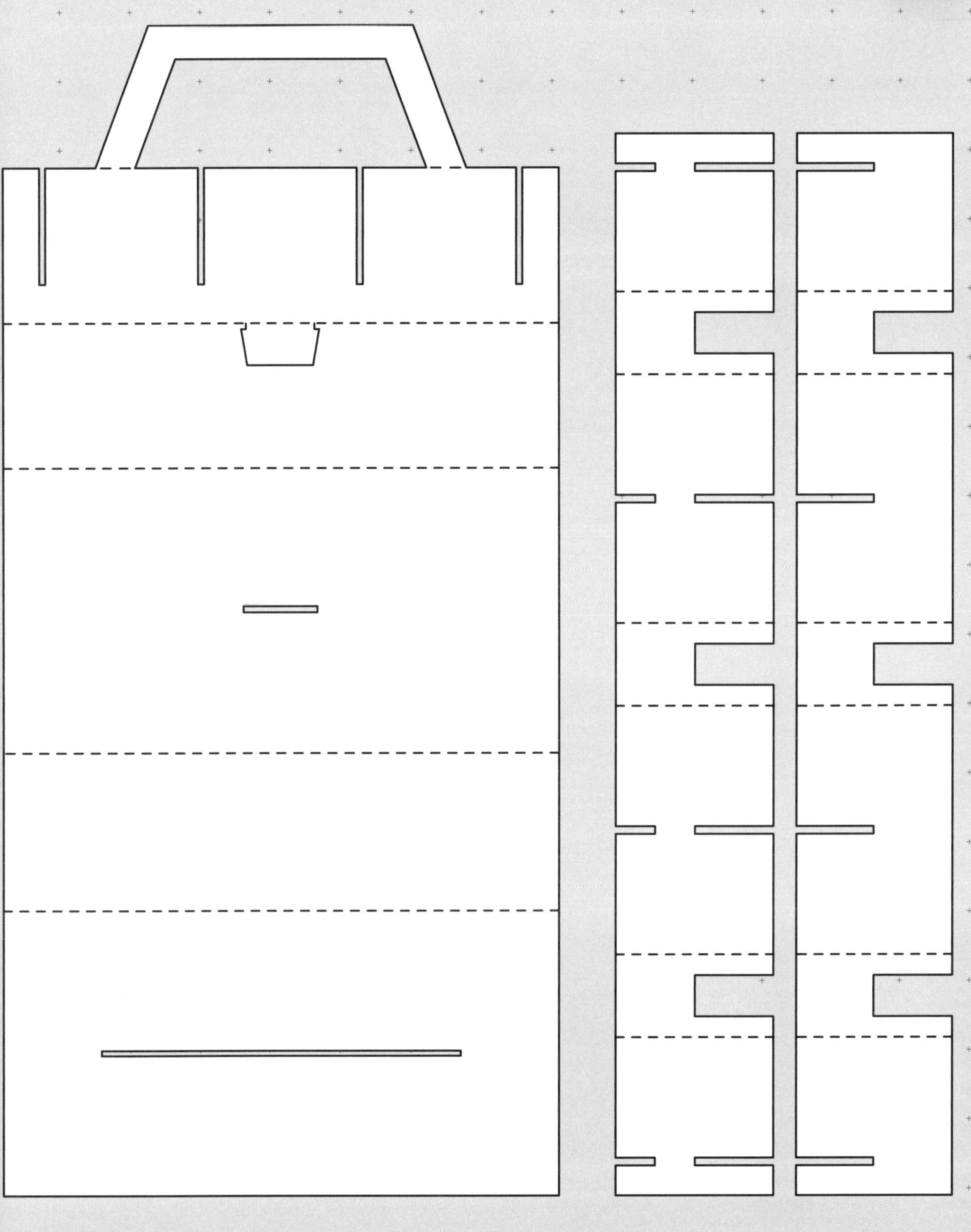

FUNAZUSHI

Design Shuji Hikawa

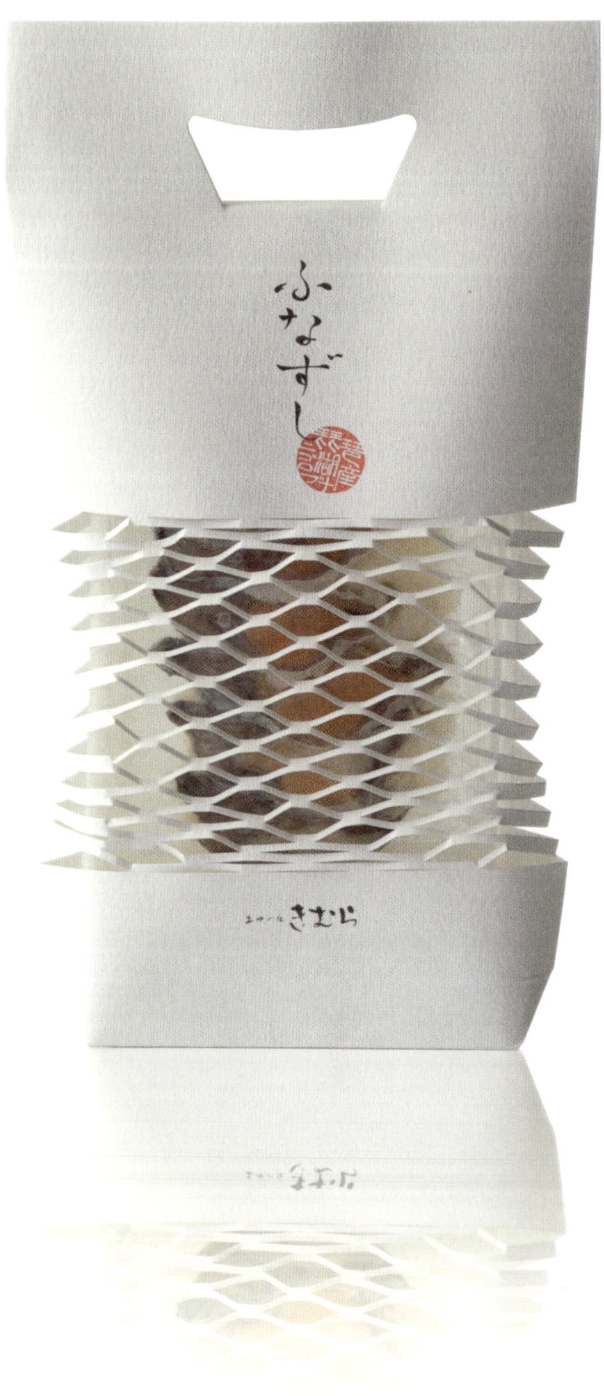

This package design gracefully shows funazushi in vacuum packing, a traditional food in Shiga prefecture of Japan. There are slits on the package and they open up when the bag is loaded. The pattern formed looks like fishing net and scales and it also reminds people of many funazushi arranged on a tub. Another thing worth noting is the handle taking the shape of a fin.

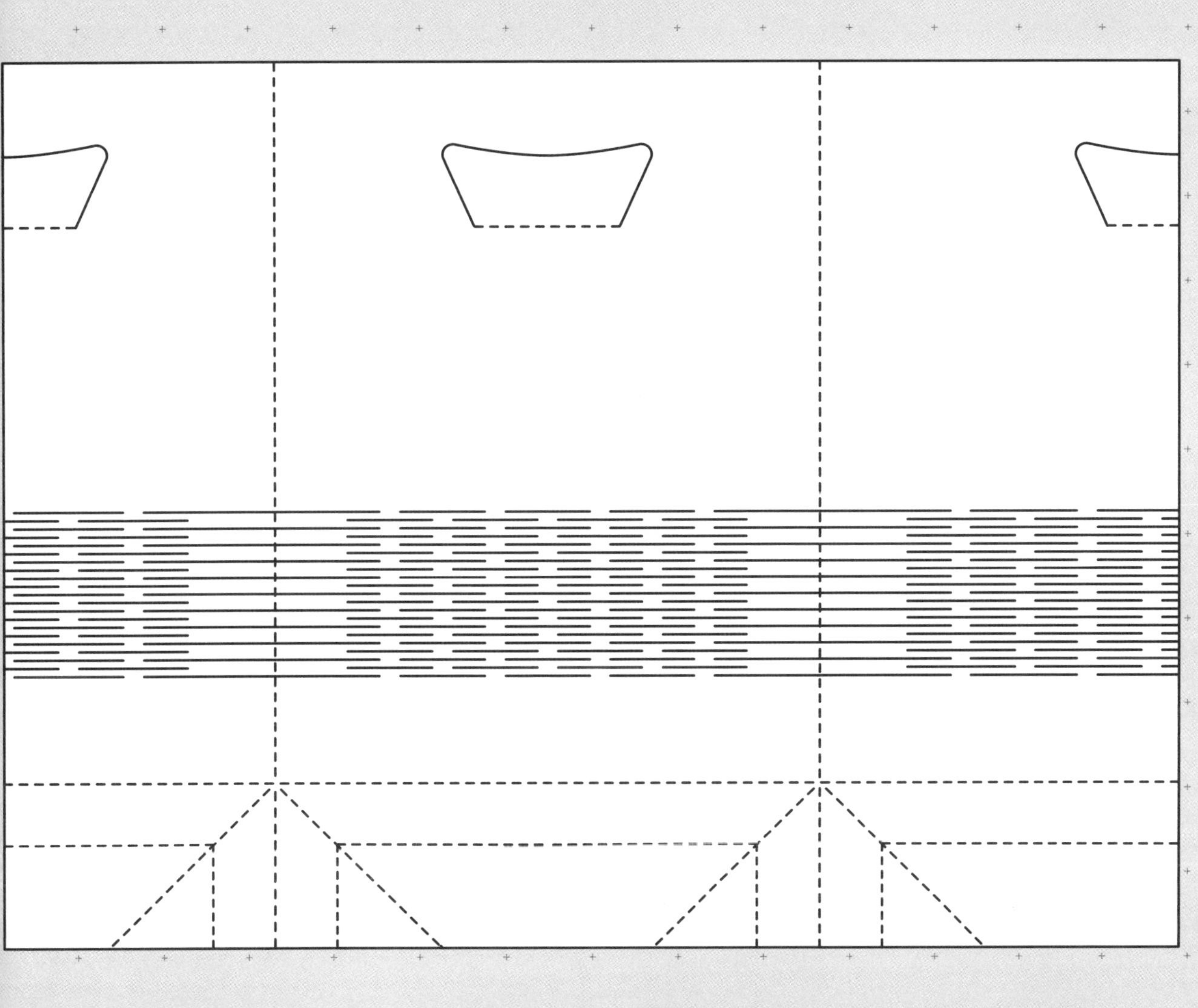

TÉ QUIERO TEA

Design **Daniela Hurtado Caicedo**

"Té Quiero" phonetically, in Spanish, can either mean "I love you" or "I want tea". Inspired by this, the designer created a package that provokes the feeling of love and gives the tea packaging an emotional touch. The flower bud takes the shape of the tea that it represents, while the "blooms" unveil petals that each houses a handmade tea bag.

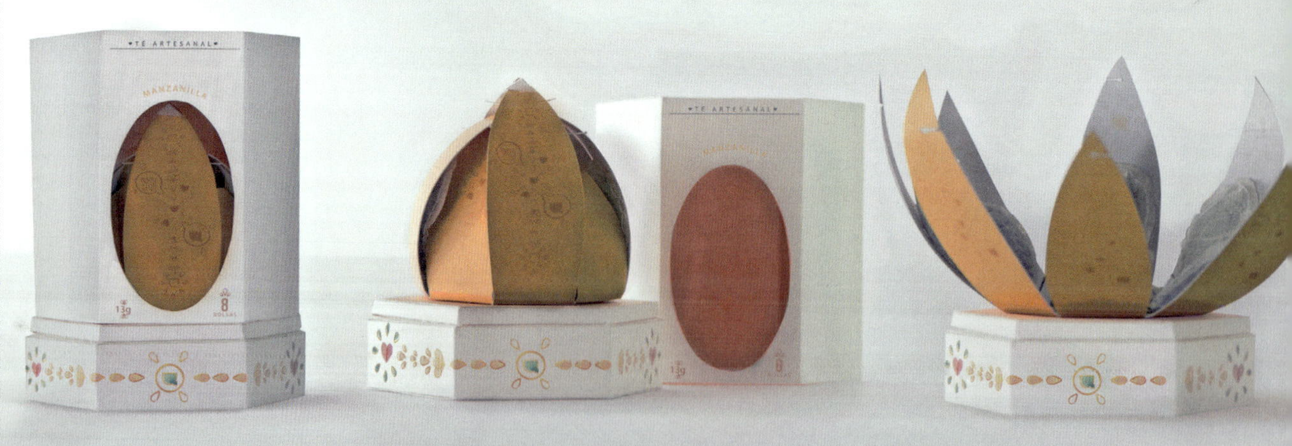

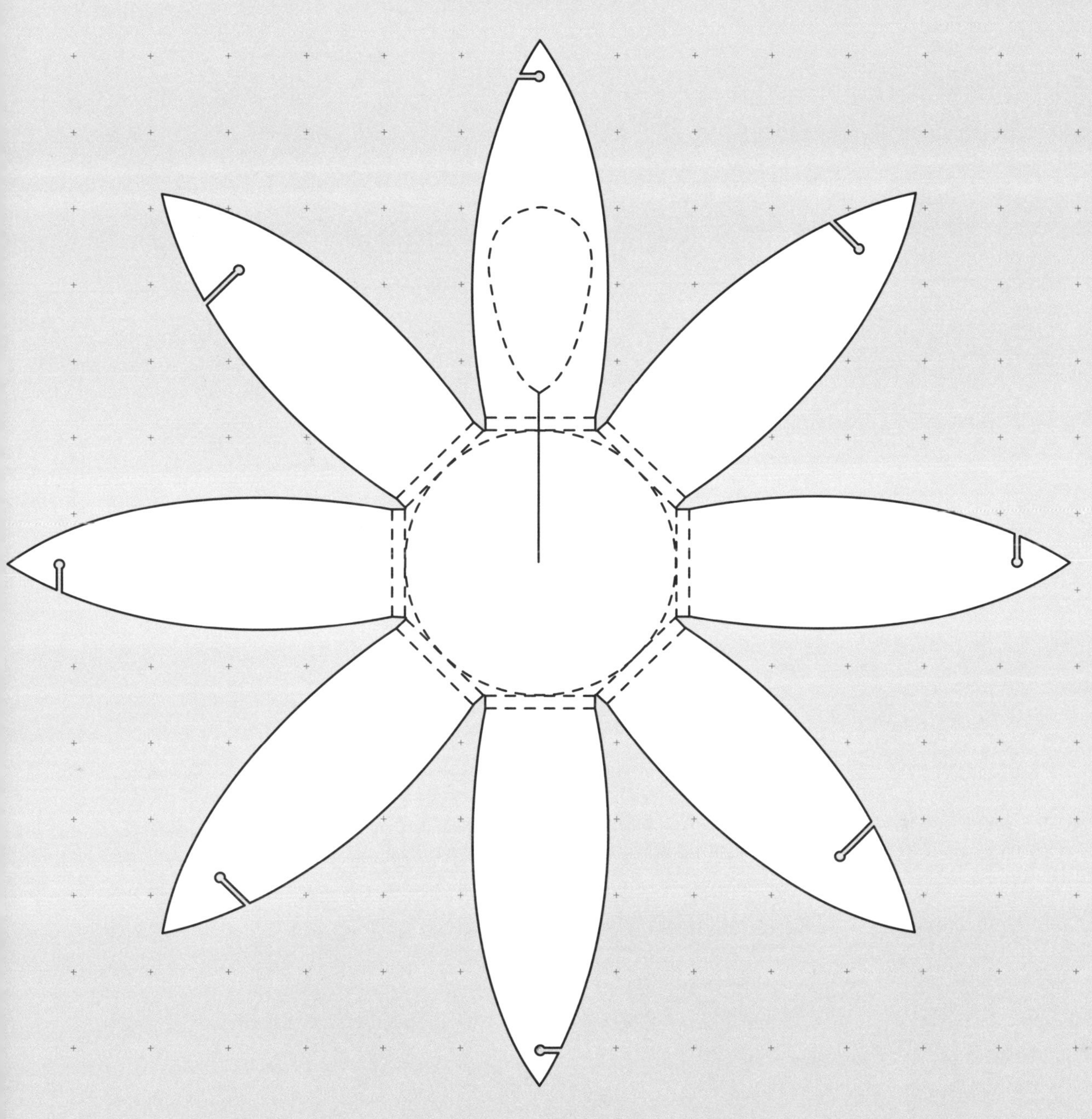

SUSHI BOX

Design **Sergio Ortiz Ruiz**

The packaging is comprised of four boxes for starters and main courses and two boxes for desserts, including corresponding wooden chopsticks and napkins. The materials chosen are from Canson, a renowned art papers producer. The idea was to create an elegant, unconventional package as a tasteful touch to the Japanese food.

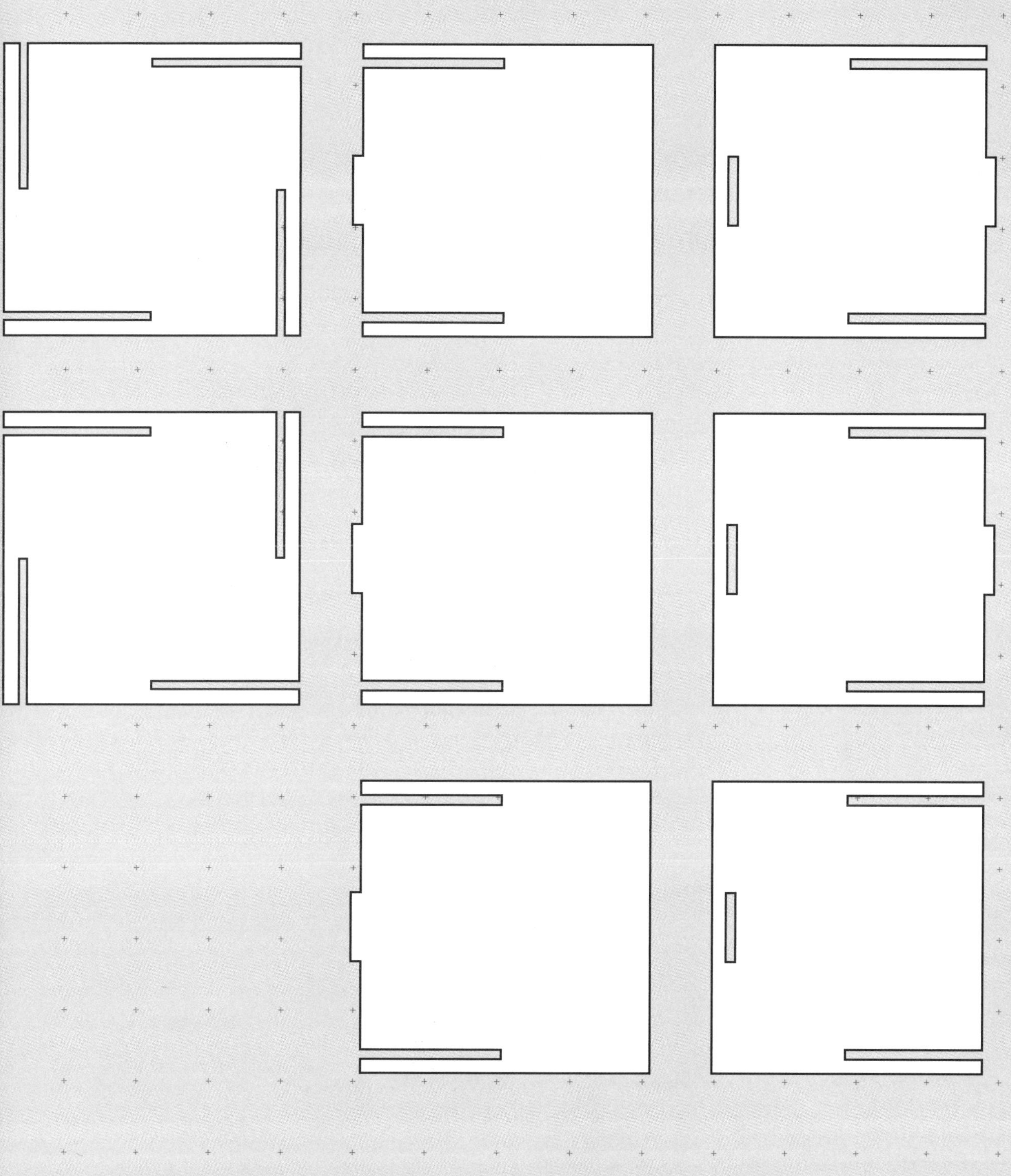

PHOTOY

Design **Sergio Ortiz Ruiz**

This is a project aimed to highlight the prestige and quality of a popular toy from the 1980s. The package is made of corrugated cardboard, fluorescent paperboard and metallic silver. It also includes two magnet closures and a hook for easy display at the point of sale.

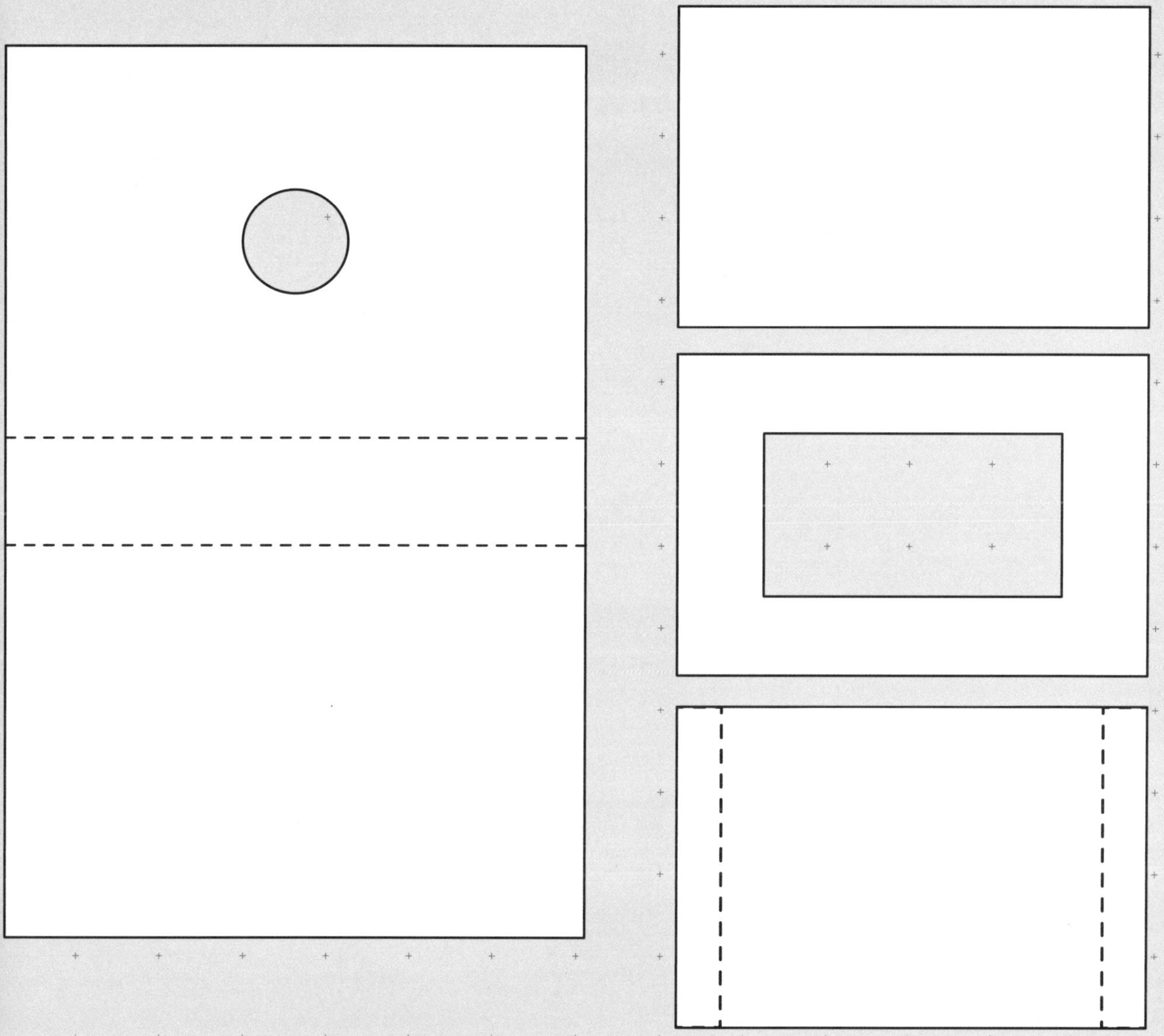

CELLPHONE PACKAGING DOCK

Design Andrew Zo

The designer believes that the unboxing ritual can enhance the brand experience. The idea of the cellphone packaging is to create a package that has a second life after unboxing. Upon opening the box, the packaging itself can be transformed into a makeshift dock.

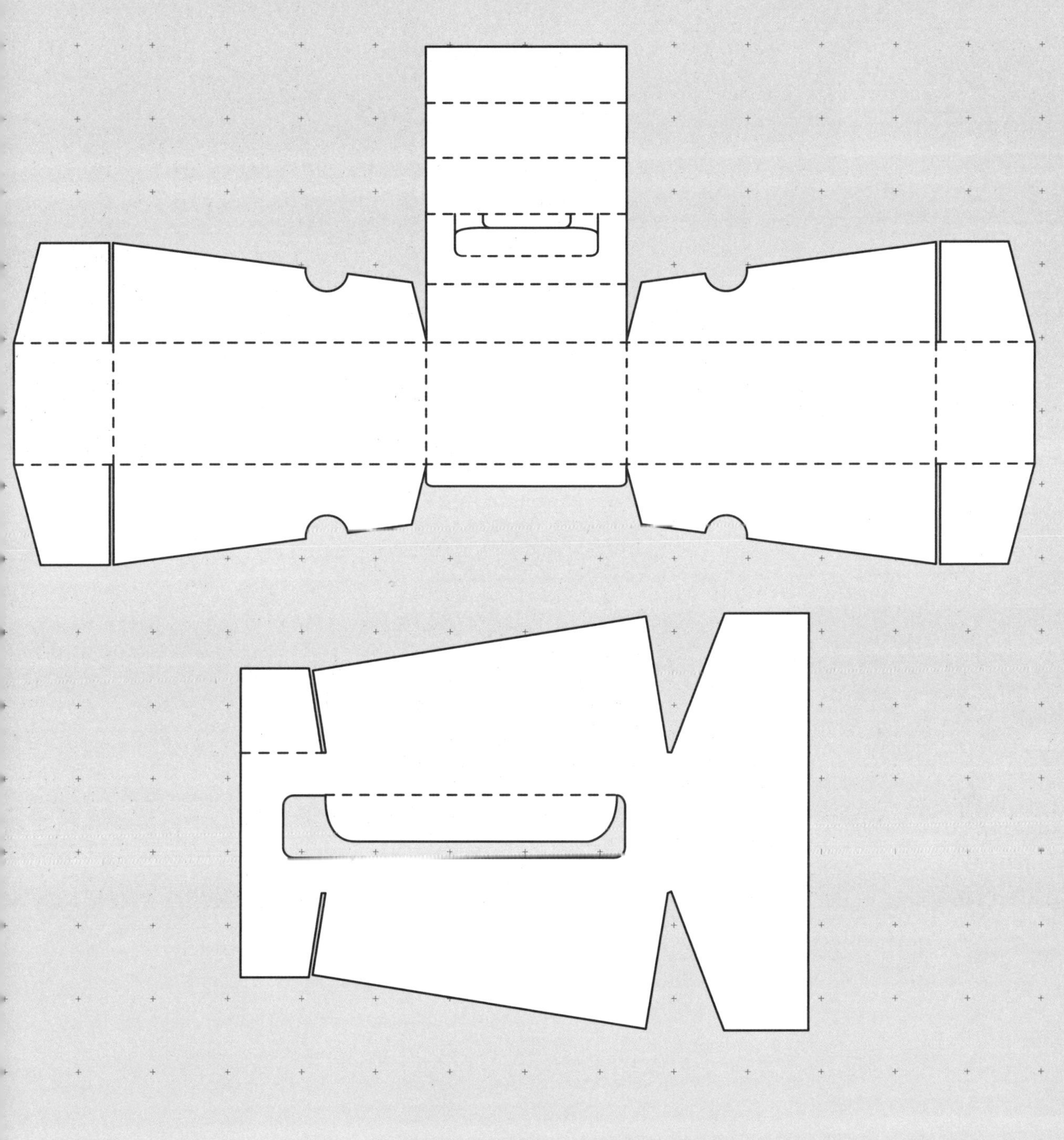

BLANC

Design　Fildel Castro

Blanc is a brand of delicacies who aims to provide an experience beyond the sense of taste. The packaging was designed to reflect the luxury brand's core values: innovation, elegance and excellence.

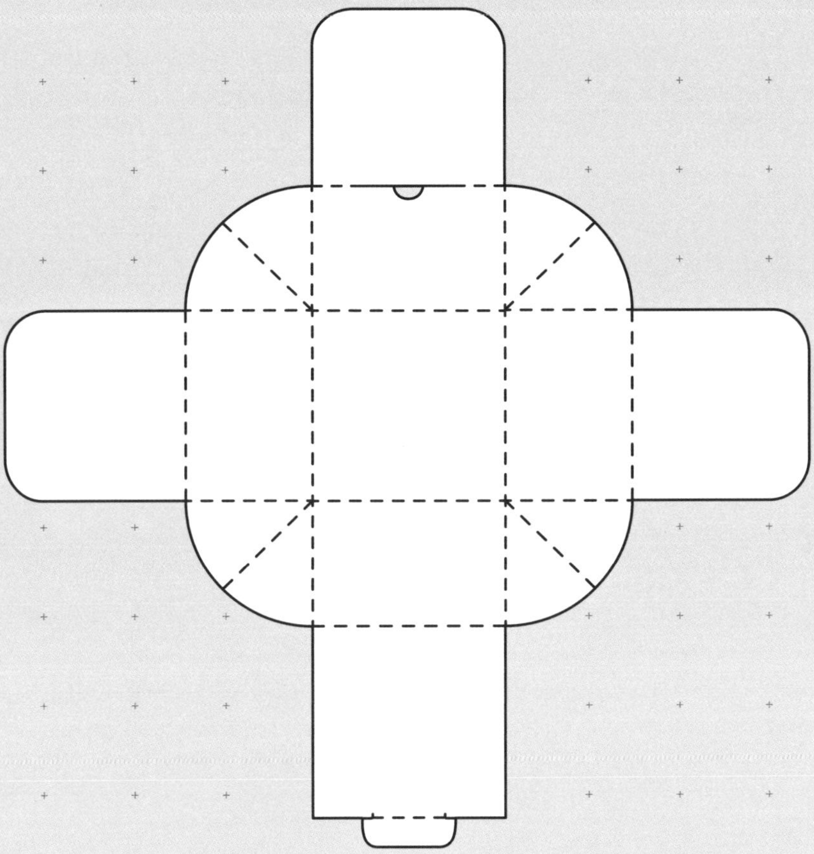

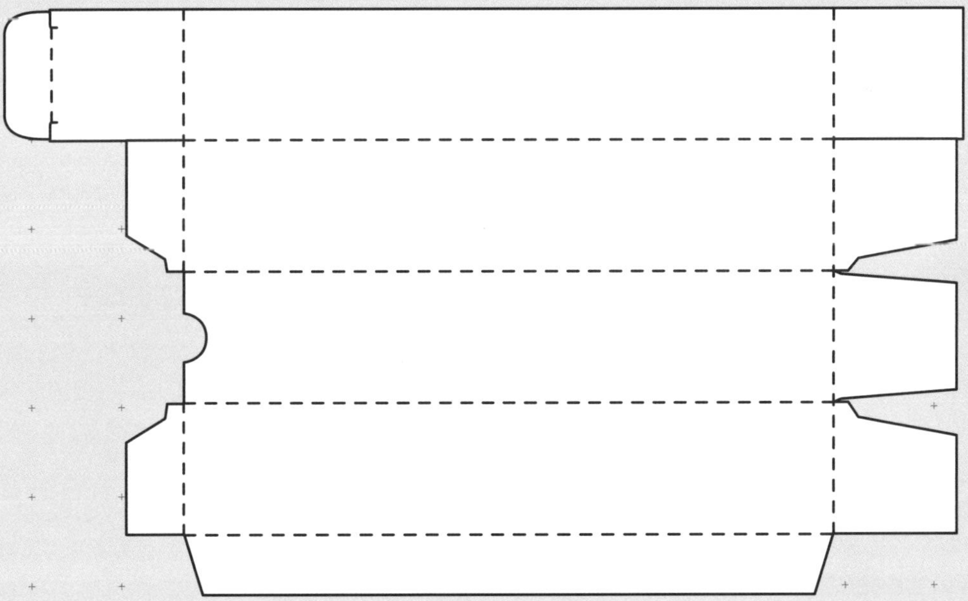

OLDWHEEL FARM CREAM & SUGAR

Design **Cedrik Ferrer**

Oldwheel Farm is a fictional business that produces contemporary food products based on the classic and organic values. An original packaging structure has been developed for one of their products, where it shows an interpretation of vintage milk can. The goals are to incorporate Oldwheel's classic values in a contemporary form through their products, and to come up with a unique package that is original and meaningful.

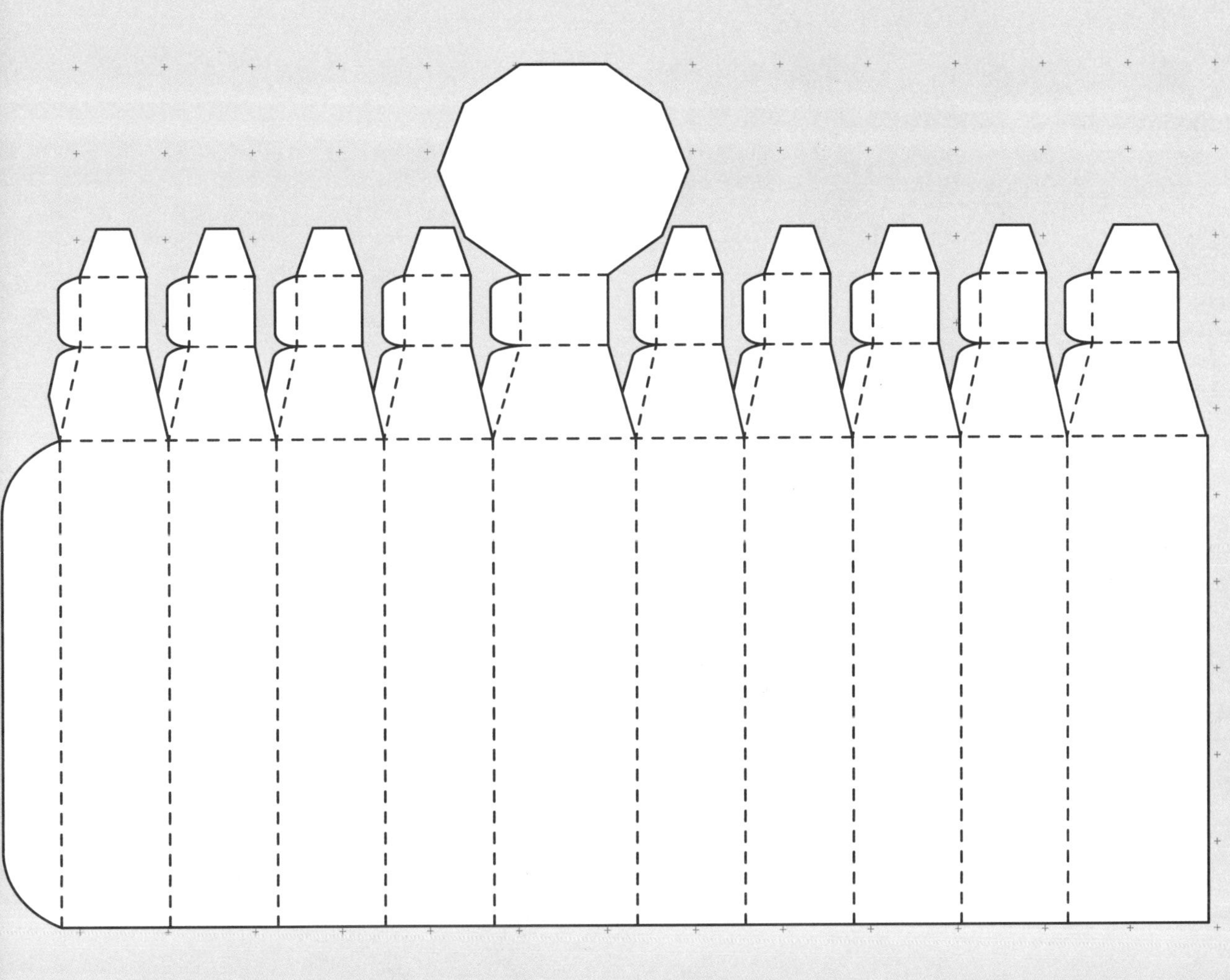

KOALA BEER & KANGAROOT BEER

Design **Charlotte Olsen**

The designer applied a handmade style inspired by Australian aboriginal art in designing the beer package. The colour palette was not a casual choice but a representation of Australia's iconic blue sea and orange desert.

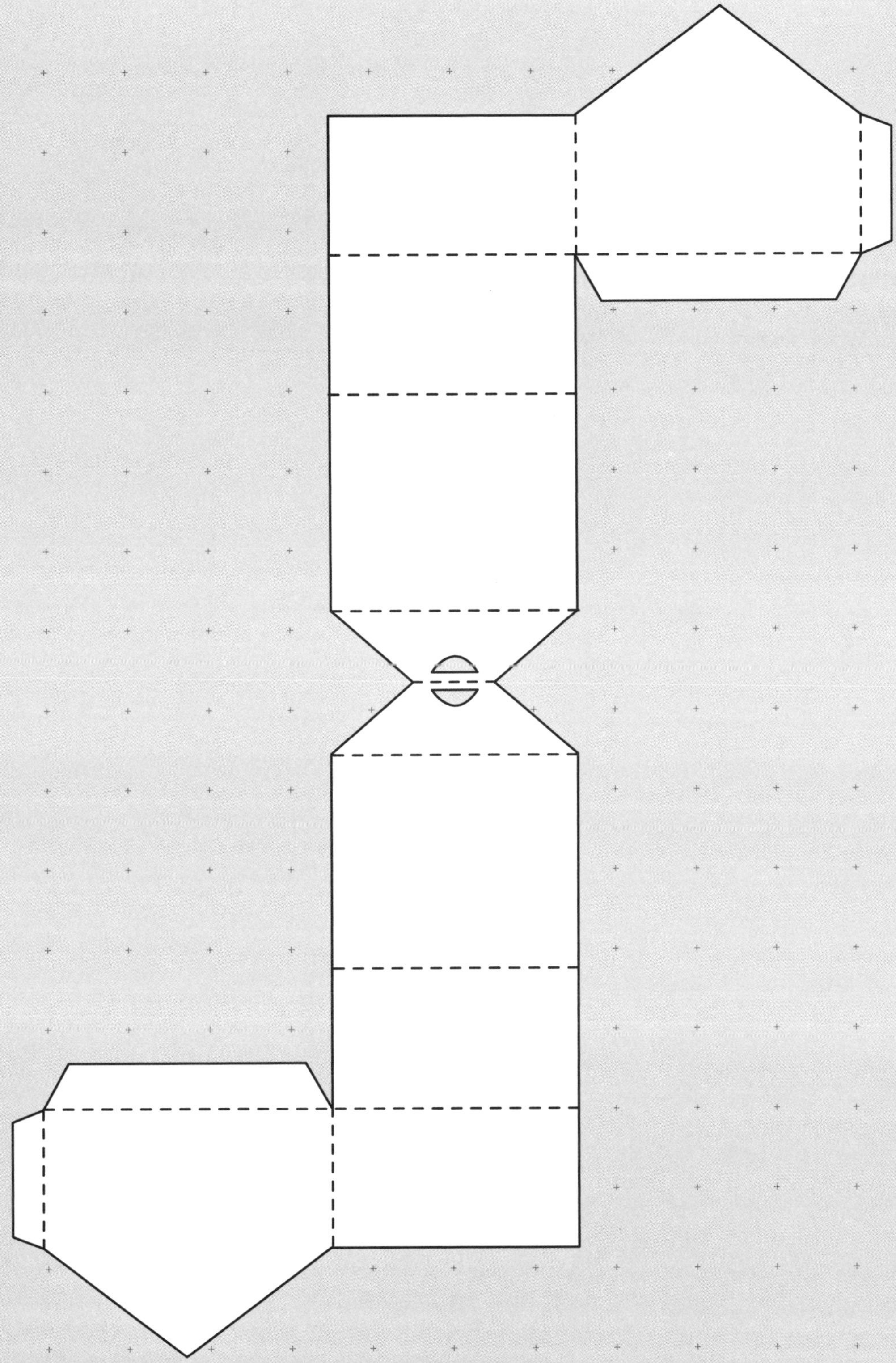

COCONUT WATER PACKAGE

Design **Ankur Sahay, Sabyasachi Kuila**

The objective was to promote packaged coconut water which is believed to be equally hygienic and refreshing as natural coconut water. An innovative and ergonomic package that retains the aesthetics of coconuts was developed to attract younger consumers.

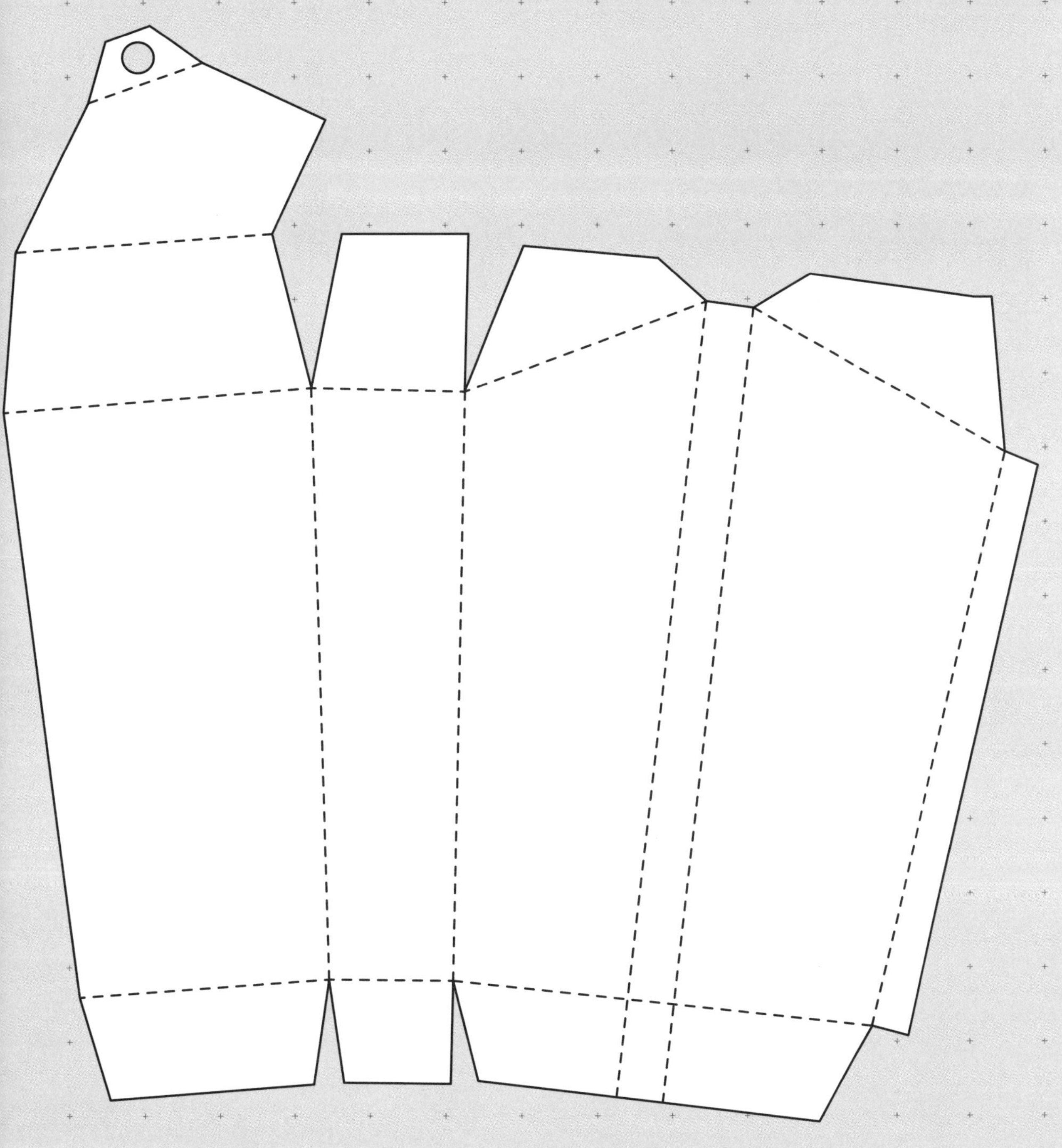

FUJIYAMA COOKIE

Design Yoko Maruyama

FUJIYAMA COOKIE is a cookie shop near Lake Kawaguchi at the foot of Mount Fuji. The logo design was inspired by Japanese brush painting and Western-style calligraphy. The package took the shape of the motif-based logo. To introduce the taste of freshly baked cookies, parts of the package are made transparent to allow the customers to see the cookies before opening the package.

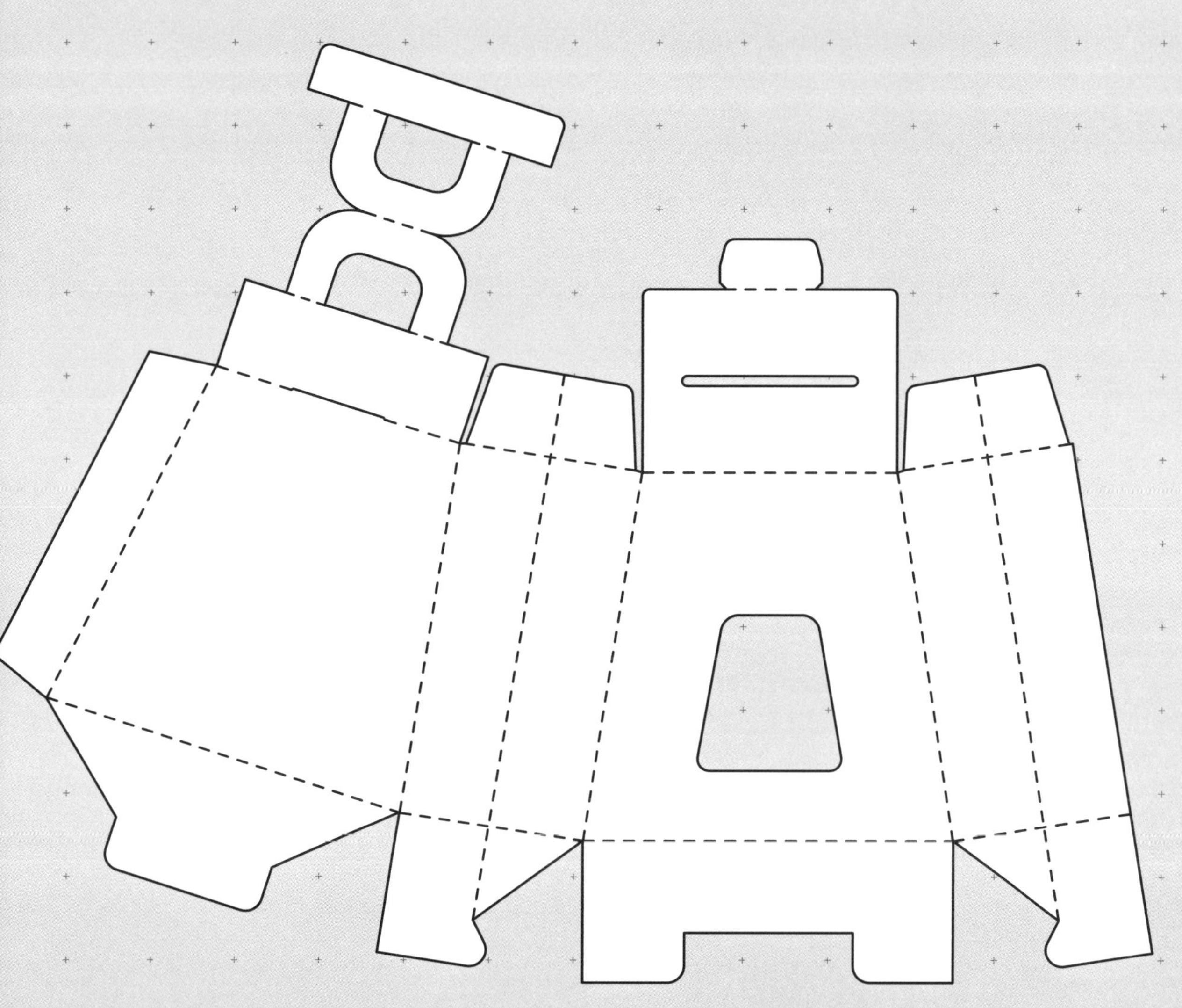

BRETT A PORTER

Design Gerlinde Gruber

Brett a Porter is a picnic box for Roughcutboard. The simple and cost-saving cut was made out of corrugated cardboard and needs no adhesive. The design offers optimal characteristics for presentation because of the open cut. The shape and material of the product can be seen and touched without opening the package. The grip hole makes way for easy carrying.

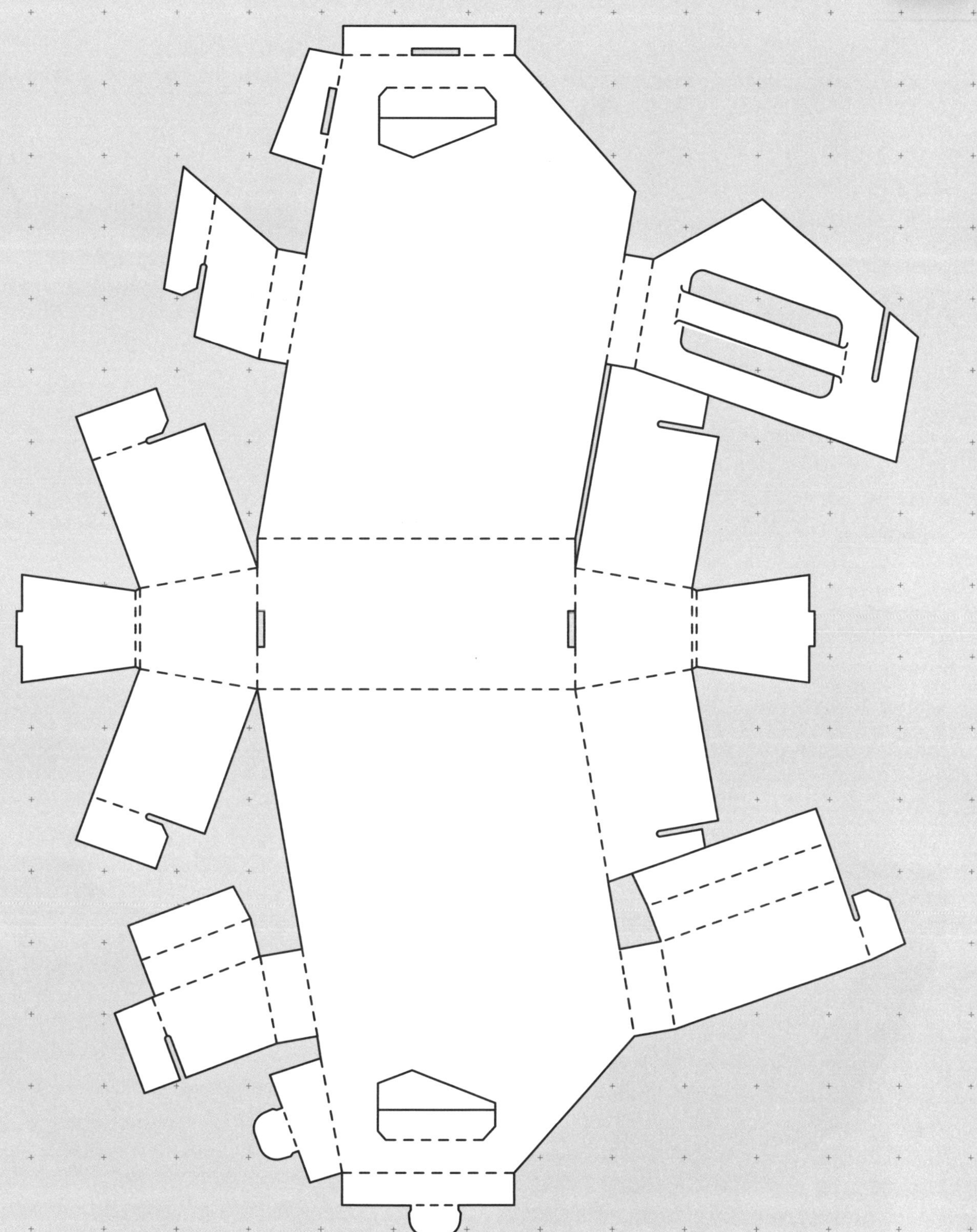

AUFSCHWUNG SWING

Design **Gerlinde Gruber**

This package was for the swing designed by Viennese designer Michael Hensel. The simple package made out of corrugated cardboard without the use of adhesive is economical. The design offers optimal characteristics for the presentation because of the open cuts, which allow the product to be viewed and touched.

KOLOR GRISSINI & DIP

Design Zsófi Ujhelyi

The task was to design a food packaging system for Kolor Bar, which holds grissini and/or chips and four types of sauce. The package had to be disposable yet eco-friendly. This disposable package was designed to be easily held in your hand and consumed for takeaway. The additional four sauce pockets could flexibly open and close to meet different needs in serving bar food.

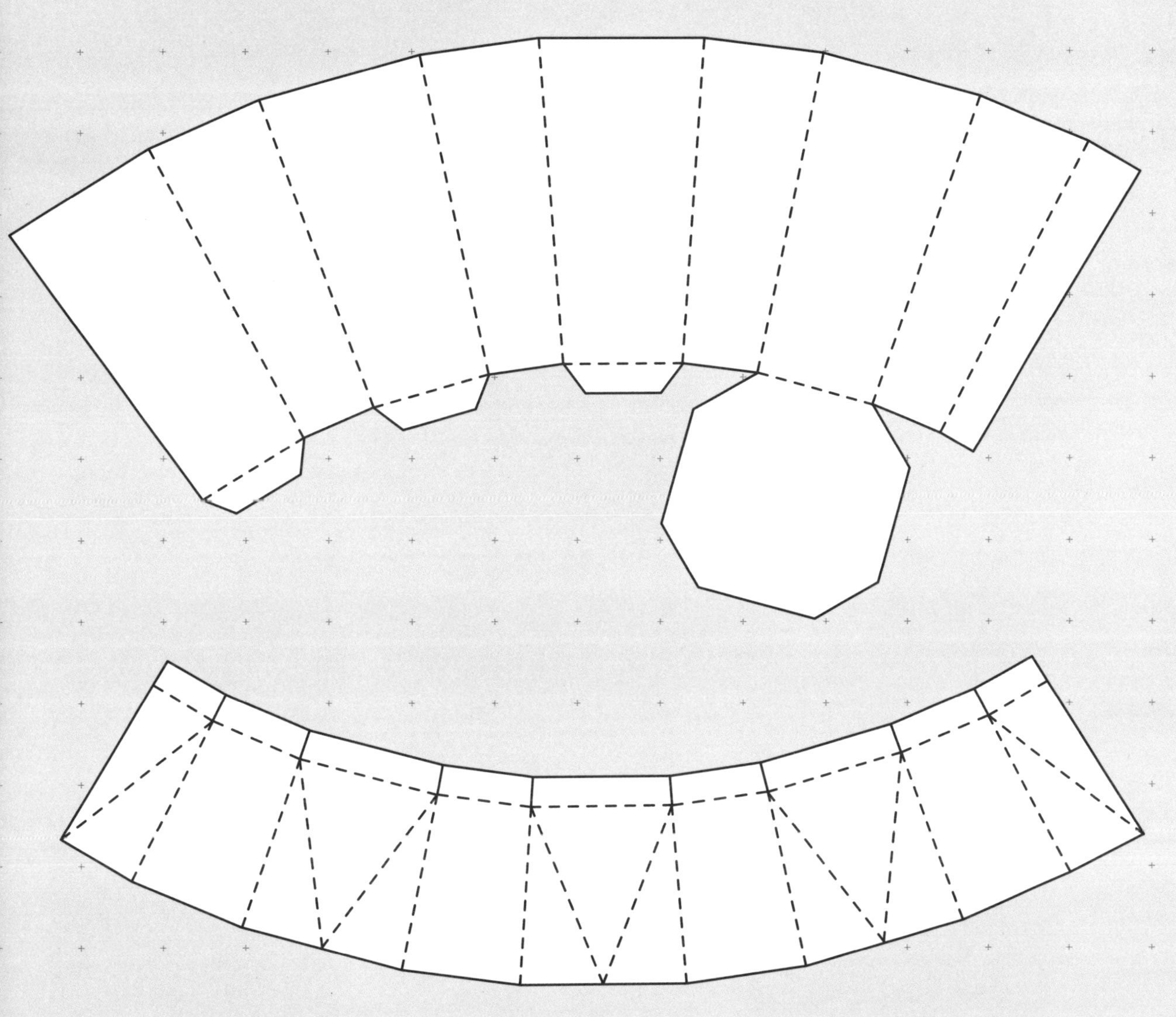

BARBOZA

Design Maksim Arbuzov

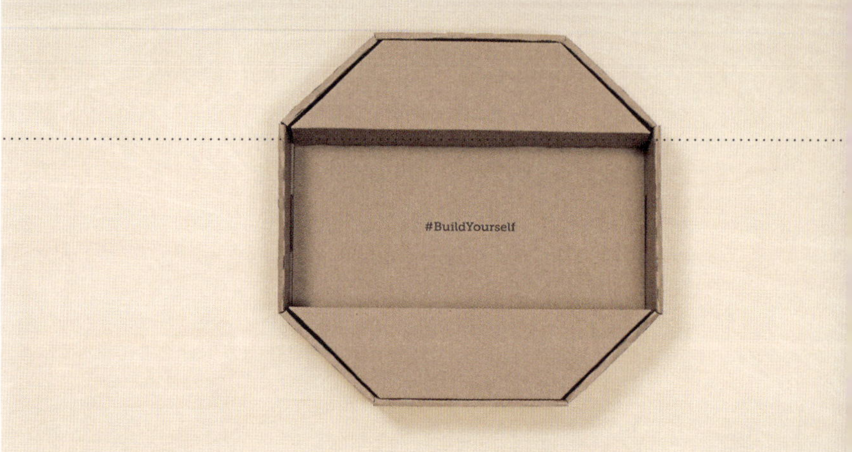

This box made with sustainable materials is 100% recyclable. The print was coloured with water-based paint and the adhesive is made from potato starch. The pure vegetable base provides a health-friendly packaging alternative to PVC bags.

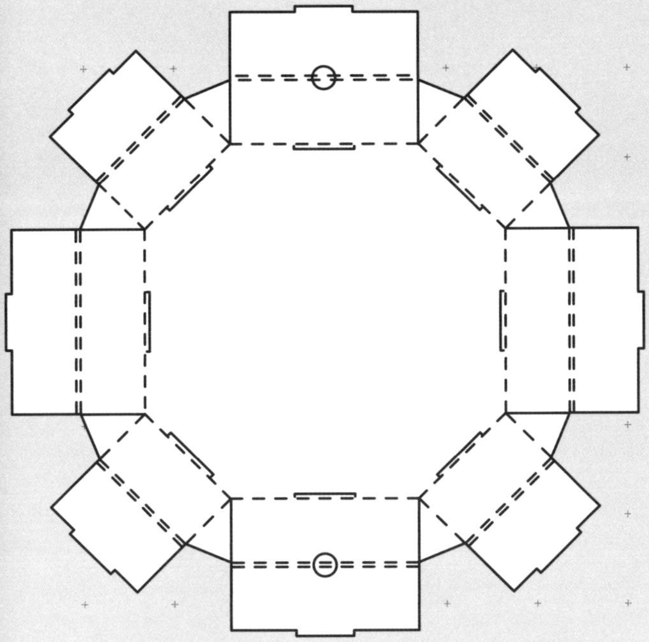

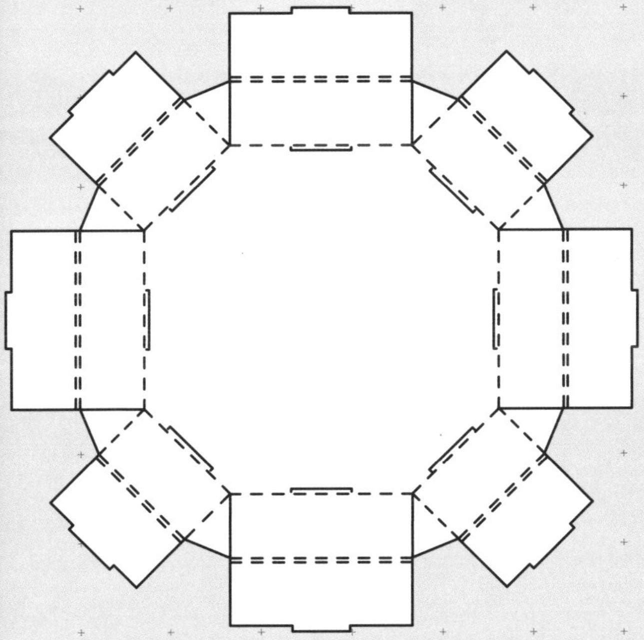

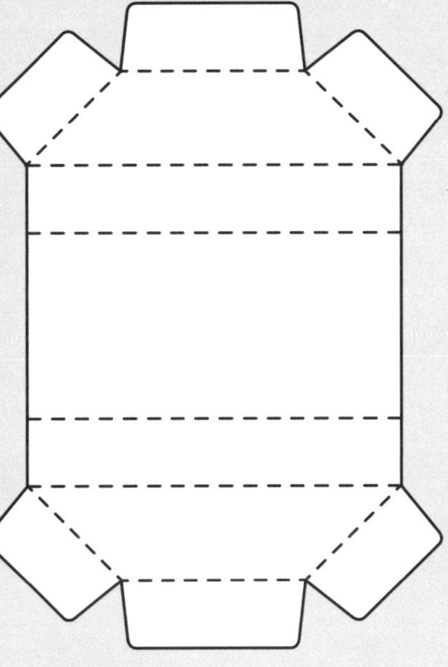

THE MESSIAH IS BACK

Design Iwona Duczmal, Daniel Naborowski

Orange the Juice is a Polish avant-garde band famed for their eclectic approach to music composition. The limited edition of their second album is packaged as a pop-up presentation box holding the CD with dedicated booklet and also a handful of toffees.

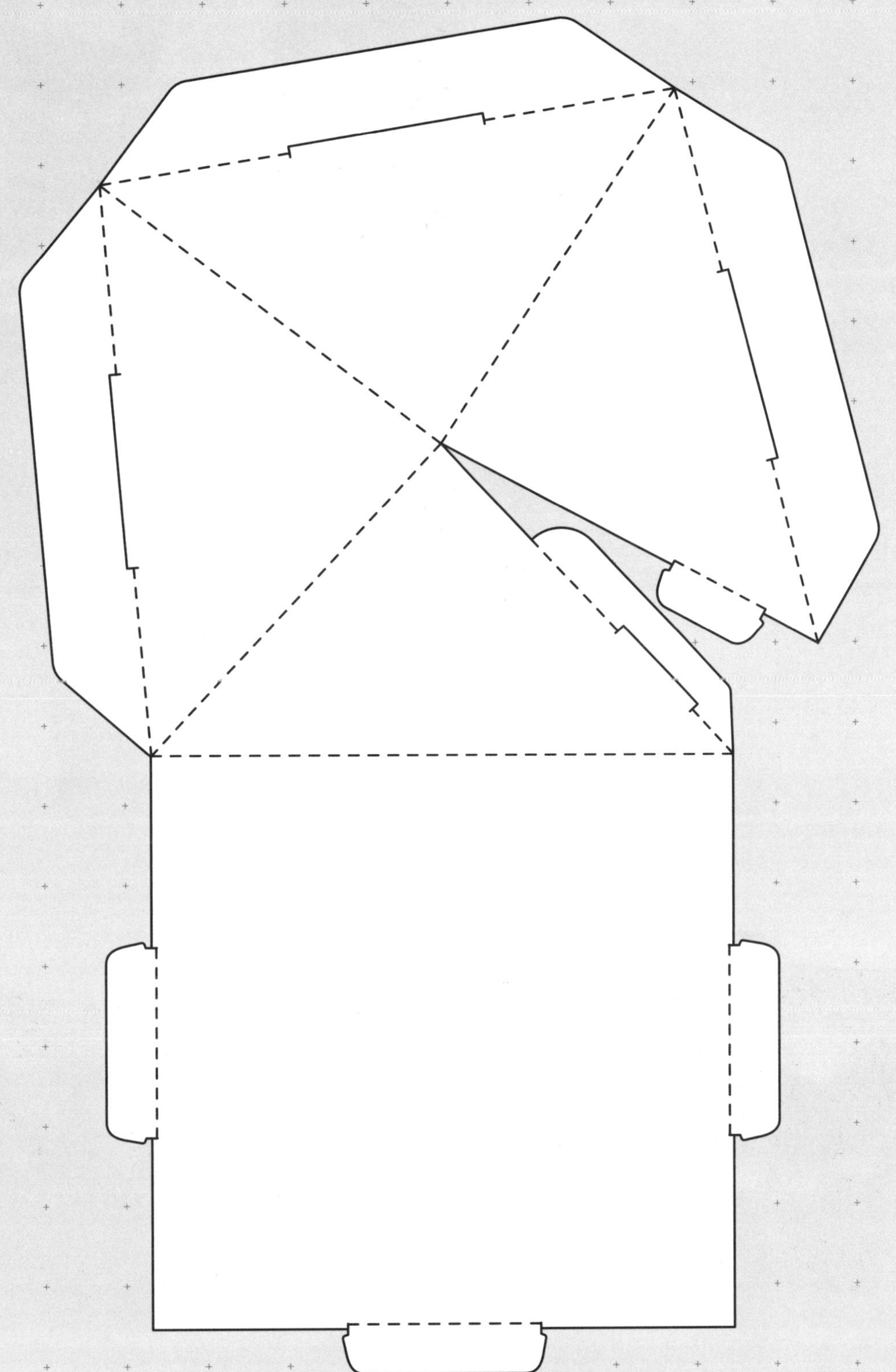

A SET OF COOKIE BOXES

Design **Agata Pietraszko**

The project presents a set of packages for tiny butter cookies. The task was to design a package inspired by something indefinite like emotions. A sip of witty humour makes it distinguishing and interesting even for a demanding consumer.

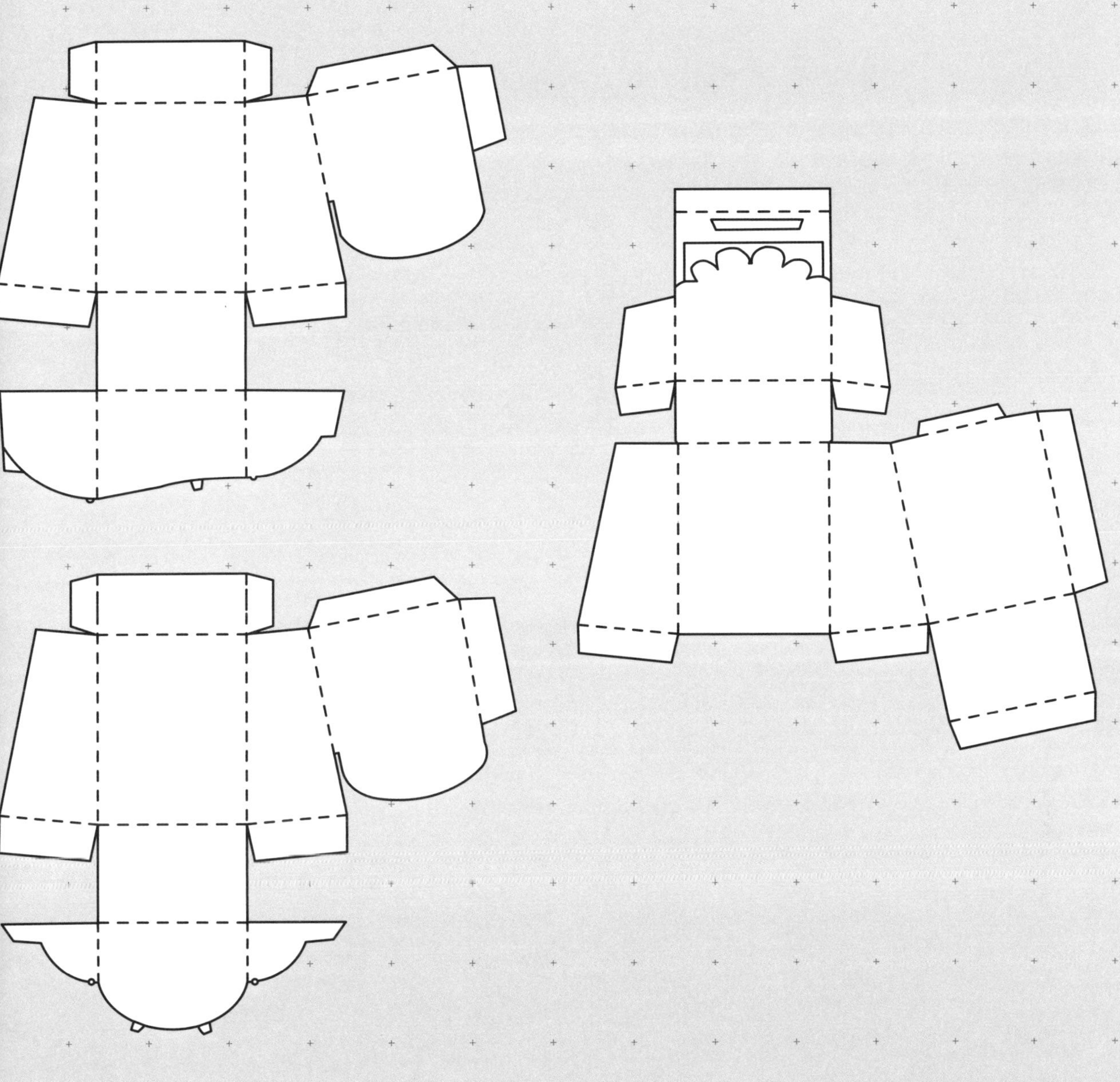

TWO EGGS FOR YOU

Design **Conor Whelan**

The idea was to create a package of two eggs, ideal for someone living on their own or someone who just wants to make a quick meal and doesn't require the standard six eggs. The designer wanted to create an interesting package that was aesthetically pleasing, functional, and simply enjoyable to hold. Each packaging features two eggs along with two easy recipes for one, which are revealed when the egg chamber is opened.

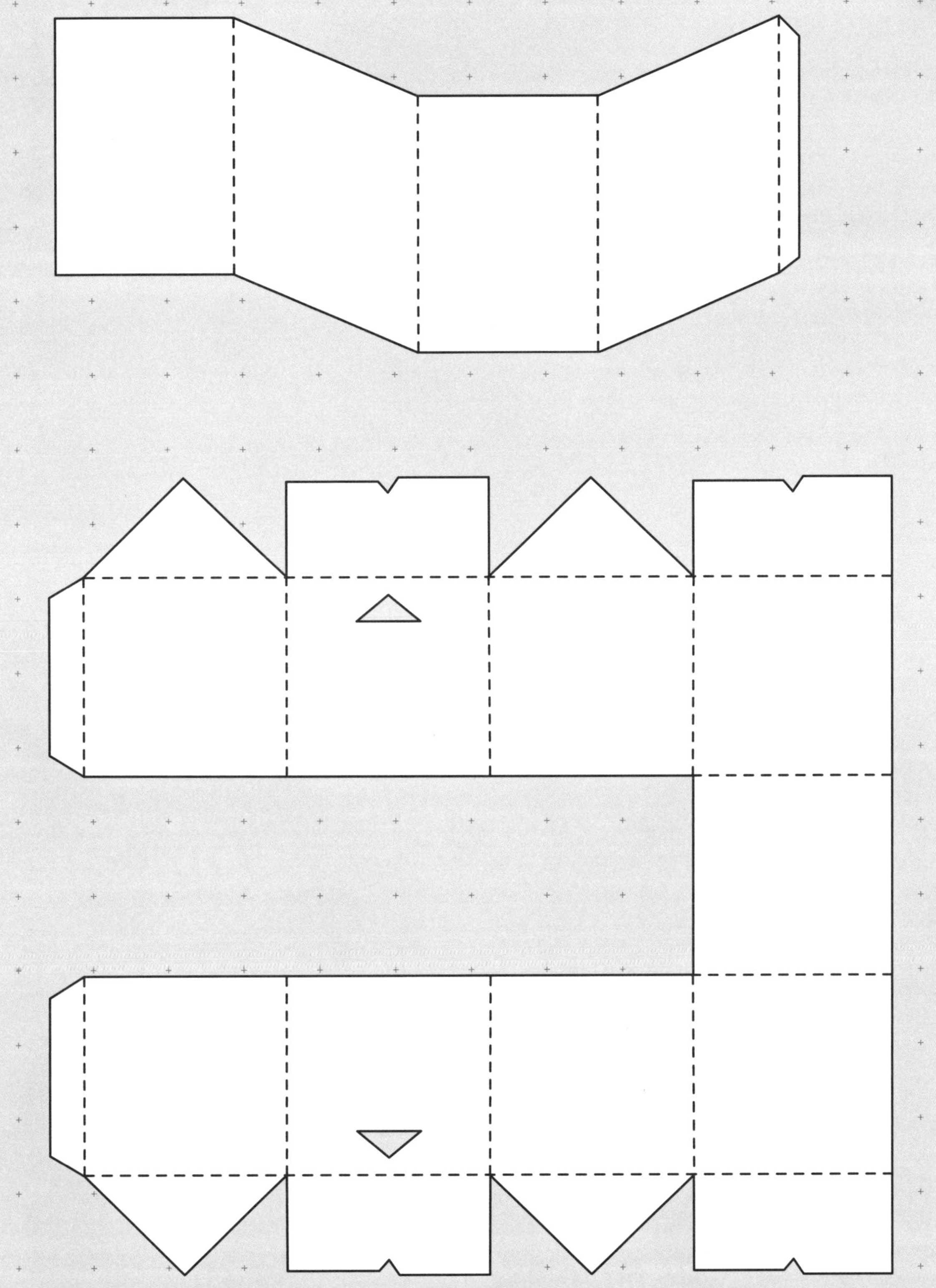

IISI PACKAGING CONCEPT

Design **Ilari Laitinen, Nikolo Kerimov**

The package can be opened with just one hand. The opening mechanism was designed using the flexibility of carton to make the content easily accessible. Its angular shape allows for a secure grip on the package, and forms a spout at the front edge making serving quick and clean.

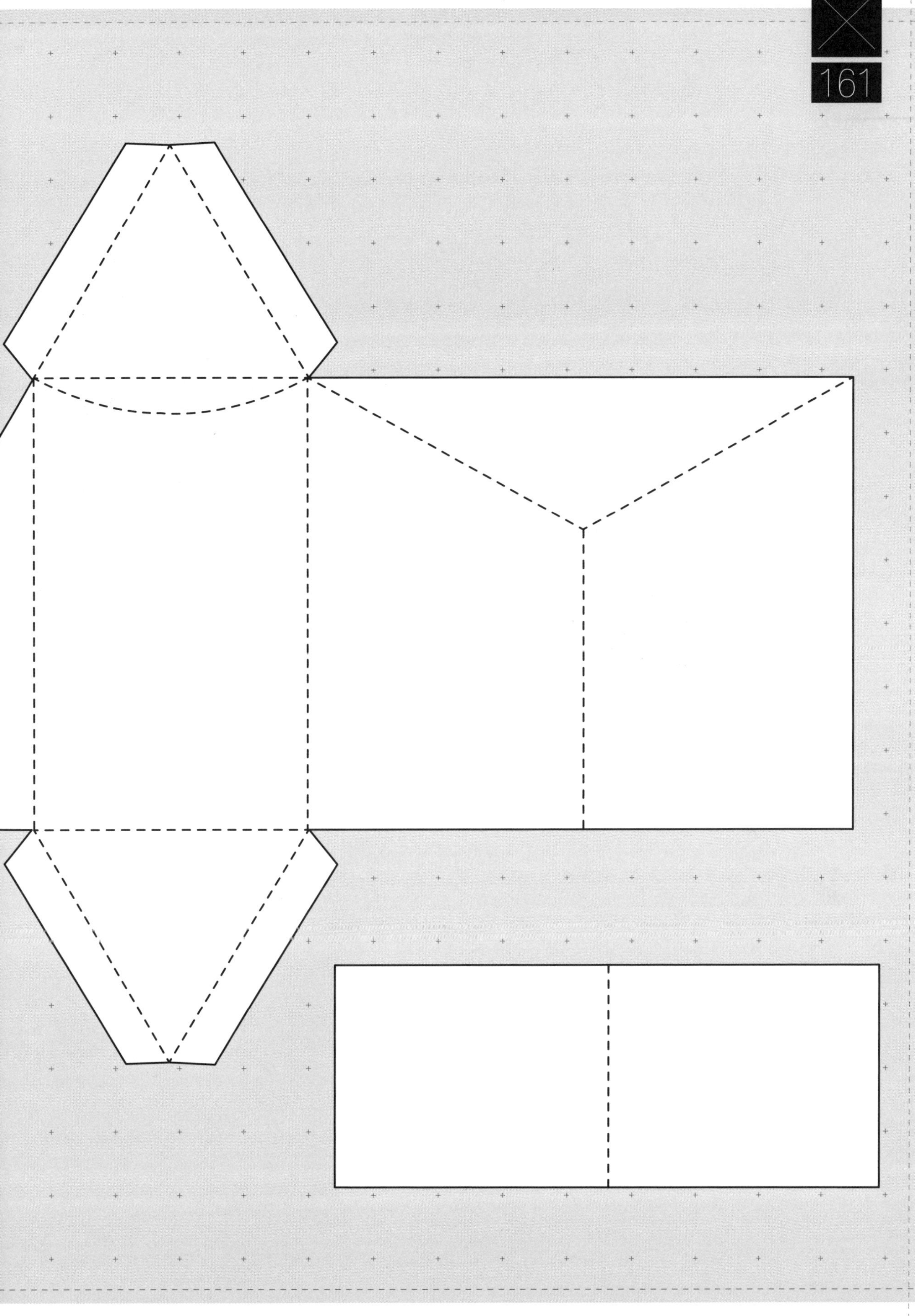

CHERRY TOMATO PACKAGE

Design **Katia Mikov**

This packaging for cherry tomatoes is based on a concept and graphic elements taken from Kotex, a brand of feminine hygiene products. The graphic elements of their packaging have been used to build a new graphic language for a different product. For example, a circle that appears as a graphic element on Kotex packaging has become a hole that is both useful for ventilation and decorative.

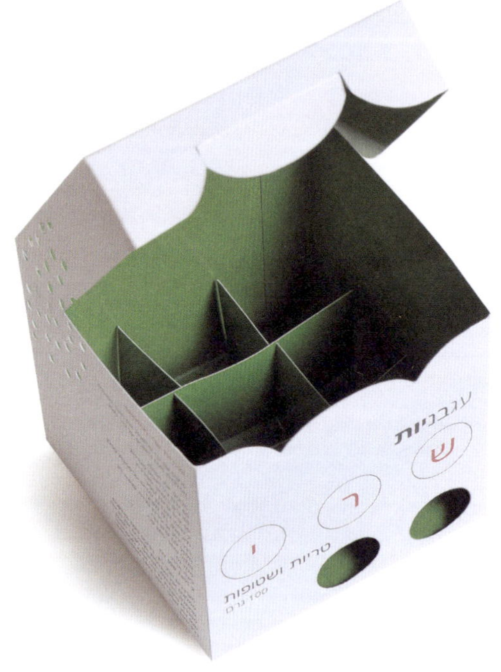

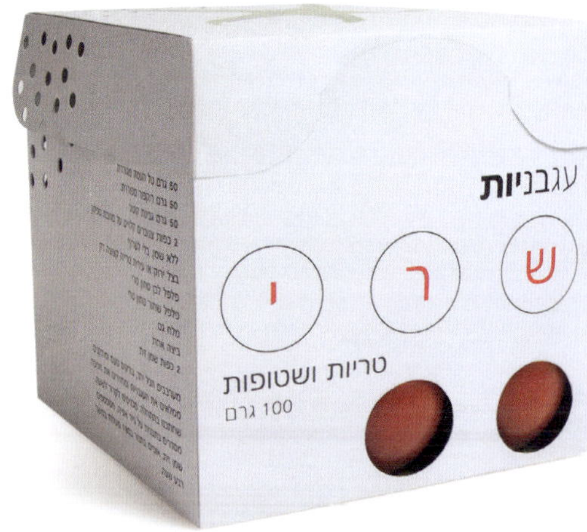

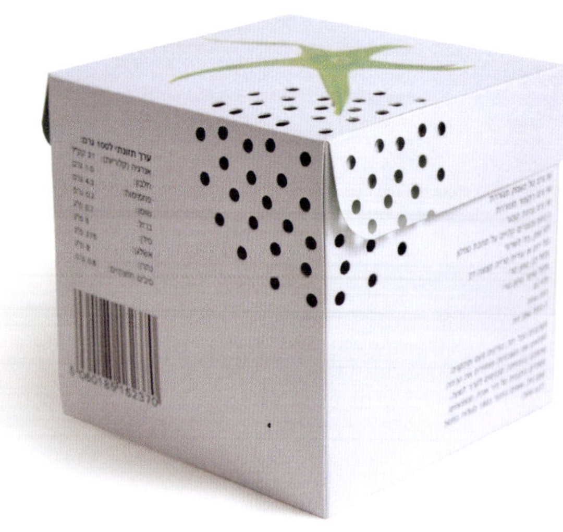

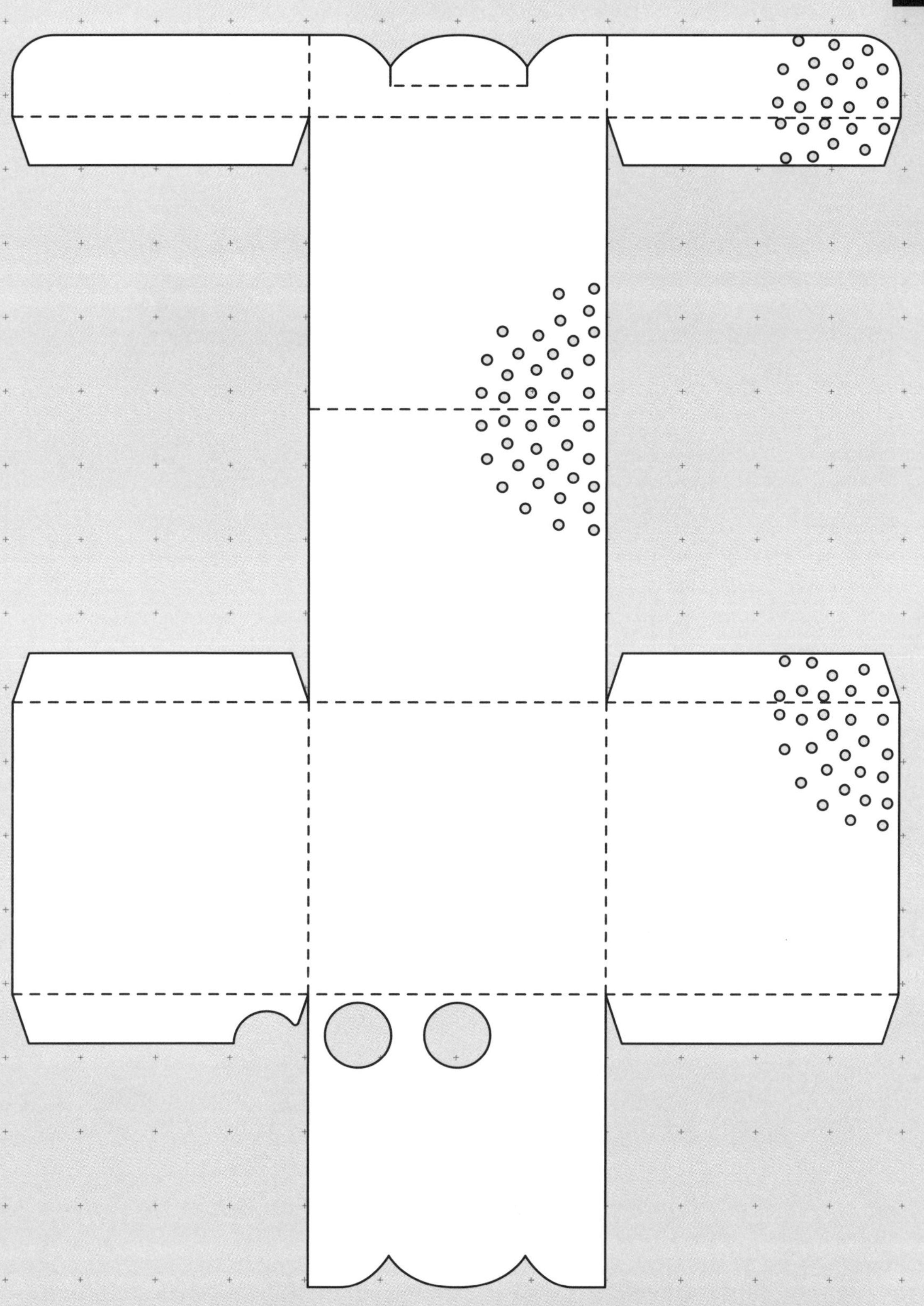

DOUBLE COOKIE PACKET

Design Juan Regueiro

This is a small packet designed to hold individual cookie portions. Its rotational symmetry allows each part to be opened independently.

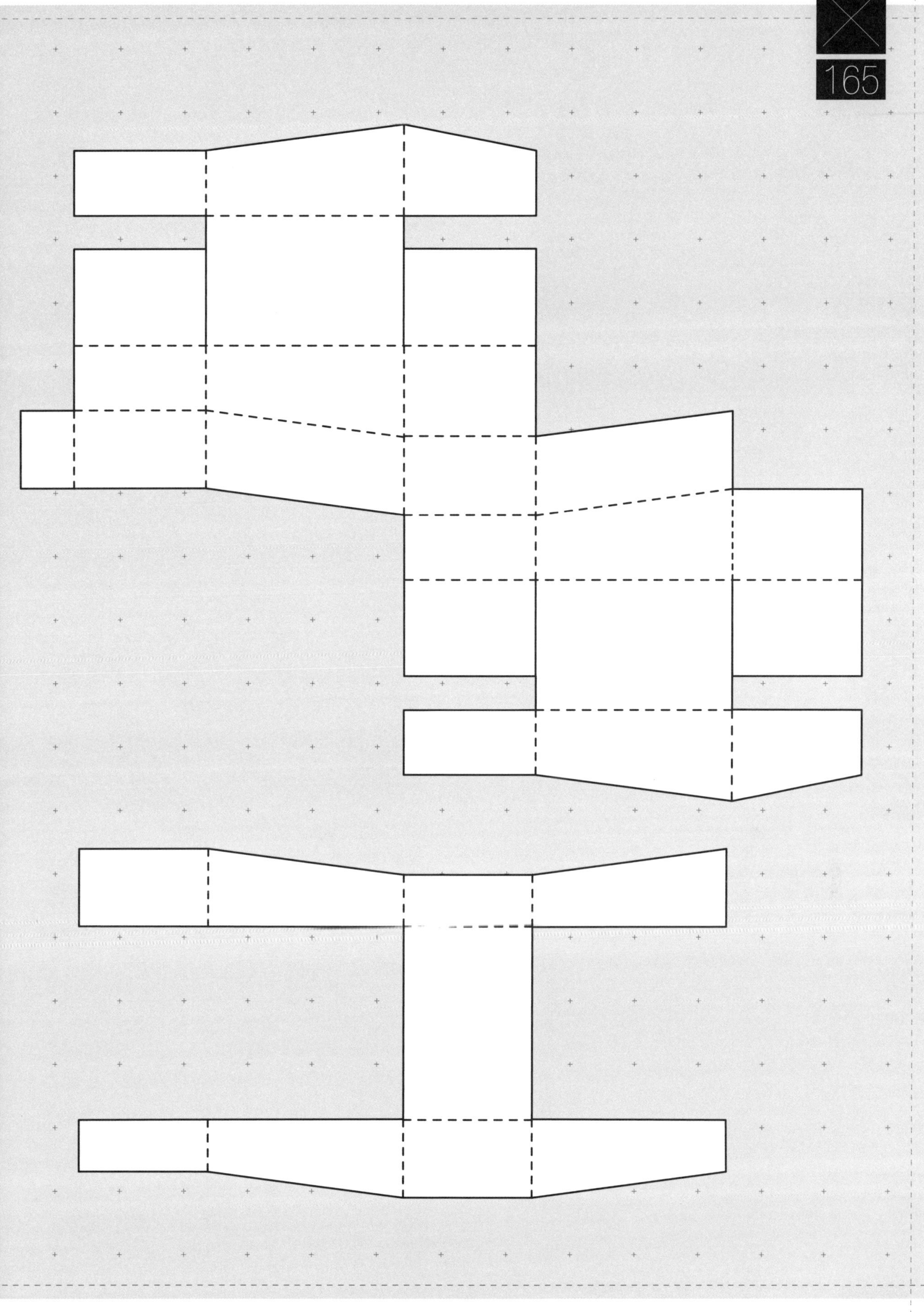

SUNFLOWER

Design Stéphanie Malak

This design is an experiment with folding paper to achieve the form of a sunflower to package sunflower seeds.

TEMARI BALL SWEETS PACKAGE

Design **Hada Tomoko**

This packet, resembling a traditional Japanese Temari ball, was the result of the designer's ambition to create a gorgeously pretty packaging design. Although the top surface is octagonal, the bottom surface is square for easy assembly.

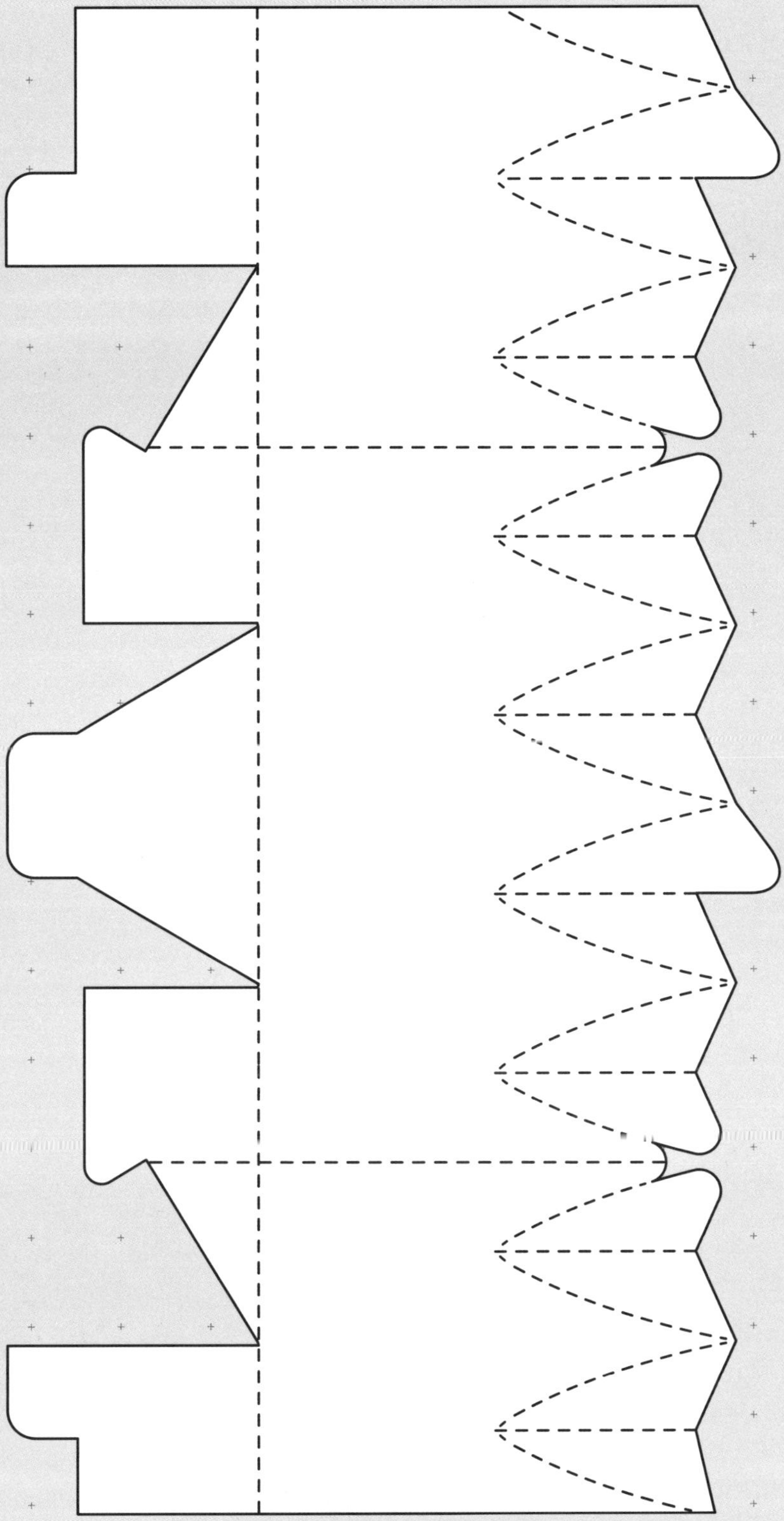

BAMBOO LEAF SWEETS PACKAGE

Design **Hada Tomoko**

This package of Japanese black candies resembles the traditional local bamboo leaf wrap. The reminiscent square-shaped box is closed with a grass string that encourages user interaction.

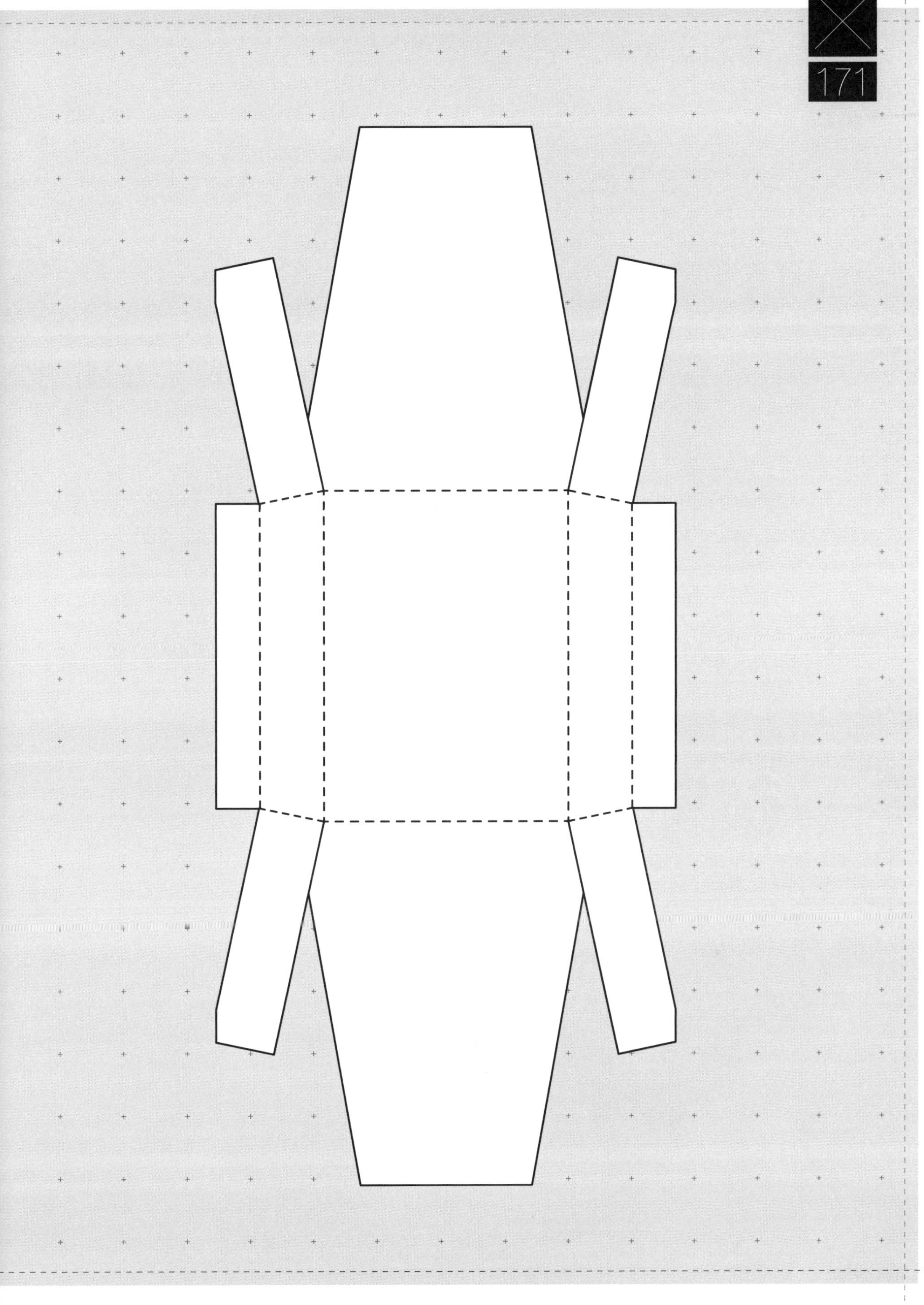

GRASS PACKAGE

Design Assaf Yogev

Inspired by Frank Loyed Wright's Falling Water and the attempt to combine architecture with nature, the entire package is made from recycled materials. The package has an air opening to gain longer shelf life for the product. The minimalistic design and logo added a flowing "breathing" feel to the package, as well as elegance and liveliness.

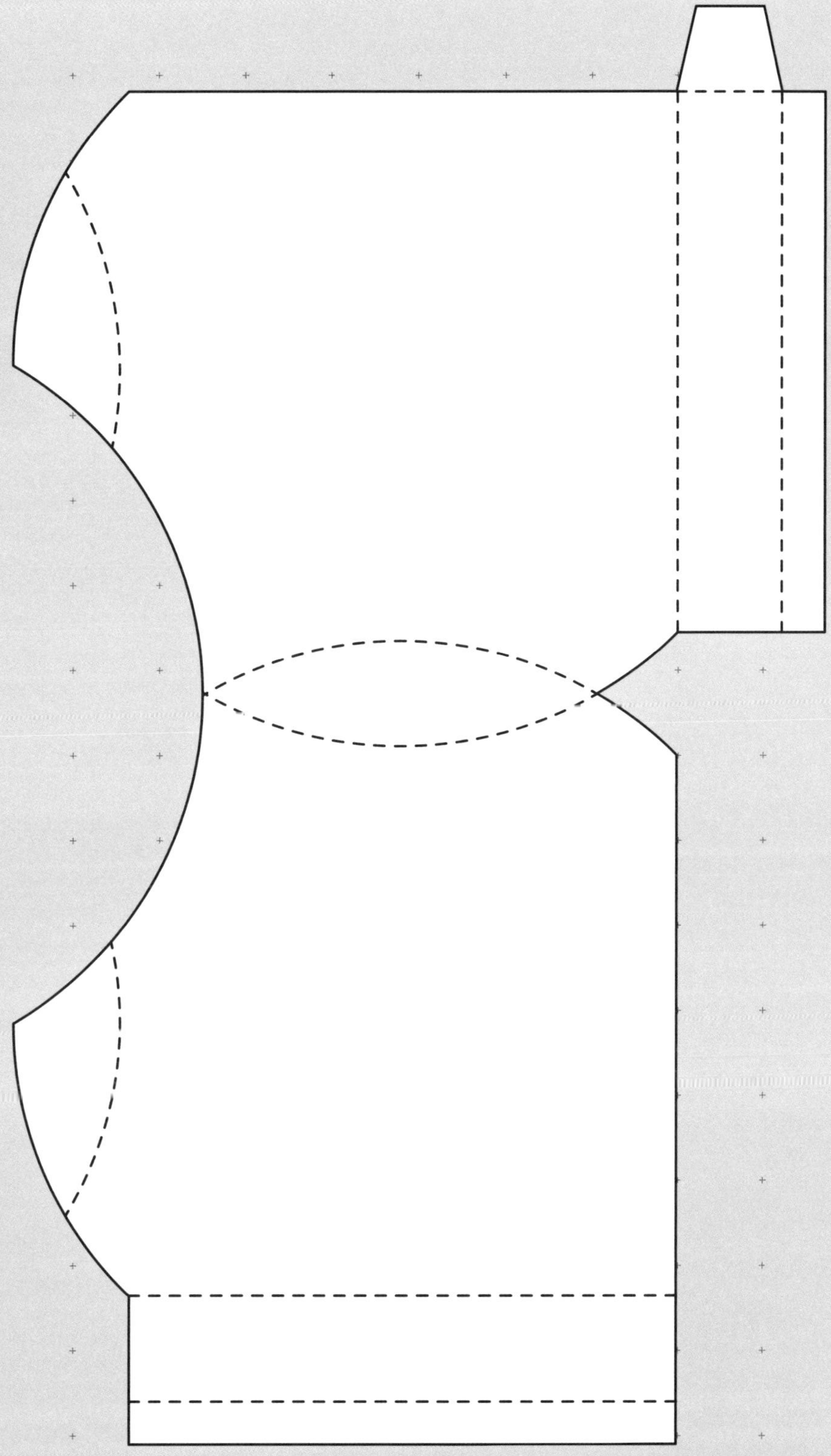

HEAL'S CANDLE

Design **Jon Hodkinson, Andrew Scrace**

Packaging design for a new range of luxury scented candles, a top tier addition to the retailer's home fragrance offer. The designers elevated the perceived value of the candles' protective packaging, achieving its luxury gift status within a 'standard packaging' budget.

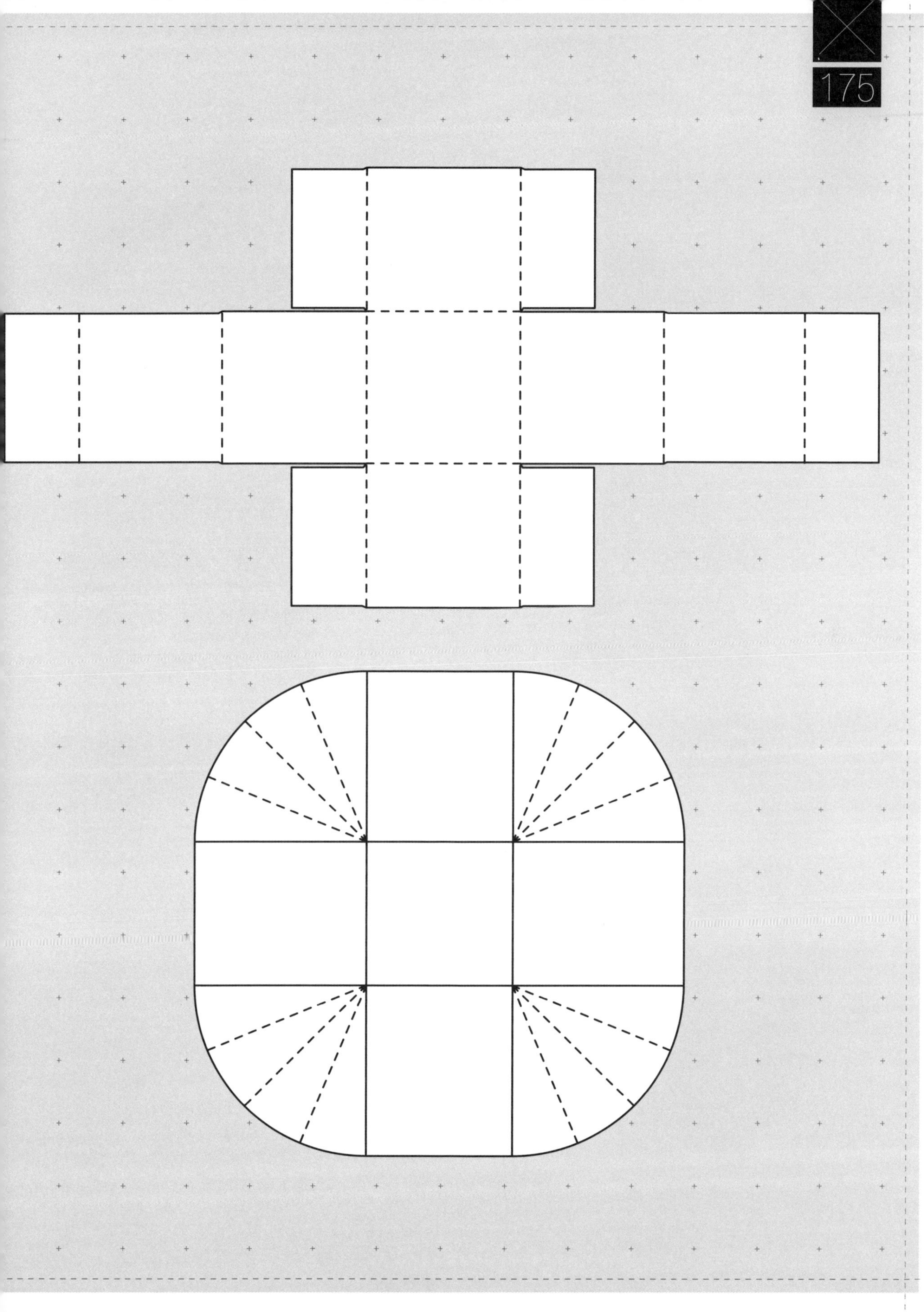

BED IDEAS

Design **Hugo Araújo, Vera Oliveira**

This versatile packaging is made from a single strip of recycled cardboard with cuts and bends and a paper sleeve printed with all the information about the lamp.

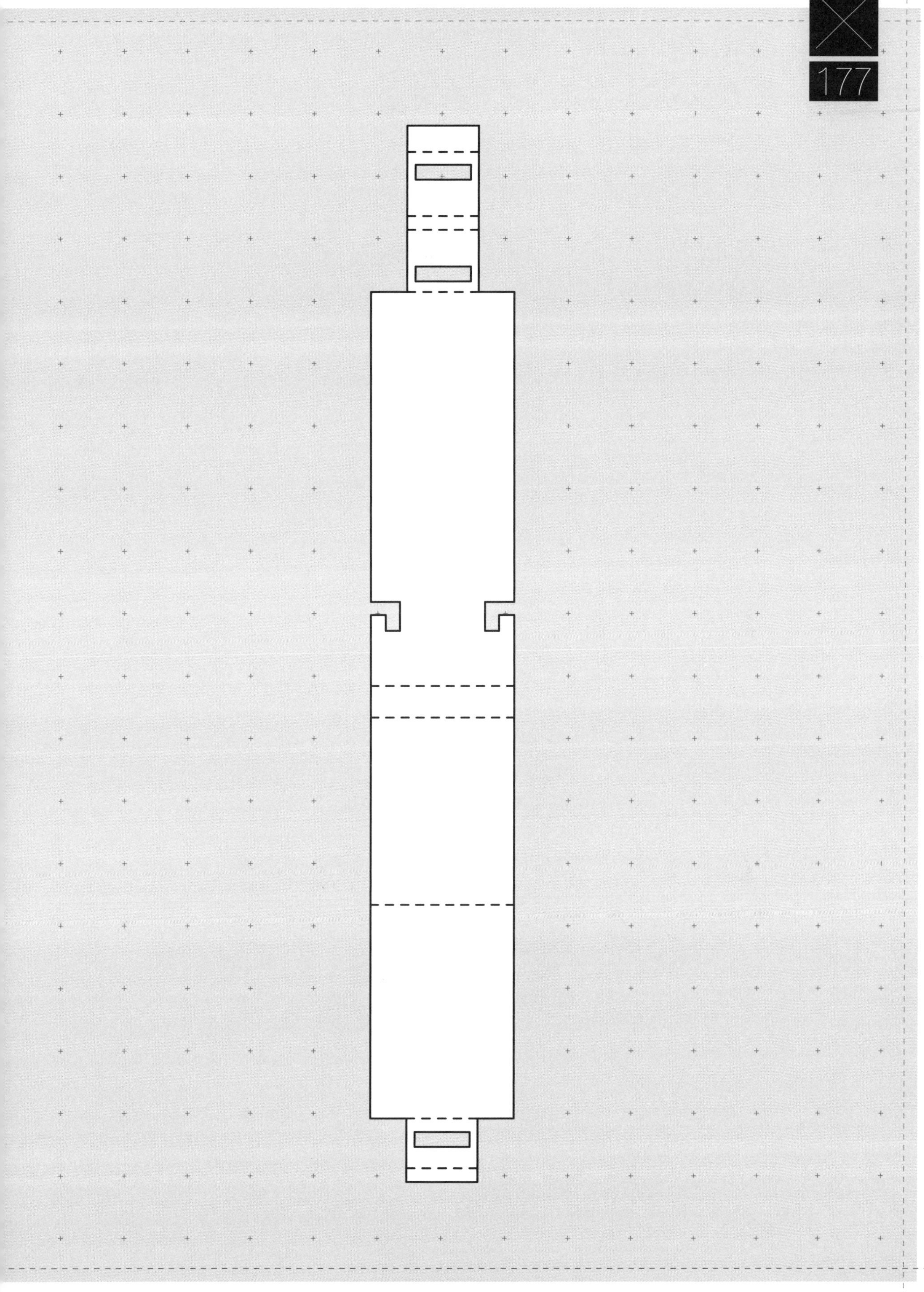

FLOWER CITY HONEY

Design **Mei Cheng Wang**

This is a concept honey package inspired by the idea of rooftop beehives in Chinatown, New York. The name "Flower City" derives from the simplified translation of the Chinese characters for "Chinatown".

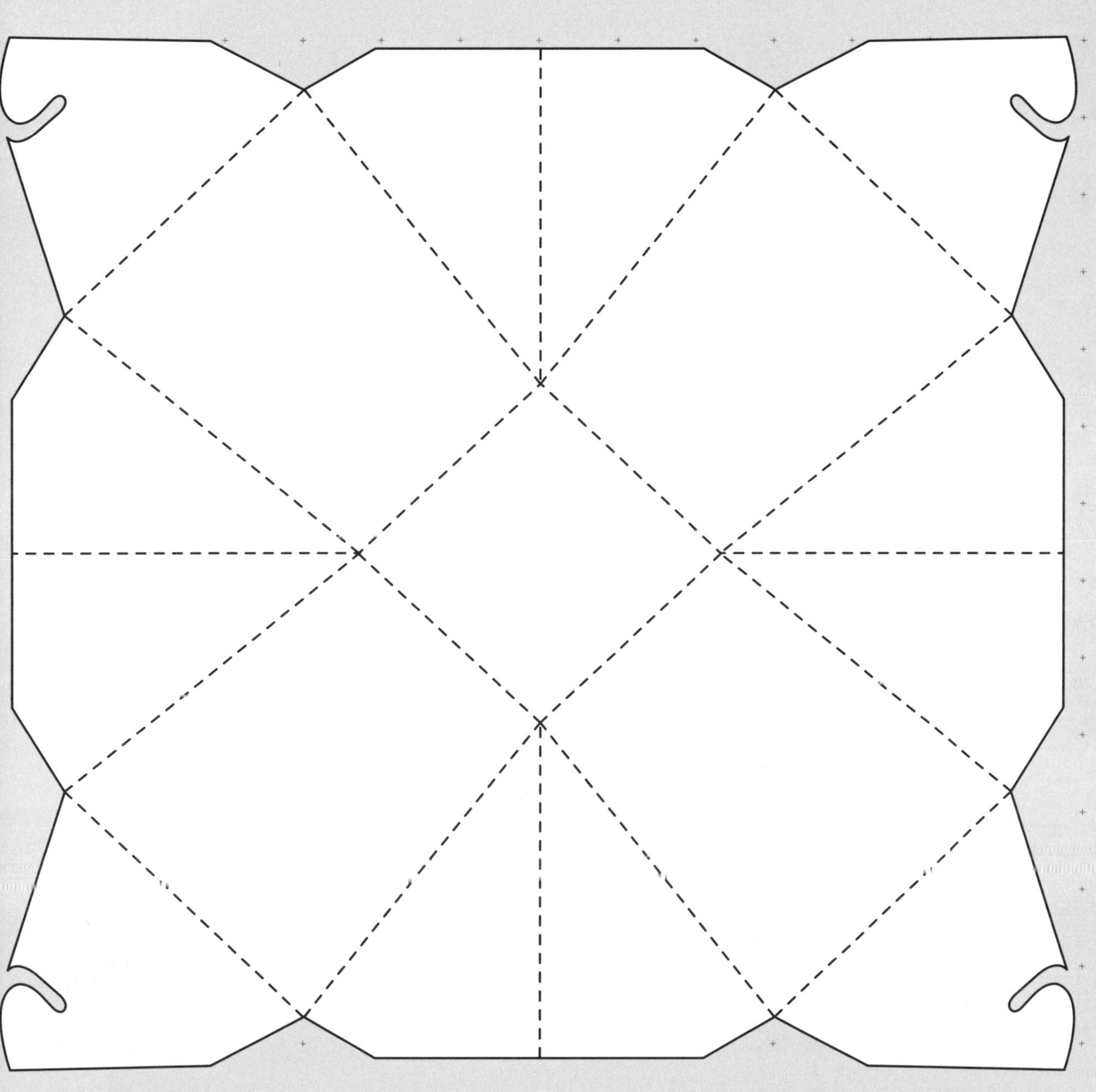

BONJOUR PHILIPPINE

Design **Julie Pirovani**

The package is made up of two inner boxes and a connective packet, mimicking the structure of an almond.

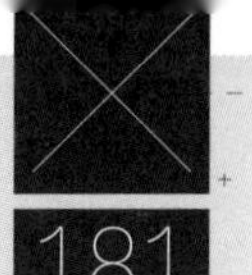

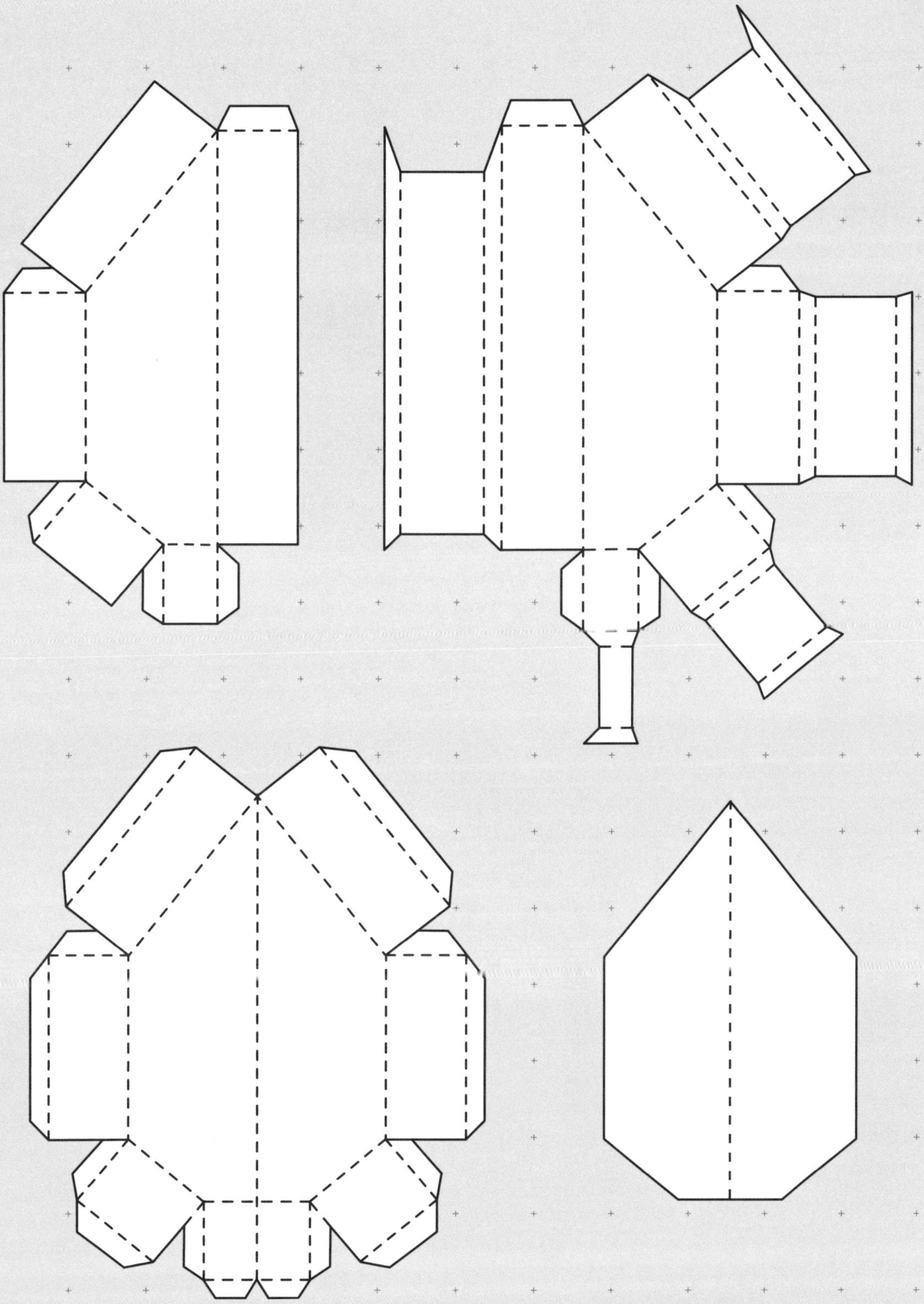

RESTORING

Design **Marta Gintere**

Restoring is a series of skin renewal products. The micro world of Kombucha black tea ferment—the main component of this product line—is very impressive with its various organisms which are visible in the shapes of extended and compressed dots and tubes. This visual language was taken as the basis for the entire packaging series.

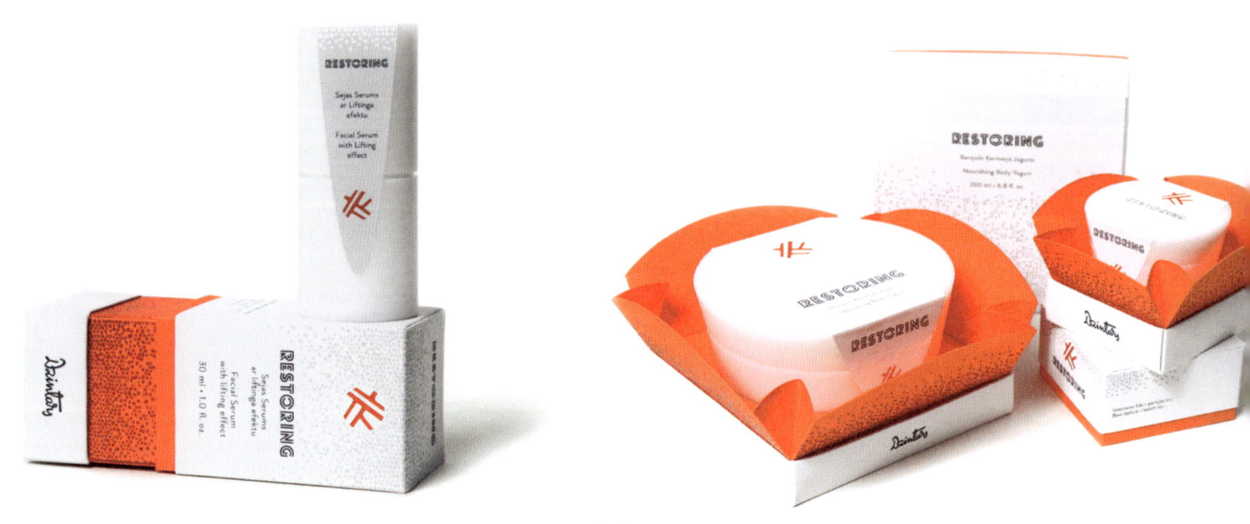

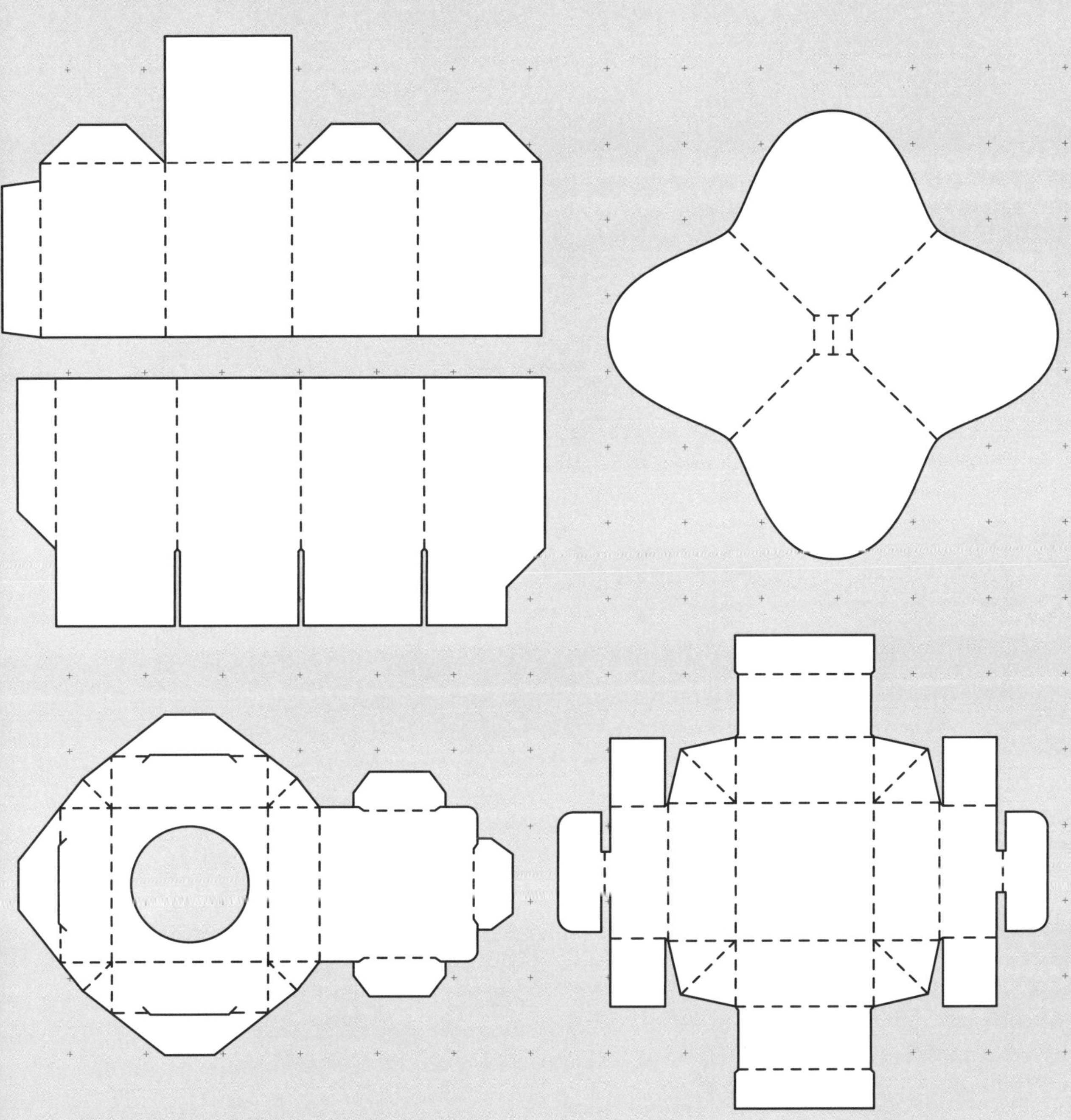

OIMU OCTAGONAL MATCHBOX

Design **Sohyun Shin**

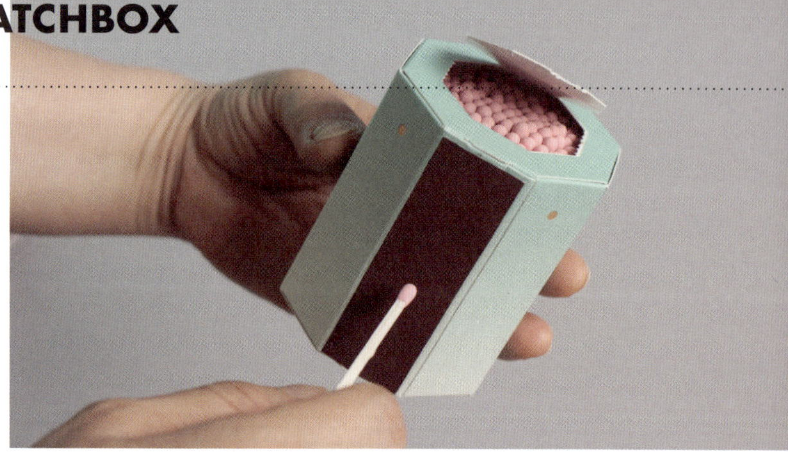

This project was made to help support the declining matches industry by redesigning the package. The lid at the top maintains the feature of the octagonal matches which is a symbolic product manufactured in Korea between the 1950's and the 2010's.

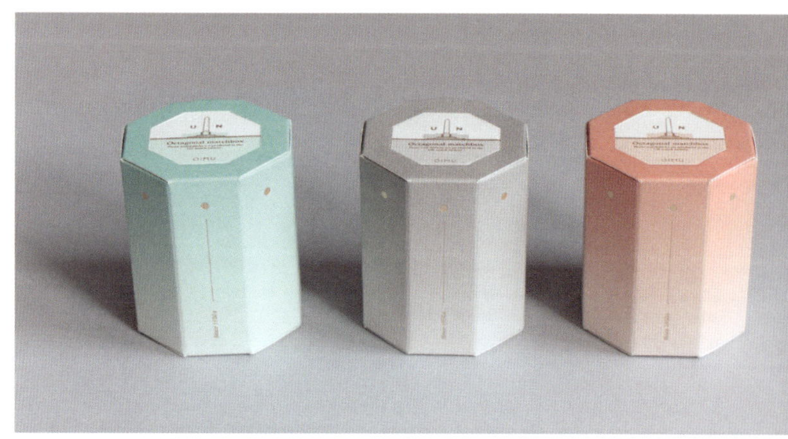

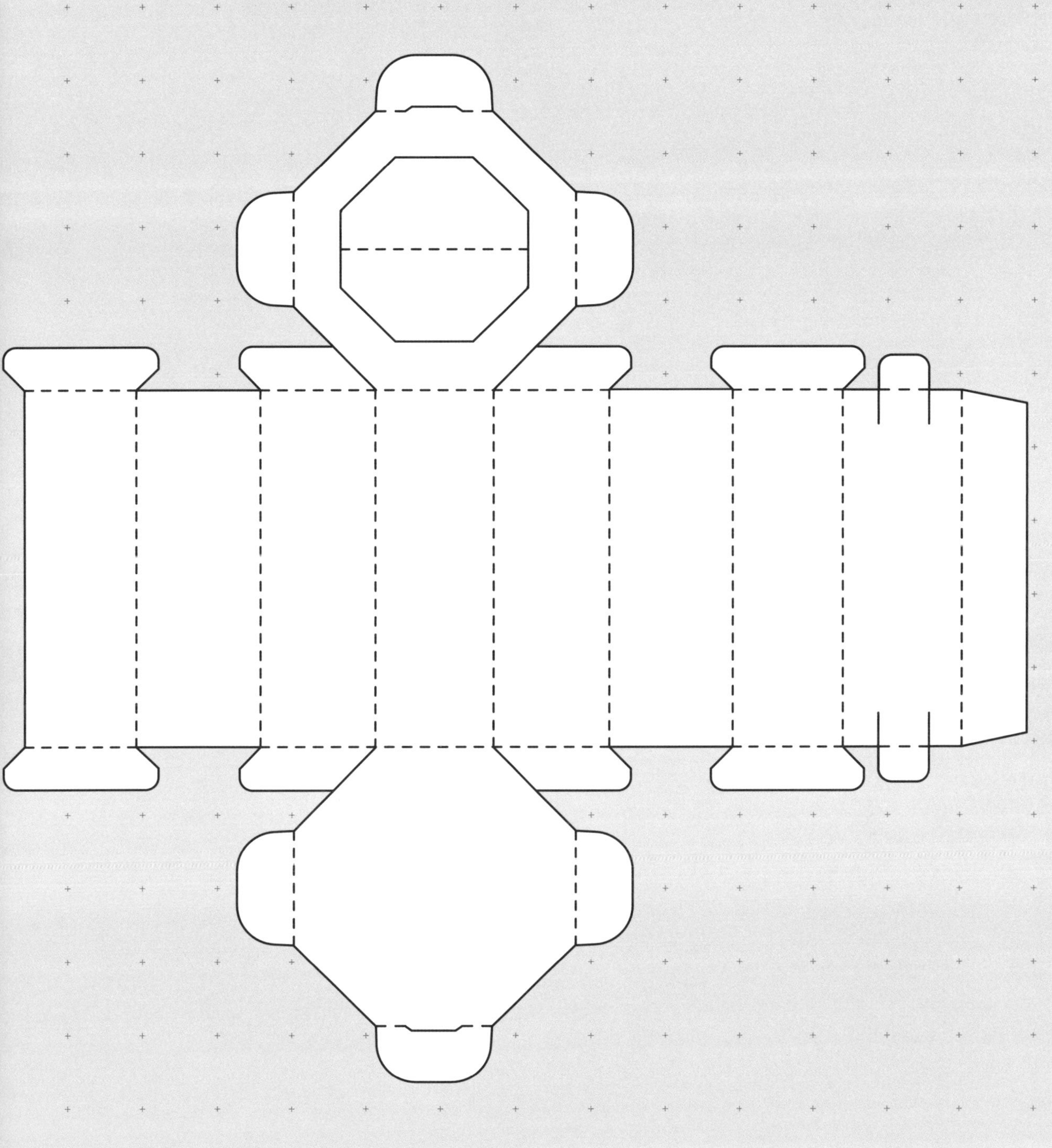

TACO OLE

Design **Guo Wei Chen**

The "Taco Ole" party pack holds 20 individually packaged tacos which are colour coded by flavors. The napkin and sauce are handily palced in the base.

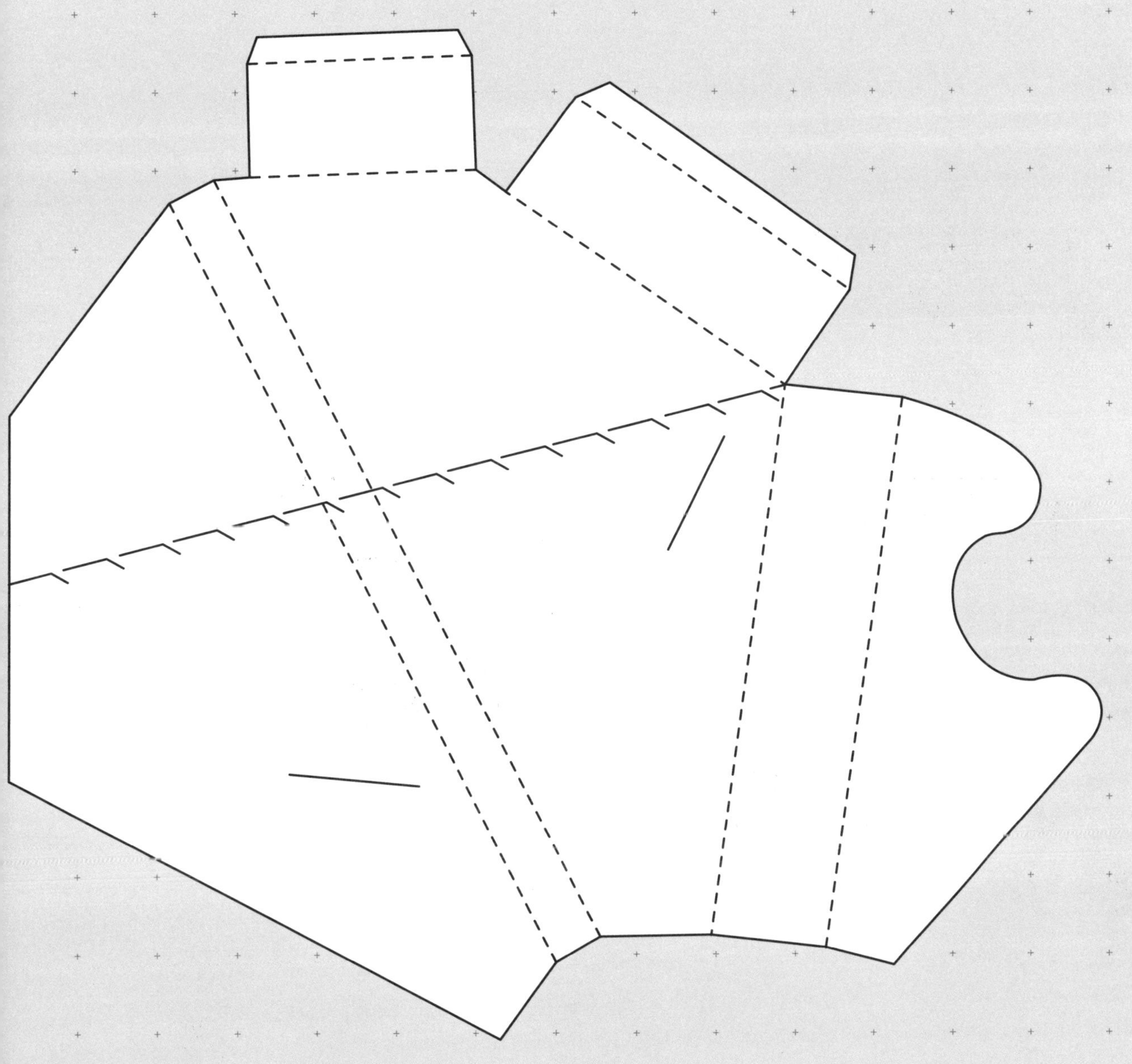

SUSHI PACKAGING CONCEPT

Design **Yannis Ampelas, Yannis Choulakis**

This project includes the packages for three courses, delivery bag, custom made chopsticks and two folded towels forming a ninja star. The concept of the shapes is building up an origami with the boxes stacked together.

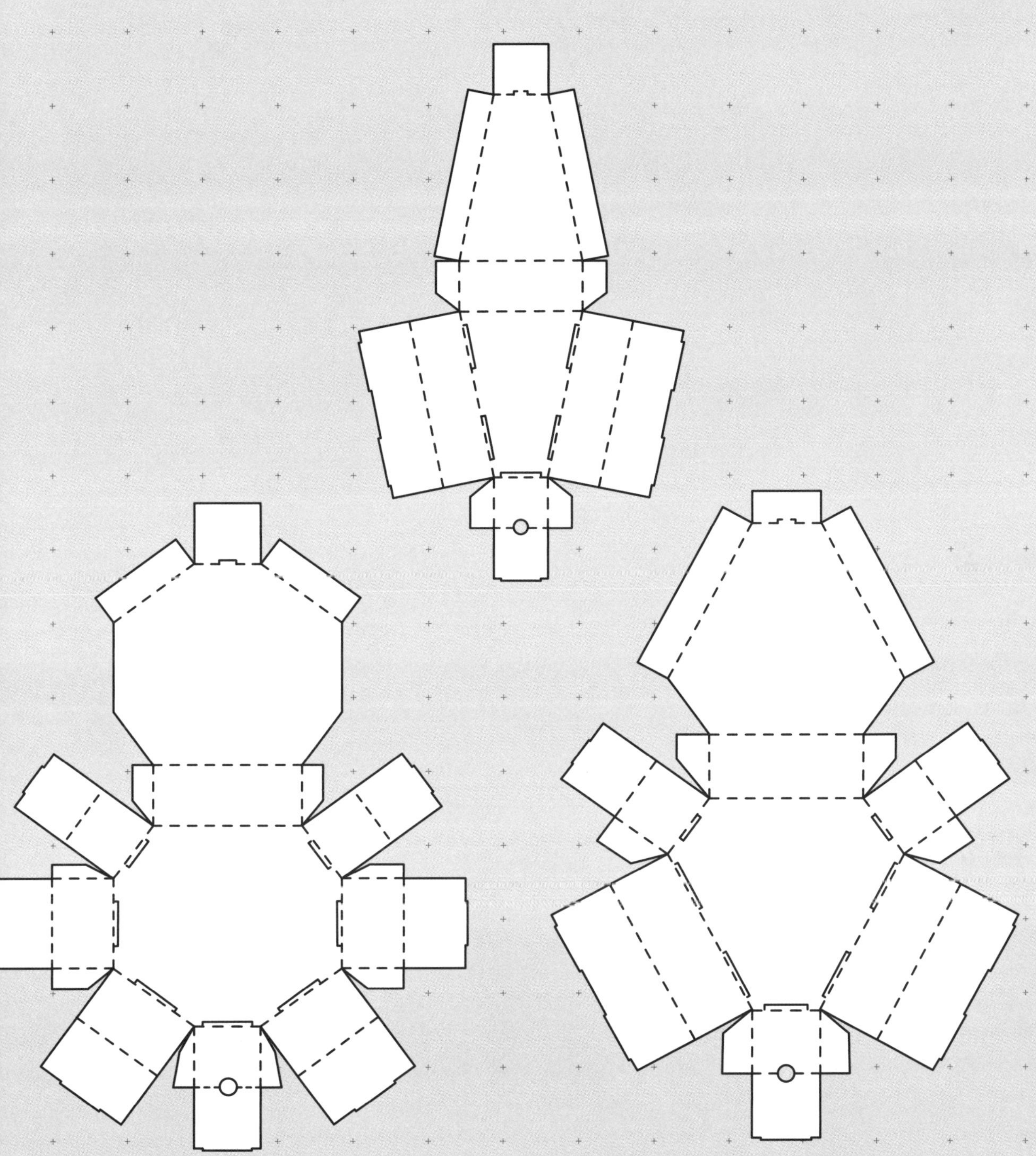

CREATIVITY

Design **Cheng Yuan Chieh**

This series of conceptual stationery packages takes structure into first consideration. The design is intended to attract children with its special structures and bright colours and more importantly stimulate them to imagine and create with colours.

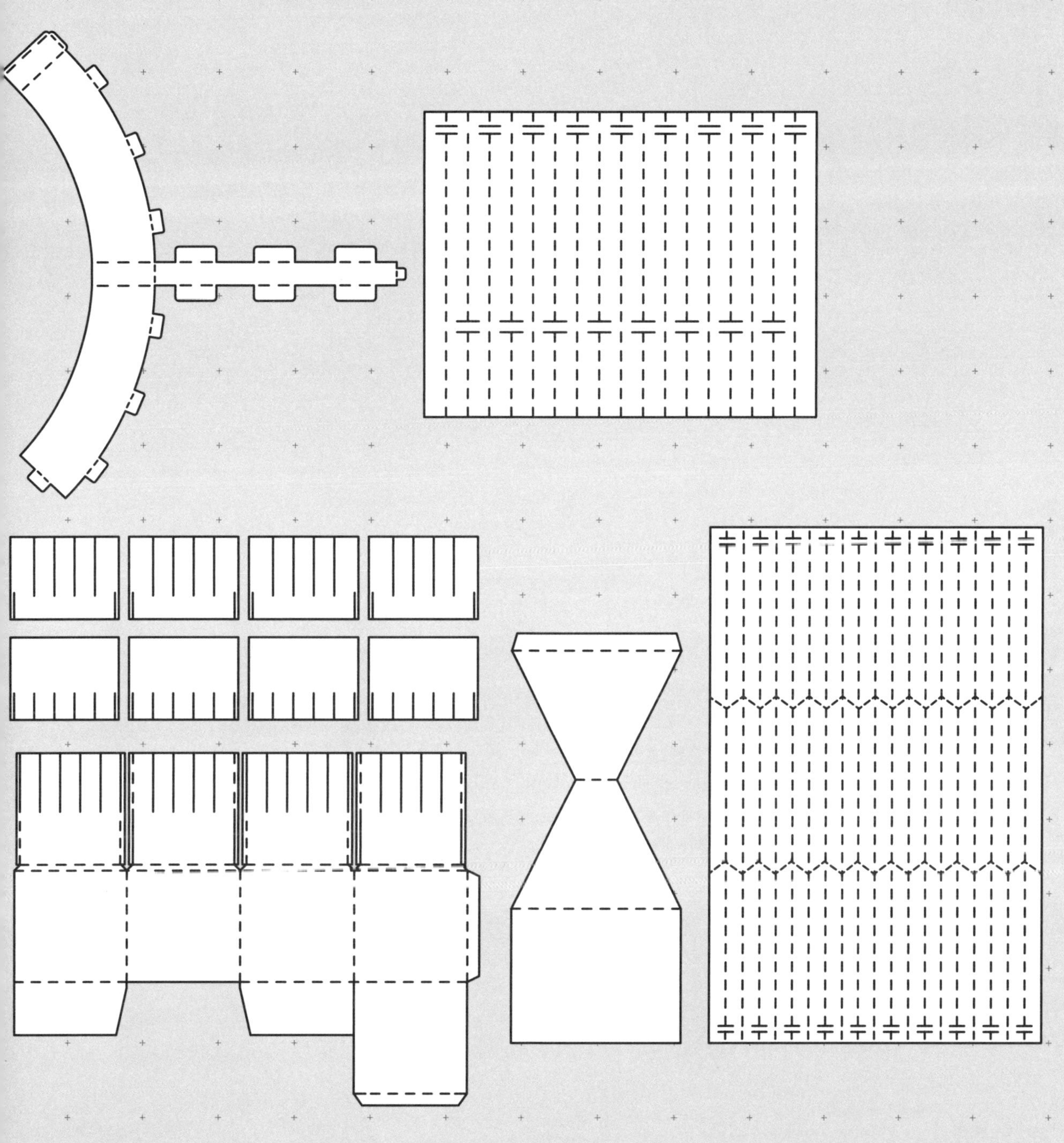

EURIPOS

Design **Trantalidi Katerina**

Euripos is a fictional company that produces tea and herbs. Euripos in Greek means good, health and usefulness. The logo is inspired by herb leaves and when the package opens it turns into leaves itself. As every flower contains pollen, in the same way each package contains revitalizing herb. The recycled paper of the package gives the product an ecological character.

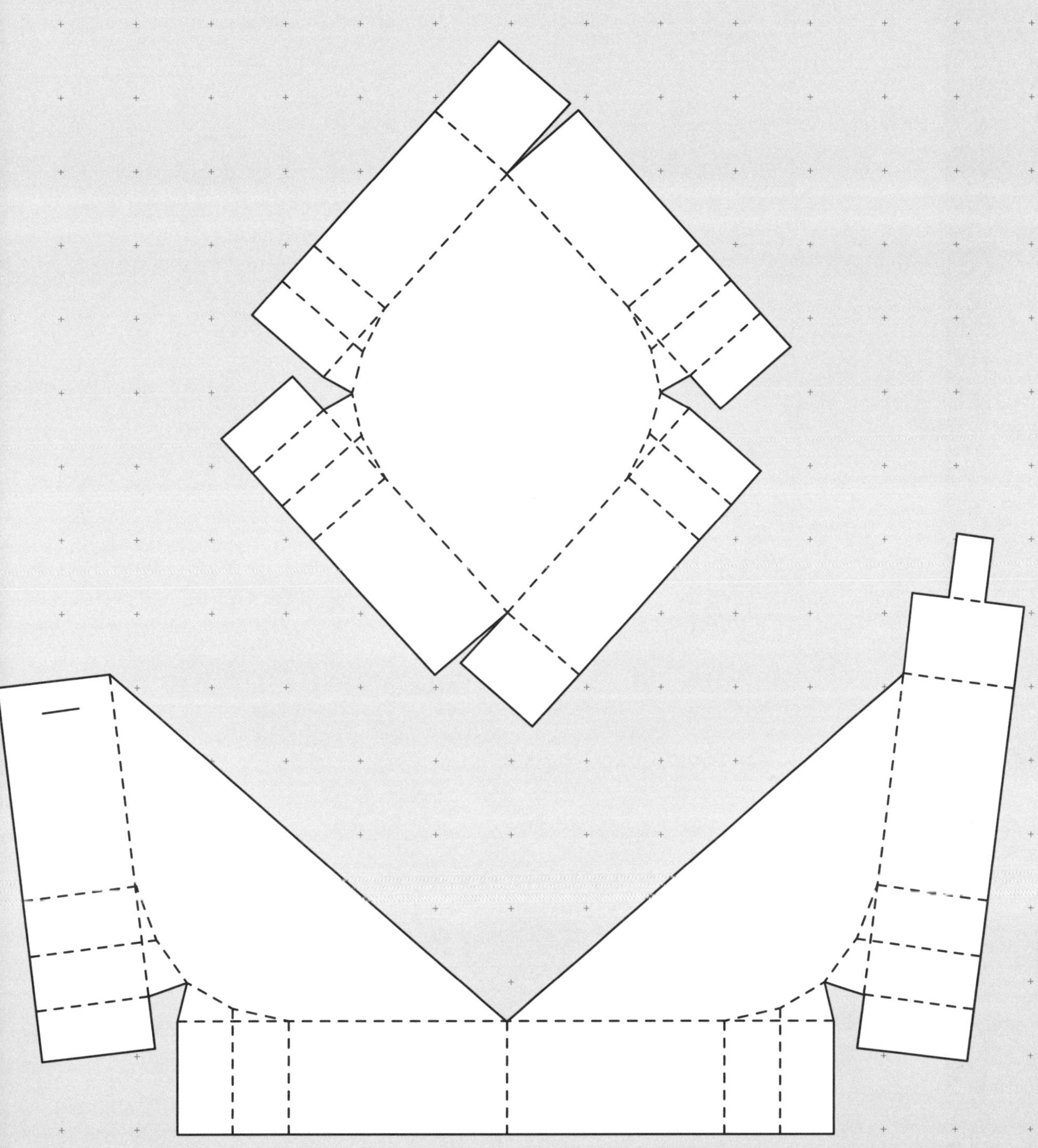

NO TEA INSIDE

Design **Nune Khachatryan**

The basic concept of this tea packaging is based on an origami worm. Each part of the worm body is packed with a different type of tea. The humorous trick of contrasting the "No Tea Inside" signs with the visible tea bag covers was meant to differentiate the brand in the market.

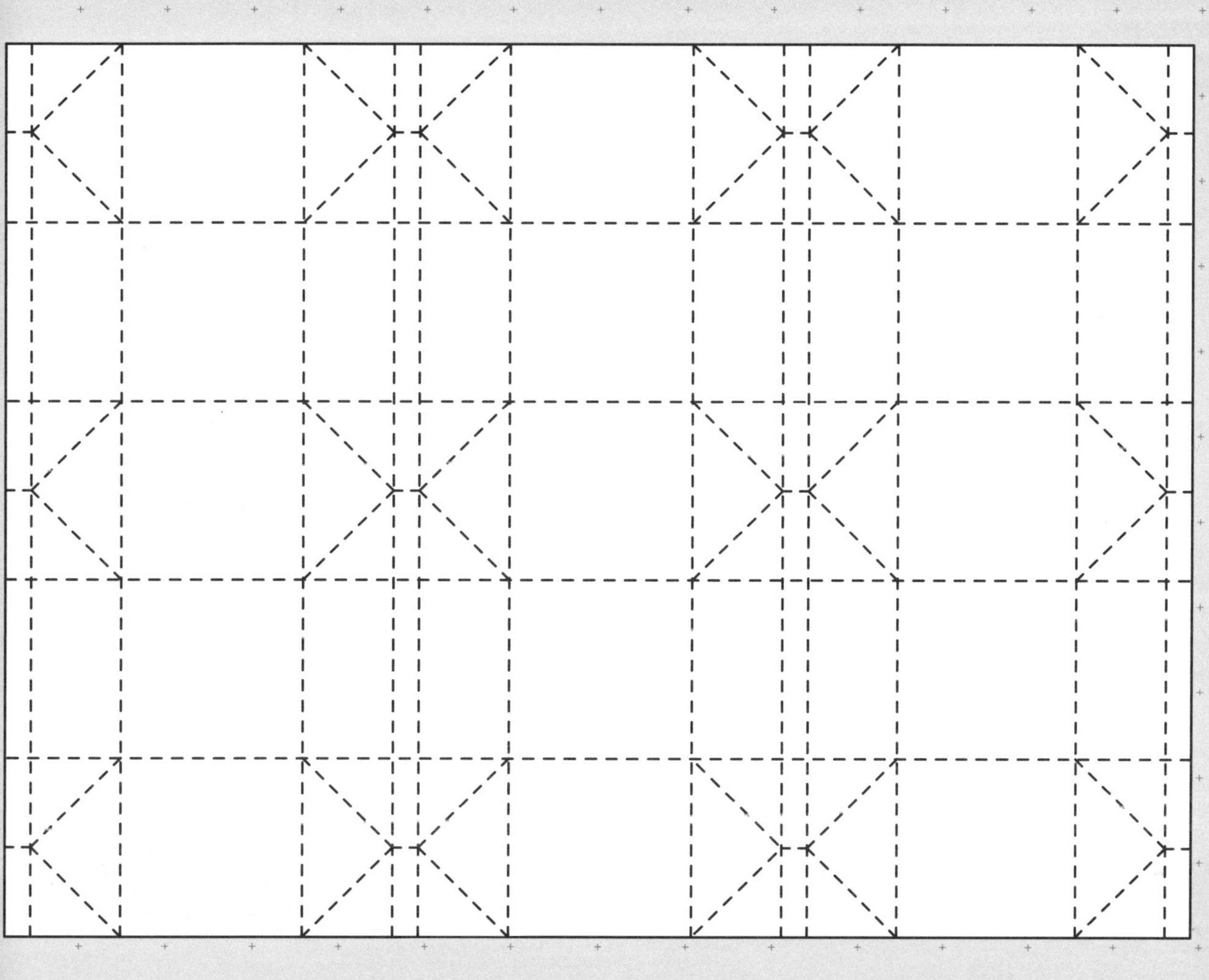

GESTURE AND PACKAGING

Design **Ângela Monteiro**

André Leroi-Gourhan in his book *Gesture and Speech* talks about a problem of regression of hand as incredibly worrying, since it's related to brain recession. This project aims to make a reflection on this issue of "unhandling", having the packaging design as primary tool. Starting from the idea of awareness of the gesture, containers were created to potentiate a new mode of human-object interaction, which goes beyond mere functional and aesthetic use of the package, and provides a sensory experience to the user.

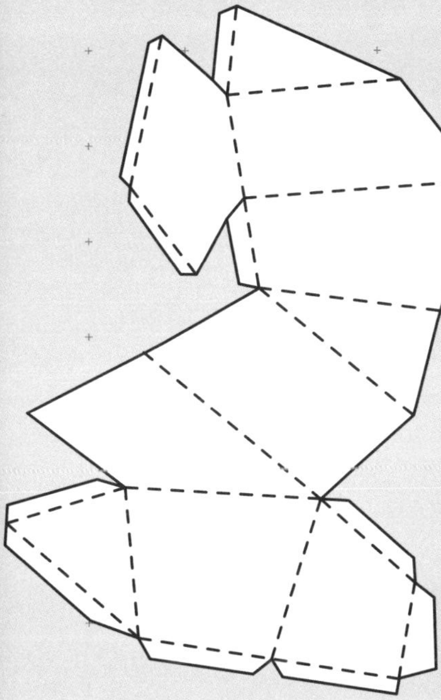

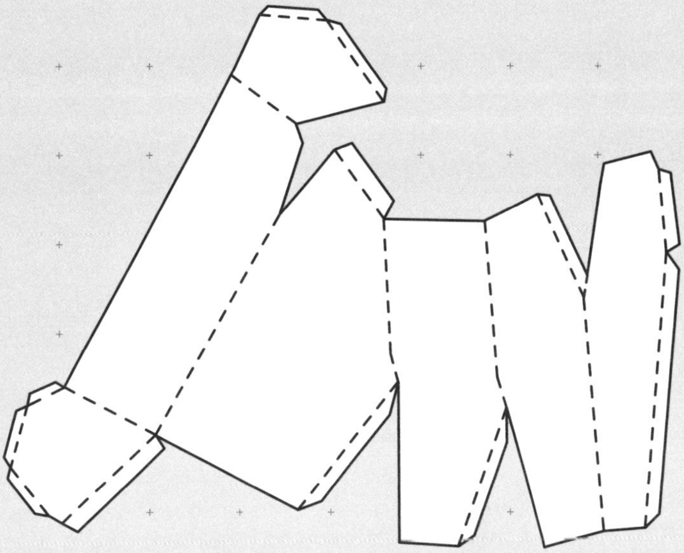

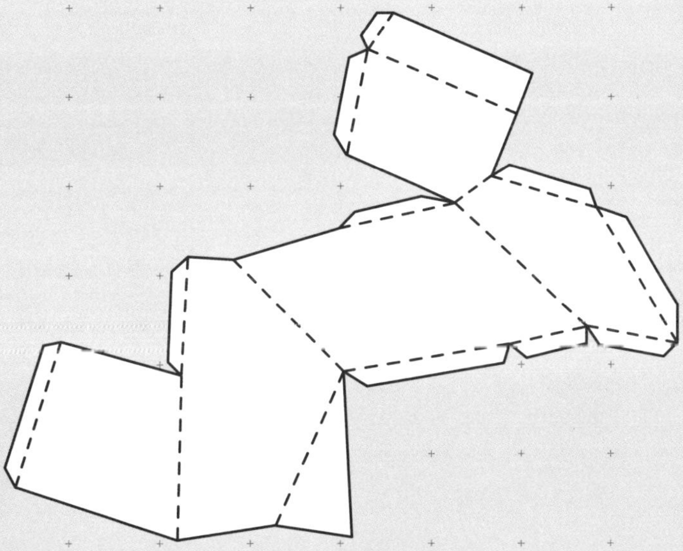

MOON CAKE FESTIVAL

Design **Yeo Wanqi**

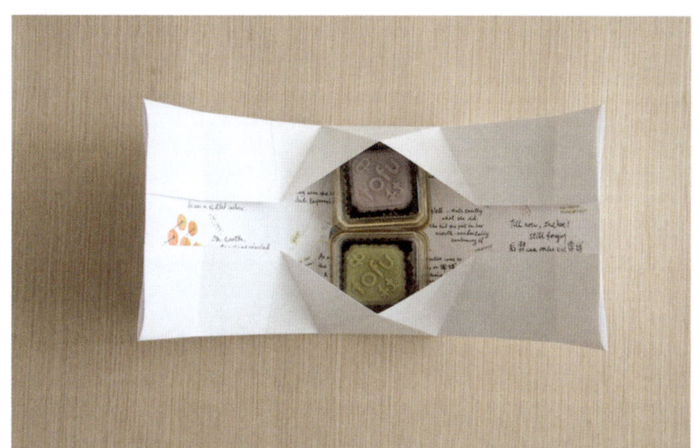

Motivated by curiosity, the designer started to investigate the origins of Mid Autumn Festival (also named Moon Cake Festival). Although the origins remain mysterious and confusing, the researching was meaningful as it turned into an interesting creation process. The collected stories have been illustrated on the foldable moon cake packaging.

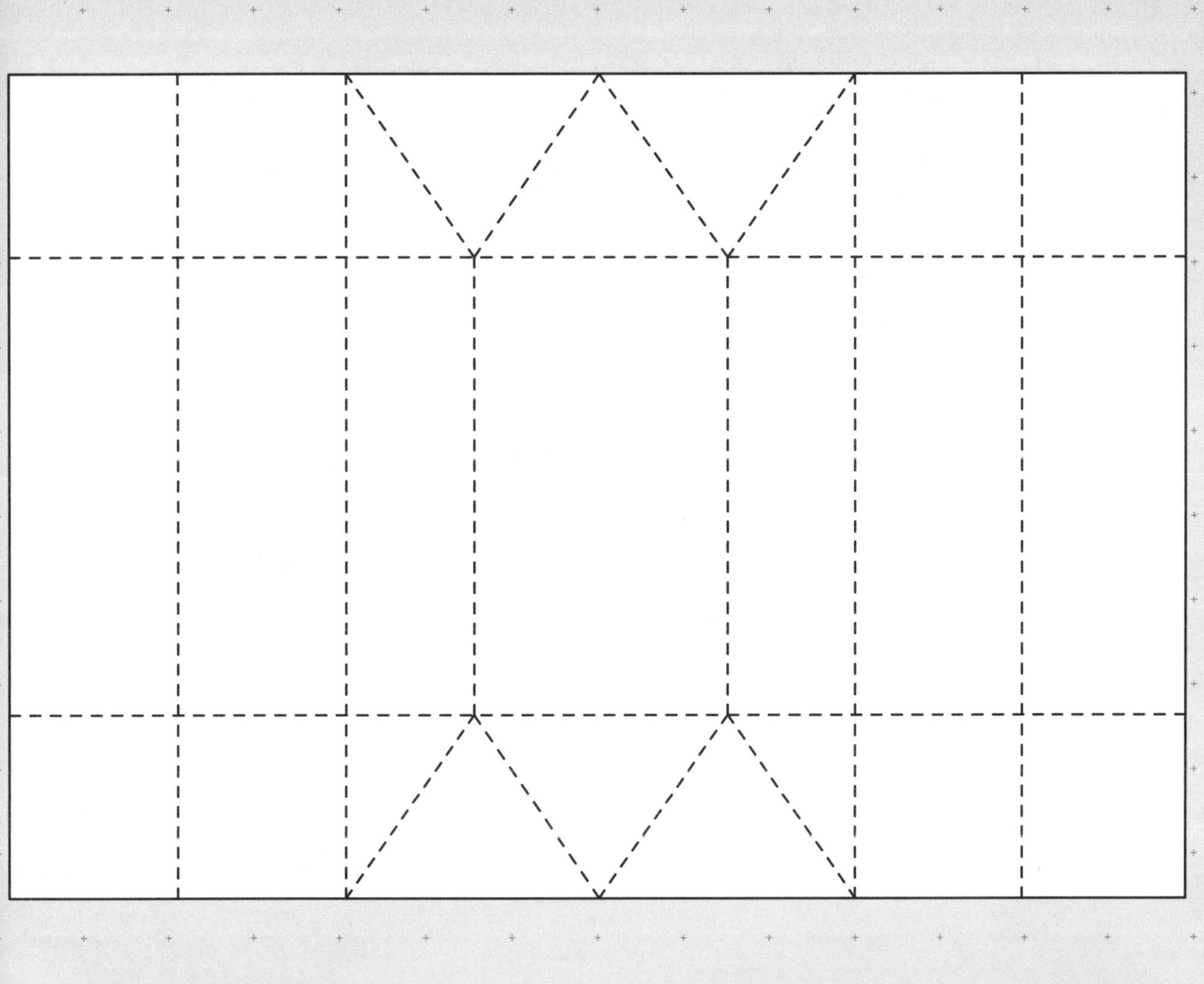

GOT ONE!! WILD MULLET CATCH

Design **Devours Bacon**

The packaging was designed to convey the joy of capturing a mullet fish in wild nature. Giving an accent on environmental protection, all the materials can be upcycled and recycled.

201

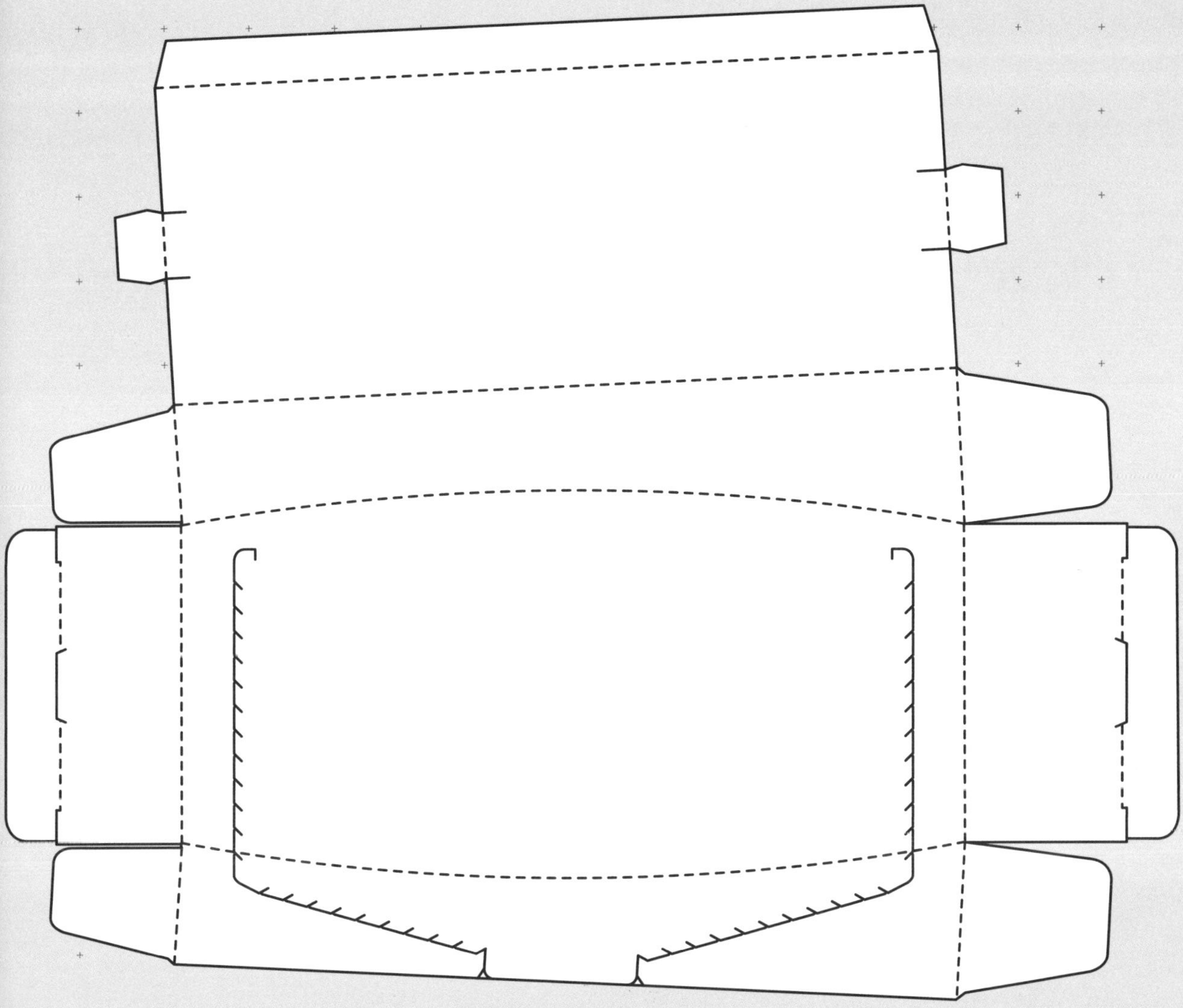

PAPER CUP CARRIER

Design **Patryk Wierzbicki**

This is a low budget packaging that enjoys surprising functionality and aesthetics. Its foldable structure saves storing space and carries firmly the cup along with the napkin, sugar sachets and stirrer.

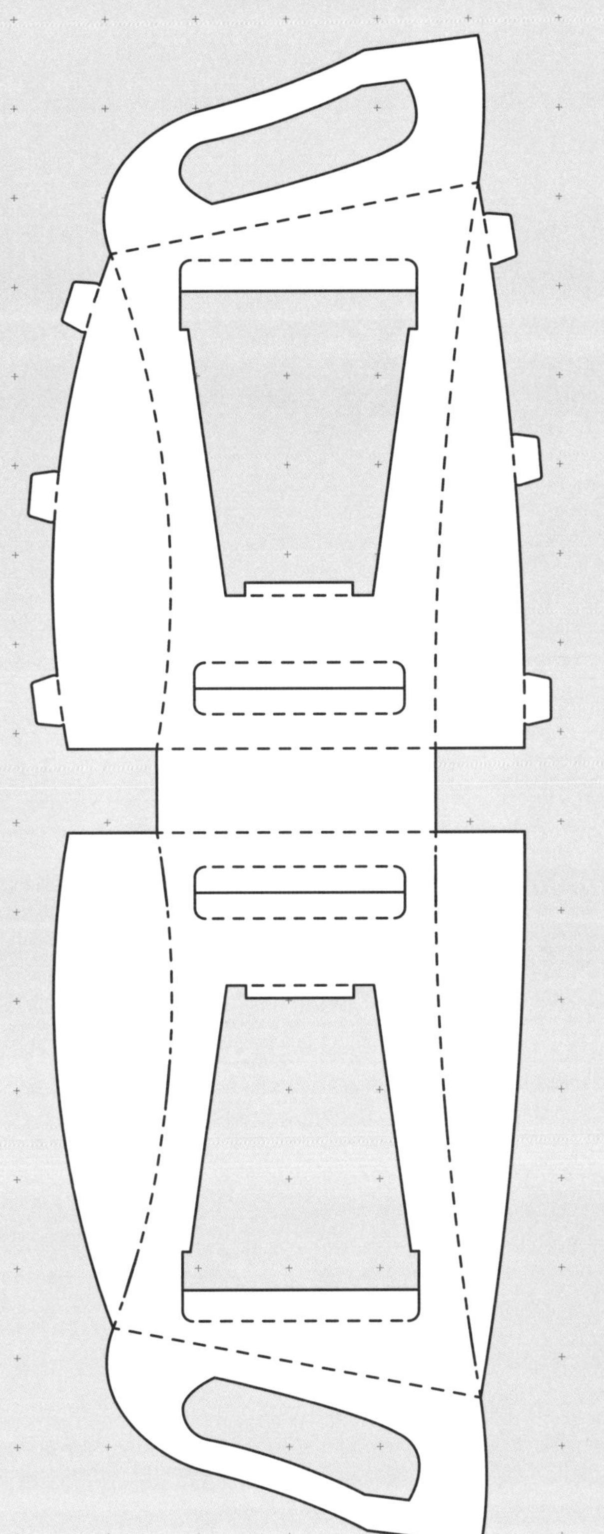

PASTA NOSTRA

Design **Patryk Wierzbicki**

The simple structure of triangular prism seems not satisfying enough for packing pasta. The designer has added a curiously twisted pyramid on the other end of the packet which thoughtfully holds basil for cooking.

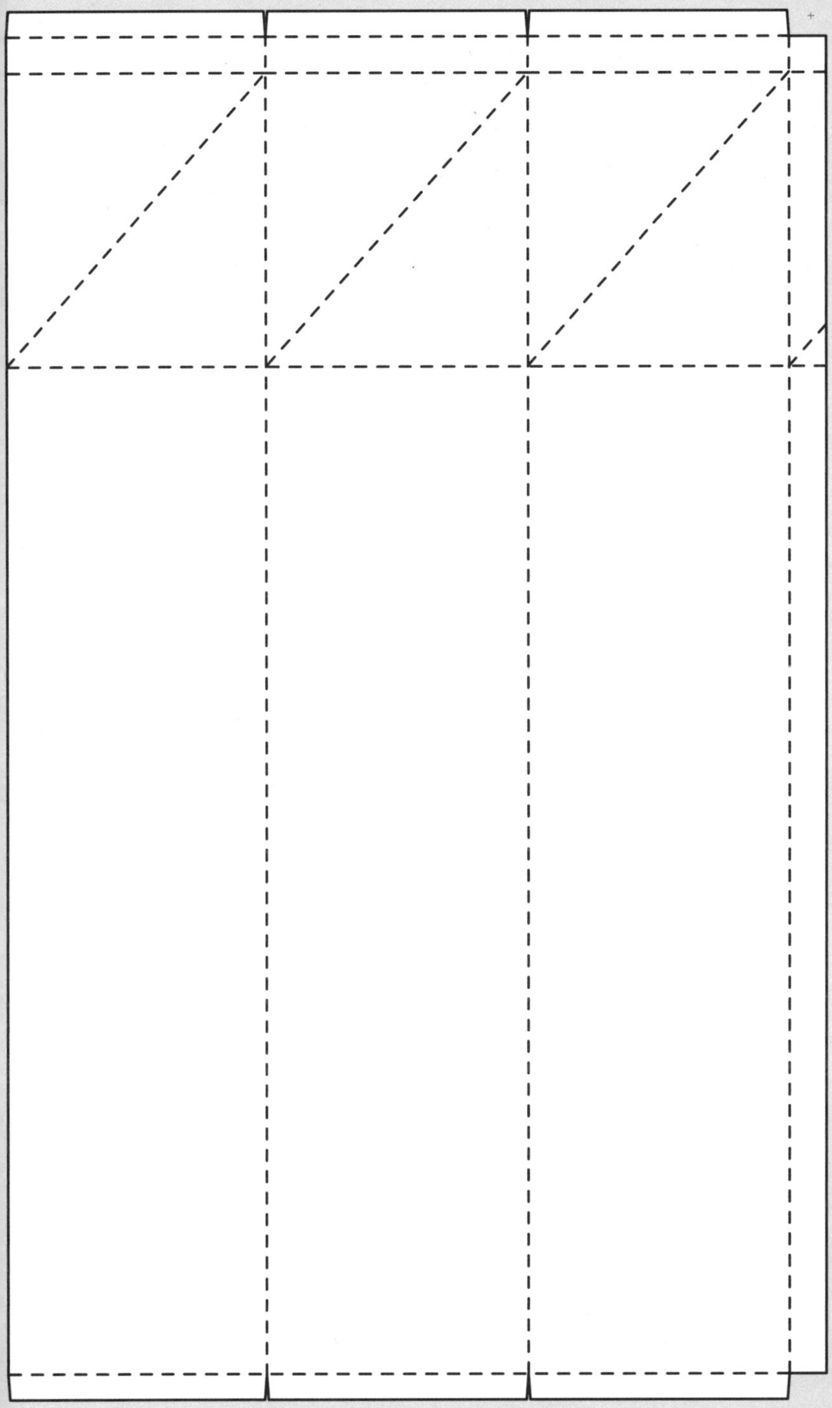

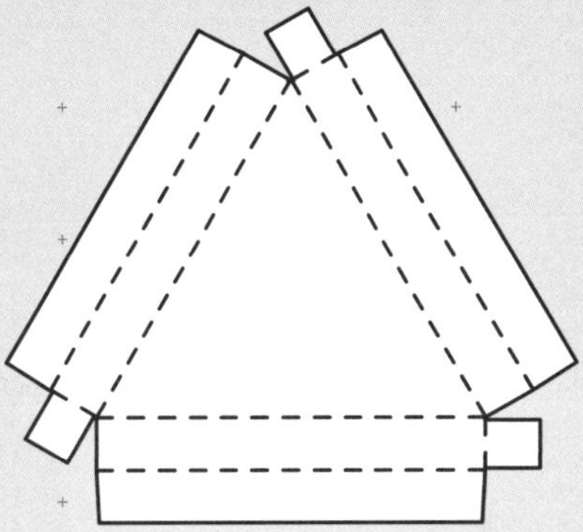

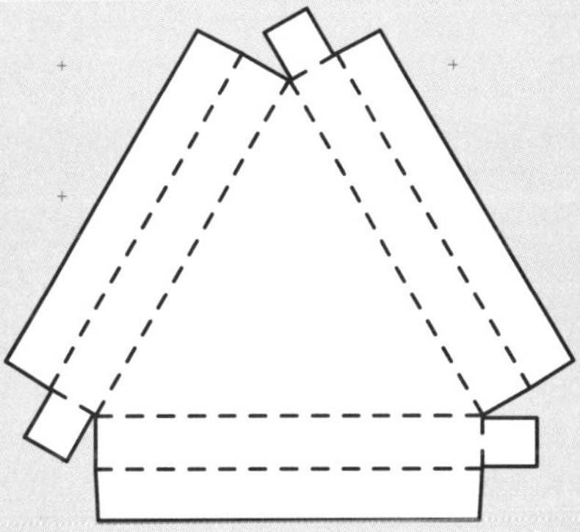

RECYCLABLE CUPS PACKAGING

Design **Alireza Jajarmi**

This is a concept project for Sur La Table's new terracotta product line. The hollowed out wooden coasters are the base of the packaging and help fasten the cups securely.

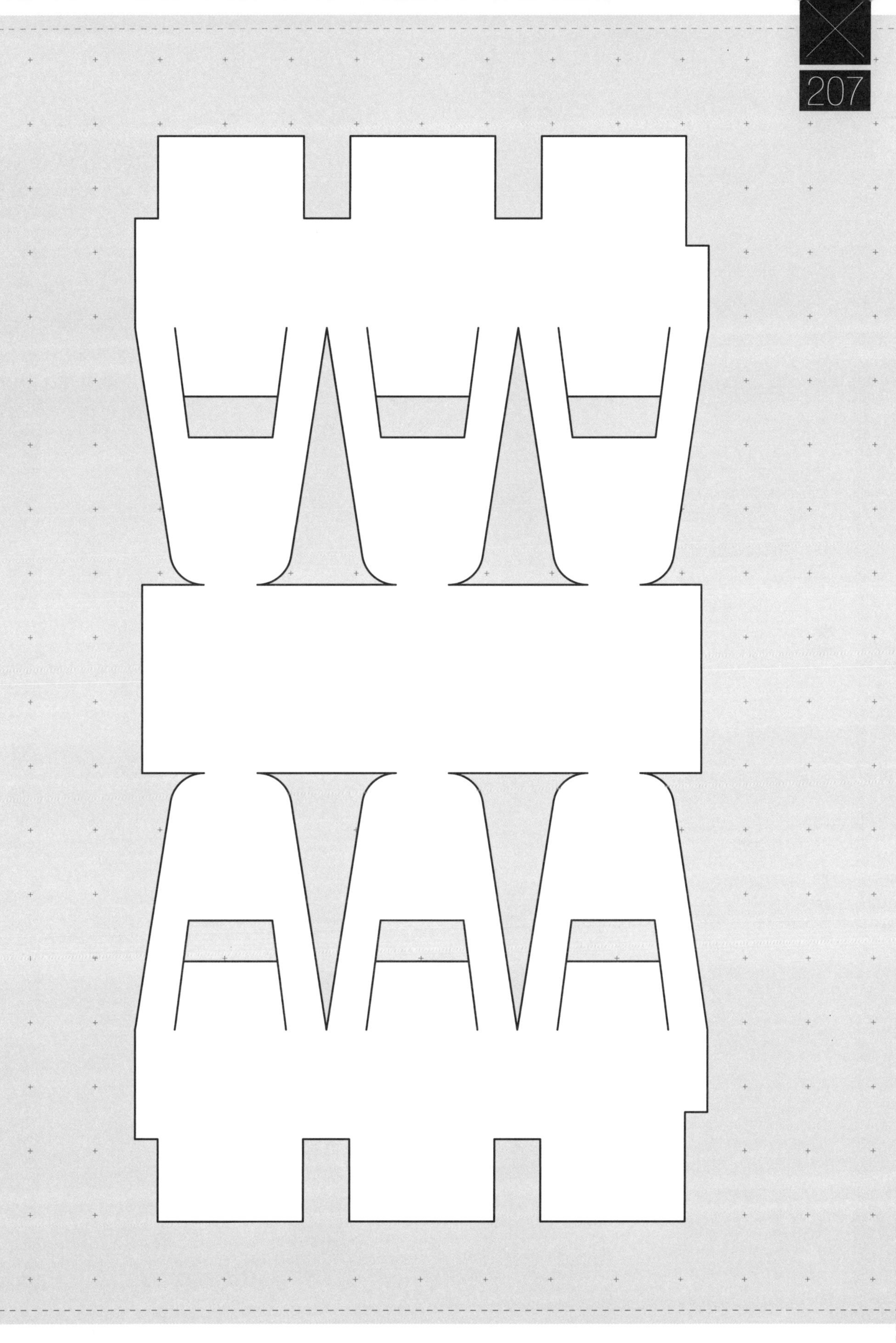

RICE BALL PACKAGE

Design **Takayuki Senzaki**

Onigiri is Japanese rice ball that imitates Japan's Holy Mountains. This rice ball shape package arouses consumer's interest and discloses the freshness through the cut-out angles.

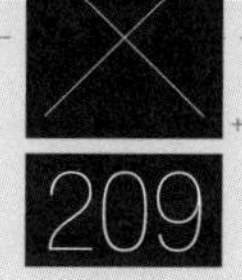

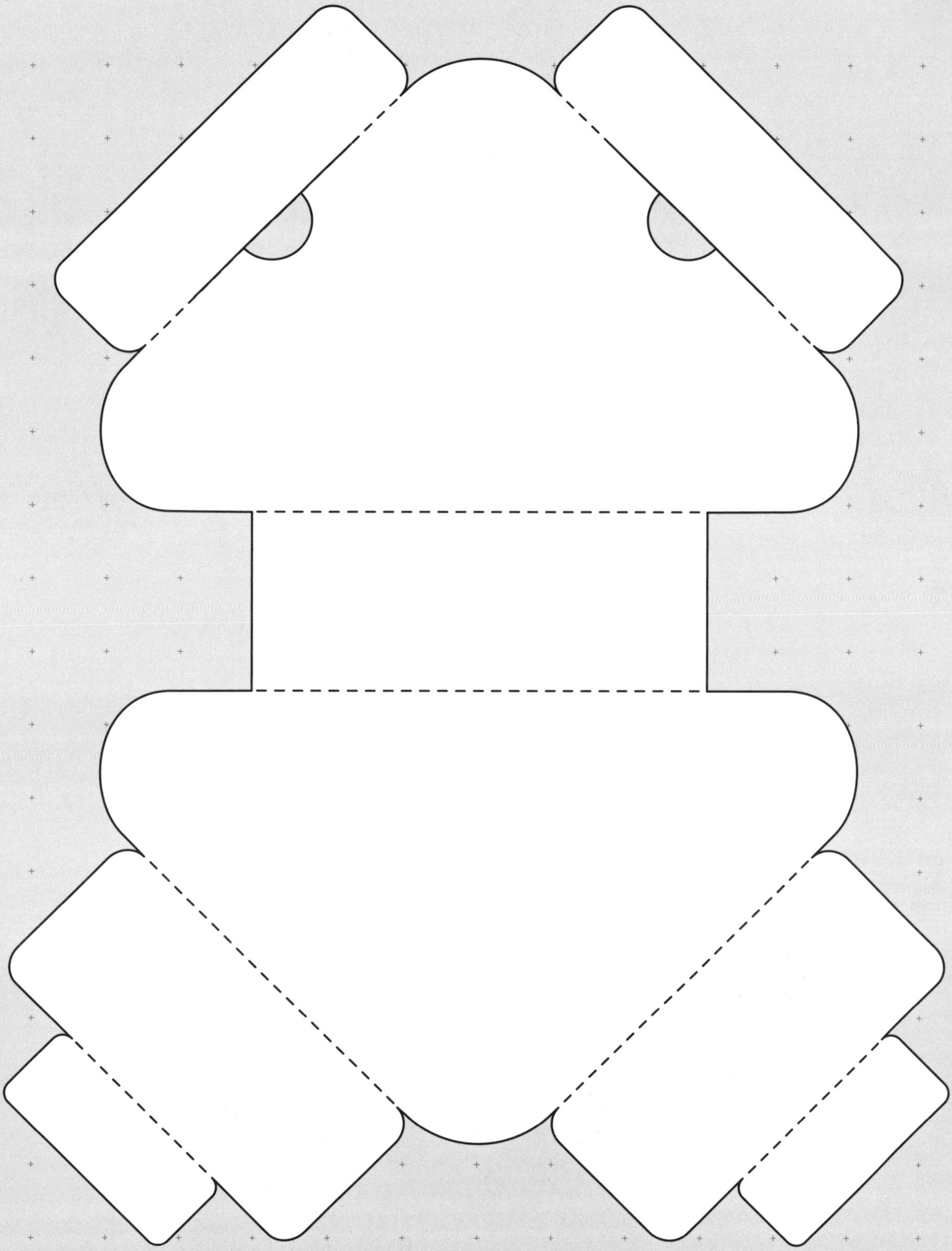

TEA PACKAGE CONCEPT

Design　Sima Boyko

The keynote of the package design and the graphic illustration is Provencal décor style. The packaging structure was delicately designed as a gift and has room reserved for some sweets that go with the tea.

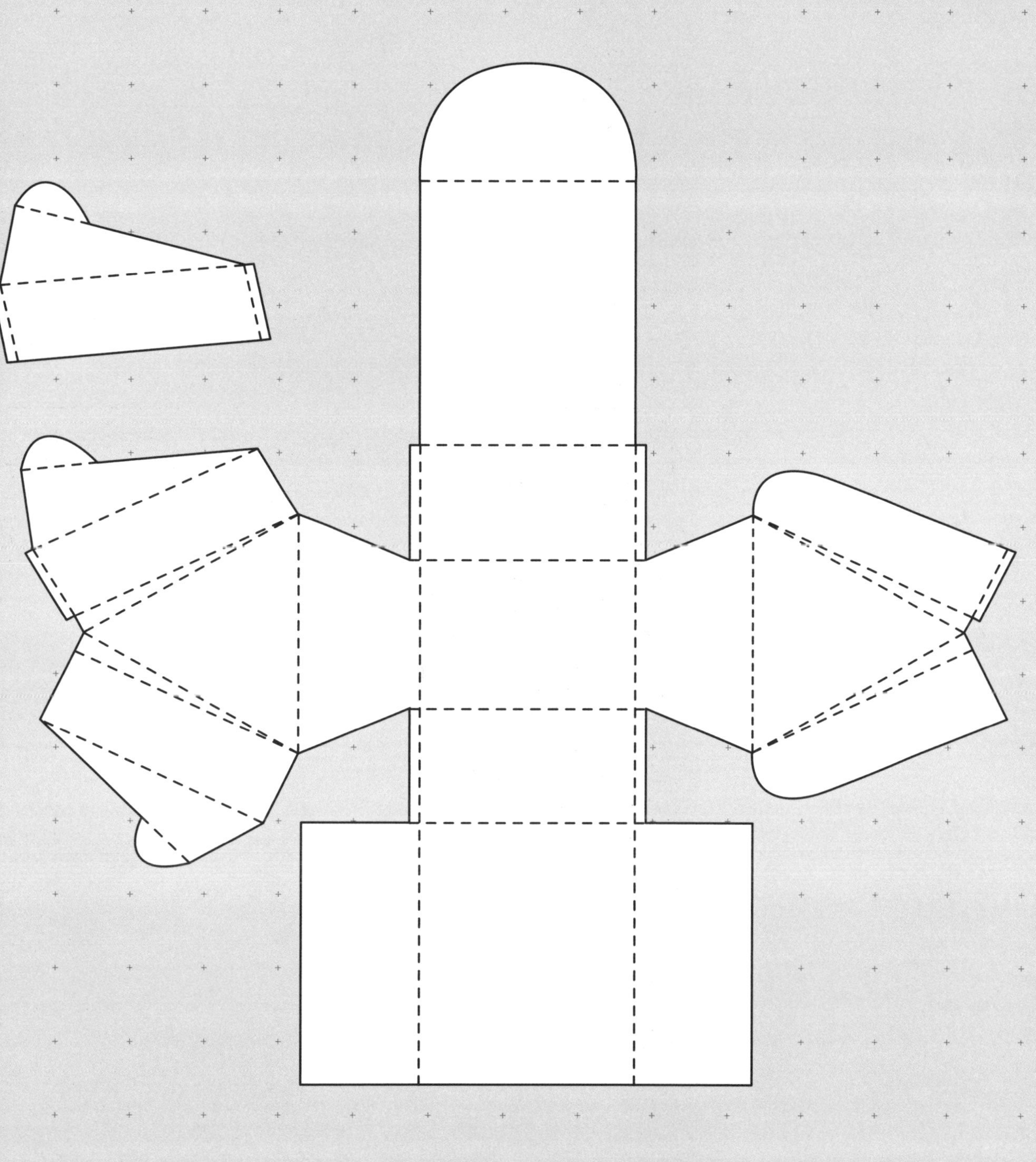

LIQUIVÉE

Design **Kissmiklos**

Instead of making a typical medicine package, the designer made these beauty vitamins a part of women's make-up kit. They should look feminine, elegant and fashionable enough to be in women's good grace.

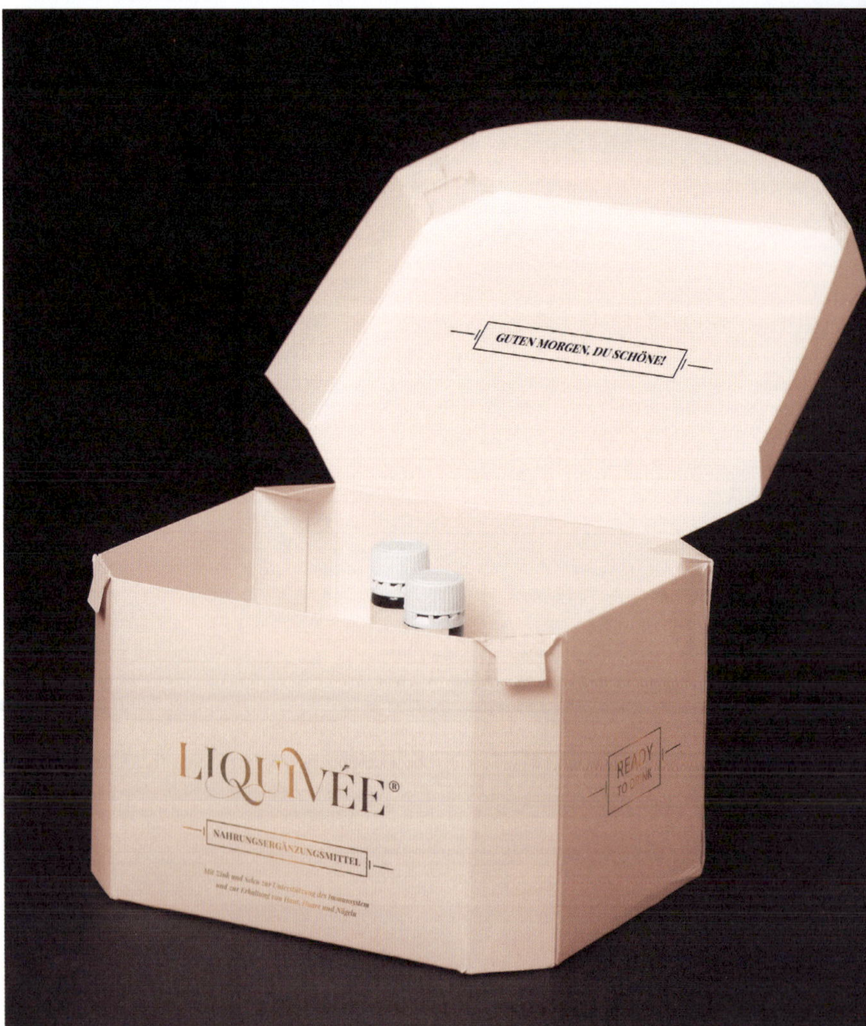

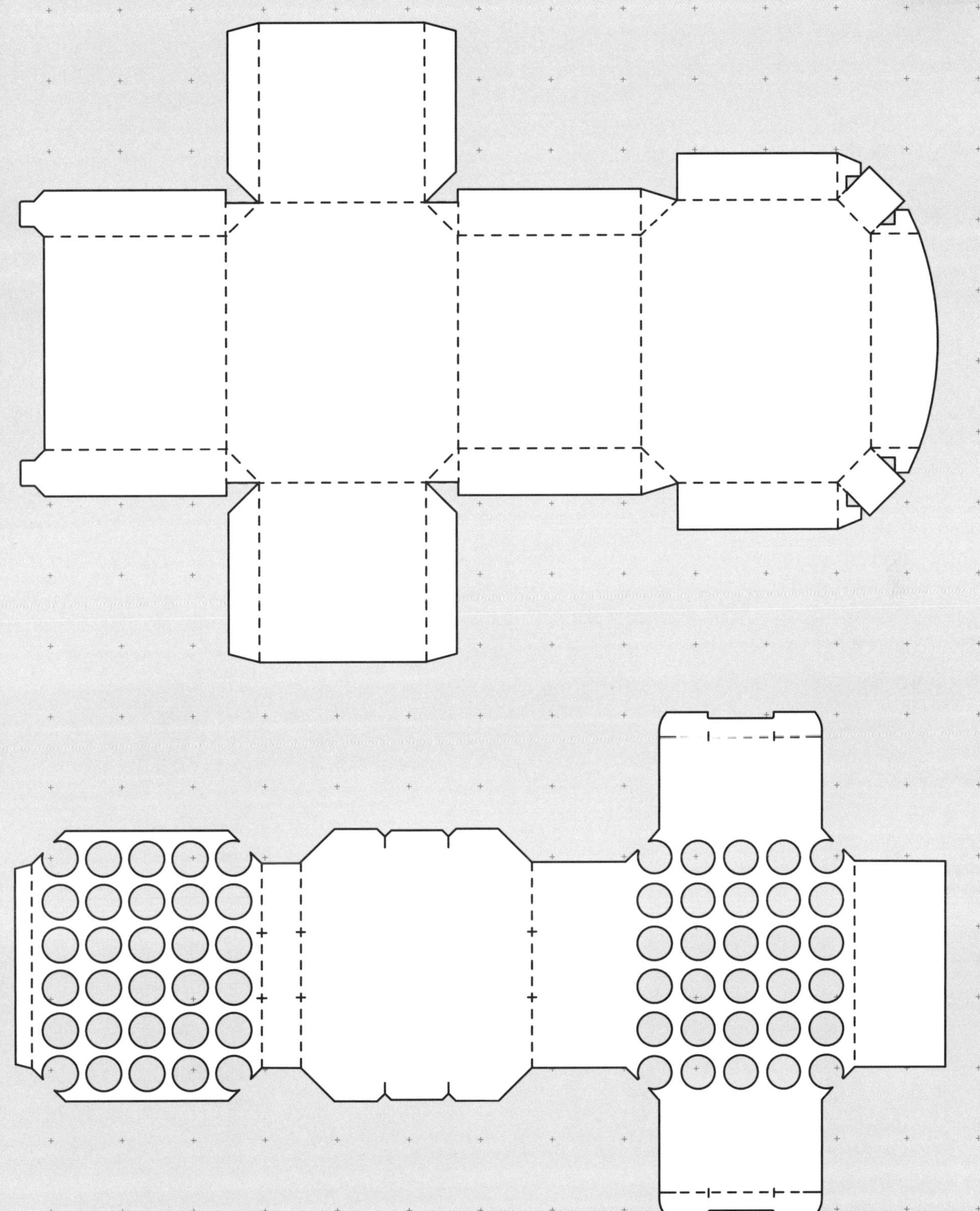

SUSTAINABLE PAINT

Design **Saerona Shin**

This conceptual project was inspired by the minimalistic approach of architect John Pawson. The designer opted for a more high-end and lightweight packaging for a paint product line. The focus on the innovative structure is a reflection on John Pawson's view about the fundamentals of art and design.

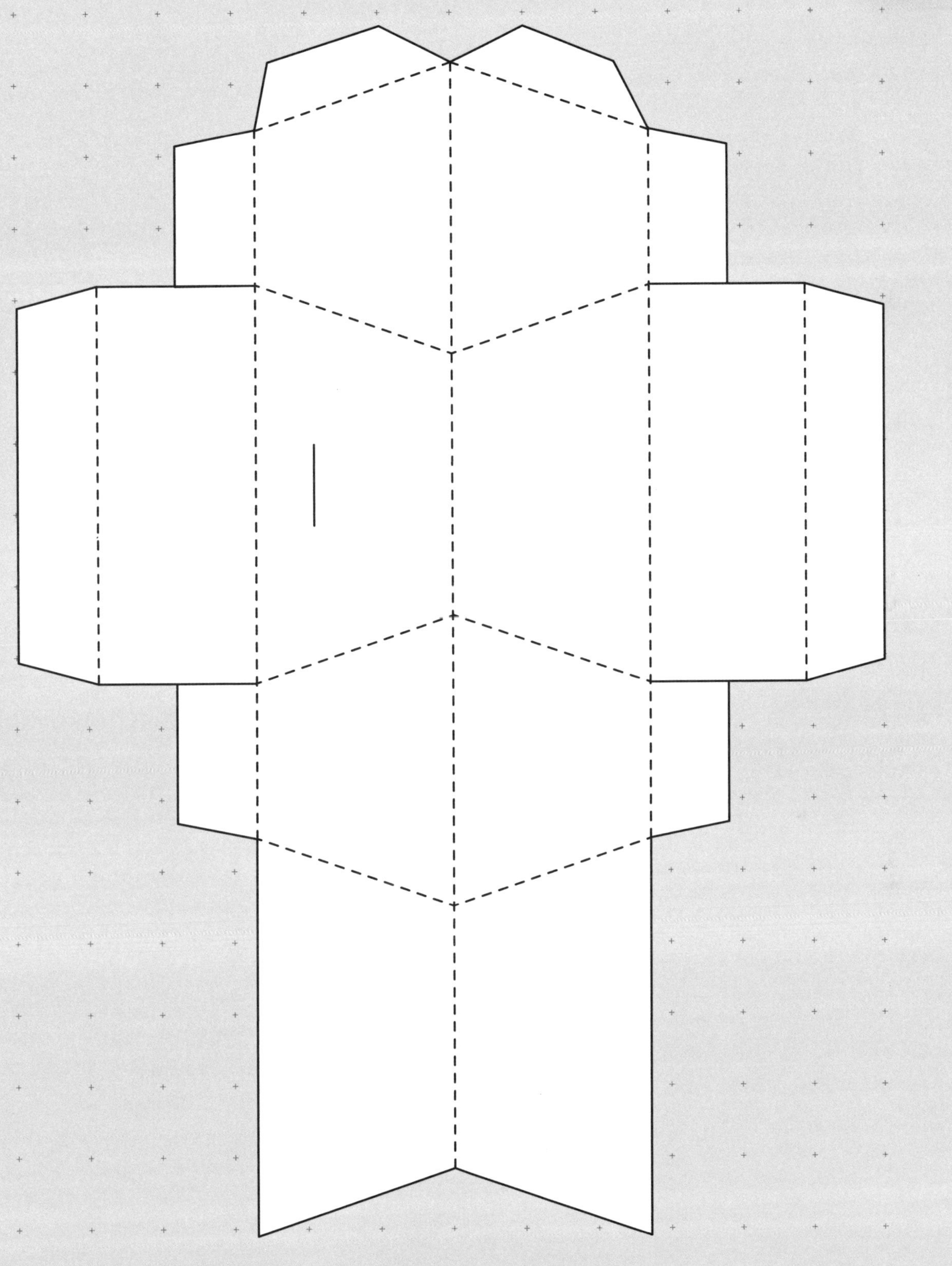

AMBROSIO

Design **Koval Lidiia**

The task was to create low profile and uncluttered packaging. The overall pointed shape of the final packaging is devised as an interesting contrast with the round candies which are visible through the transparent part. The red dot sticker indicates the opening of the packaging.

COVERT

Design **Andrea Cortes, Andrea Garza, Karla León, Arturo Soto, Denisse Carrillo**

Covert is an exclusive fashion brand. The triangle shape of the packaging was taken from the hourglass logo of the brand, for its aesthetic attribute lasts in impression. The labels on every package invite the customers to uncover the "secret" message from the brand.

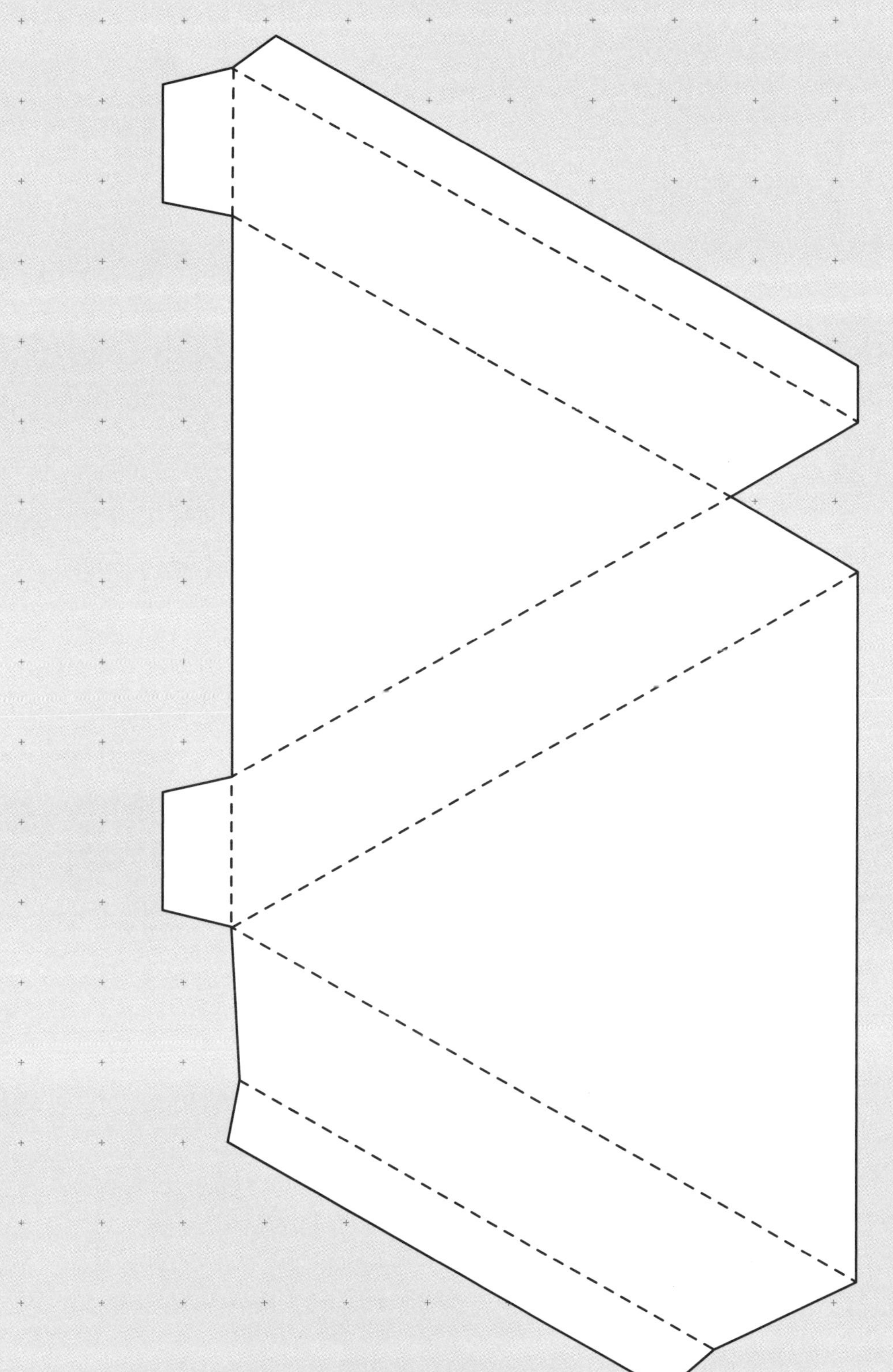

ELASTIC BAND PACKAGING

Design **Ric Bixter**

The motivation behind the packaging is to give a new life to an ordinary object sold in a pound shop. The elastic band box appears as if it is being squeezed by the band.

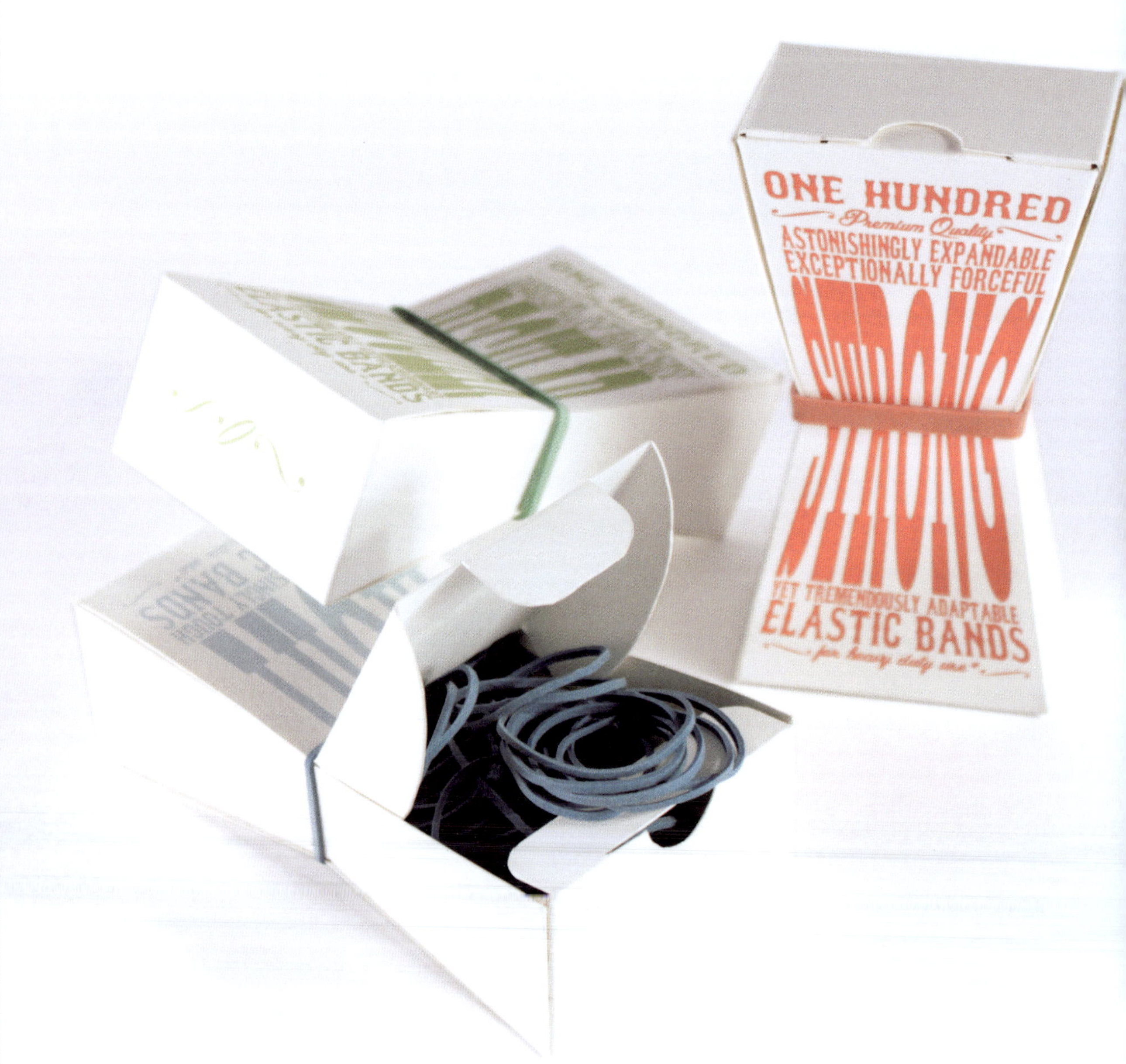

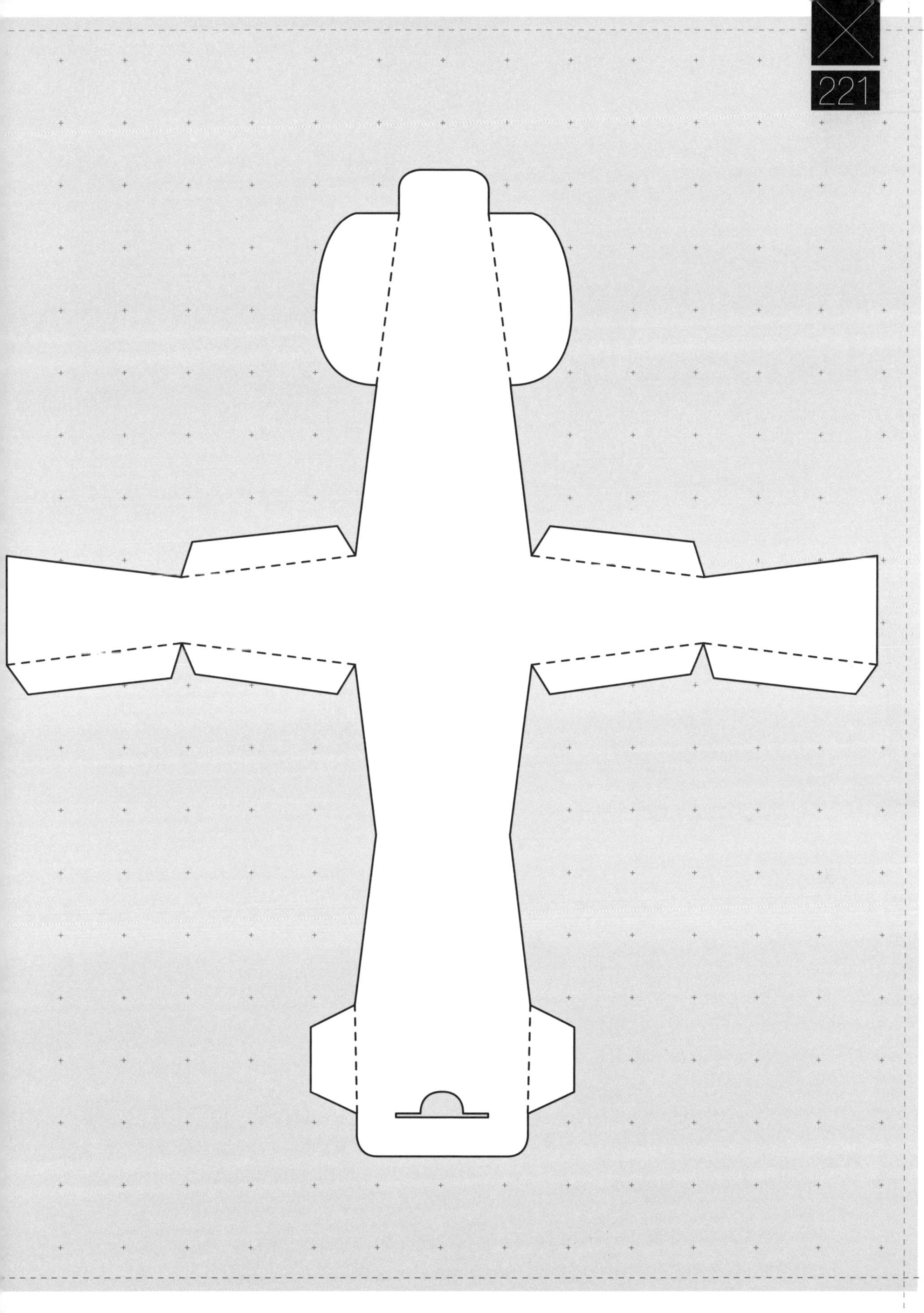

FIRST SPOON

Design **Takayuki Senzaki**

First Spoon is a special gift for babies and serves the very first meal after they are weaned. A package was custom made for the first spoon and a bowl in the form of a mother's womb.

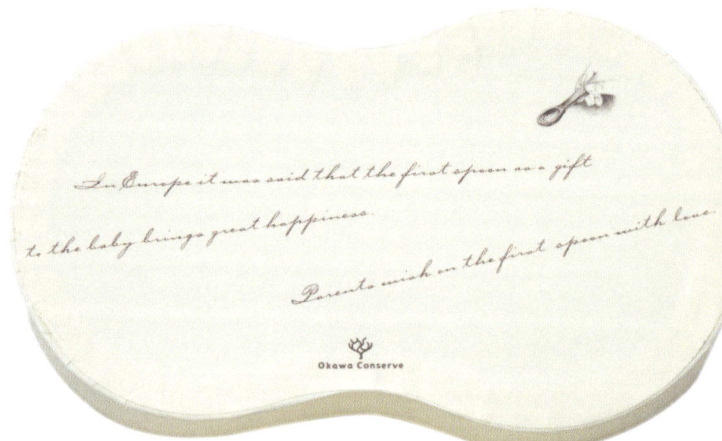

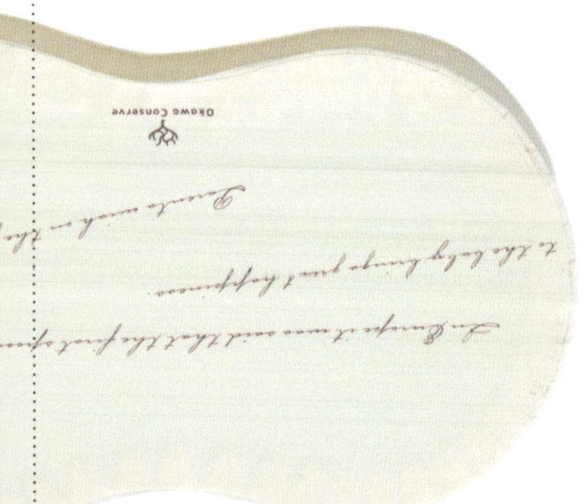

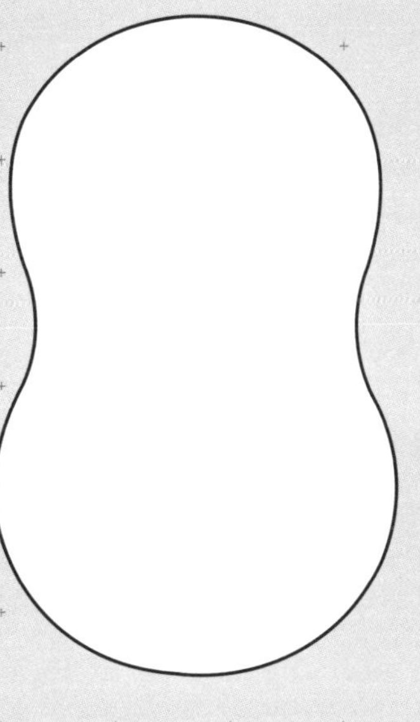

HANDCRAFT SPOON KIT

Design Takayuki Senzaki

This is a package for a handcrafted spoon kit. The craft-paper made with embossed process and staple highlights the handcraft nature of the product.

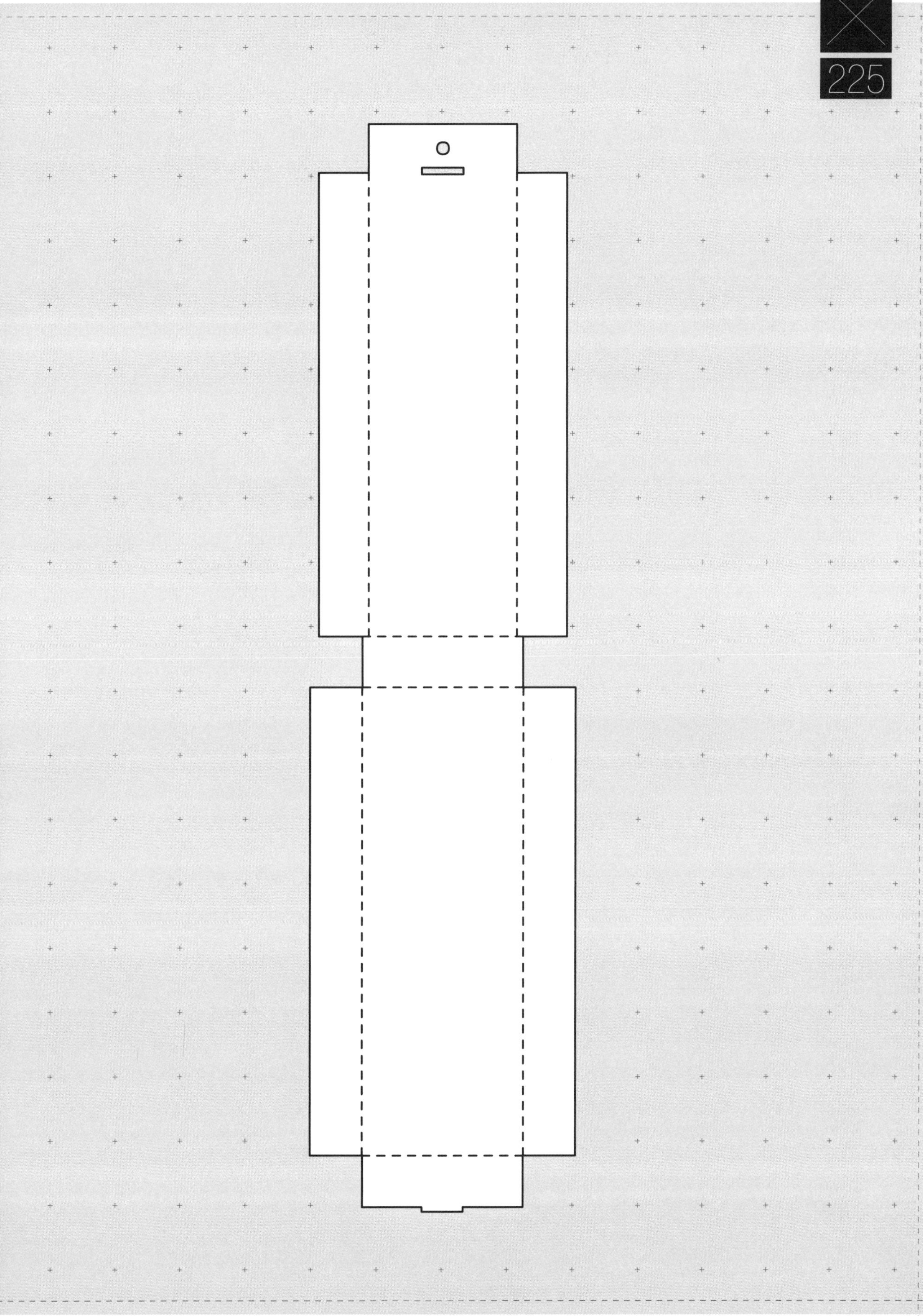

HELVETICA 50 YEARS

Design Nuno Picolo d'Almeida

The purpose of the project was to celebrate the 50 years of history of the typeface Helvetica, by making a limited edition package for the typeface. The design has borrowed the Swiss cross and the simplicity of Swiss style.

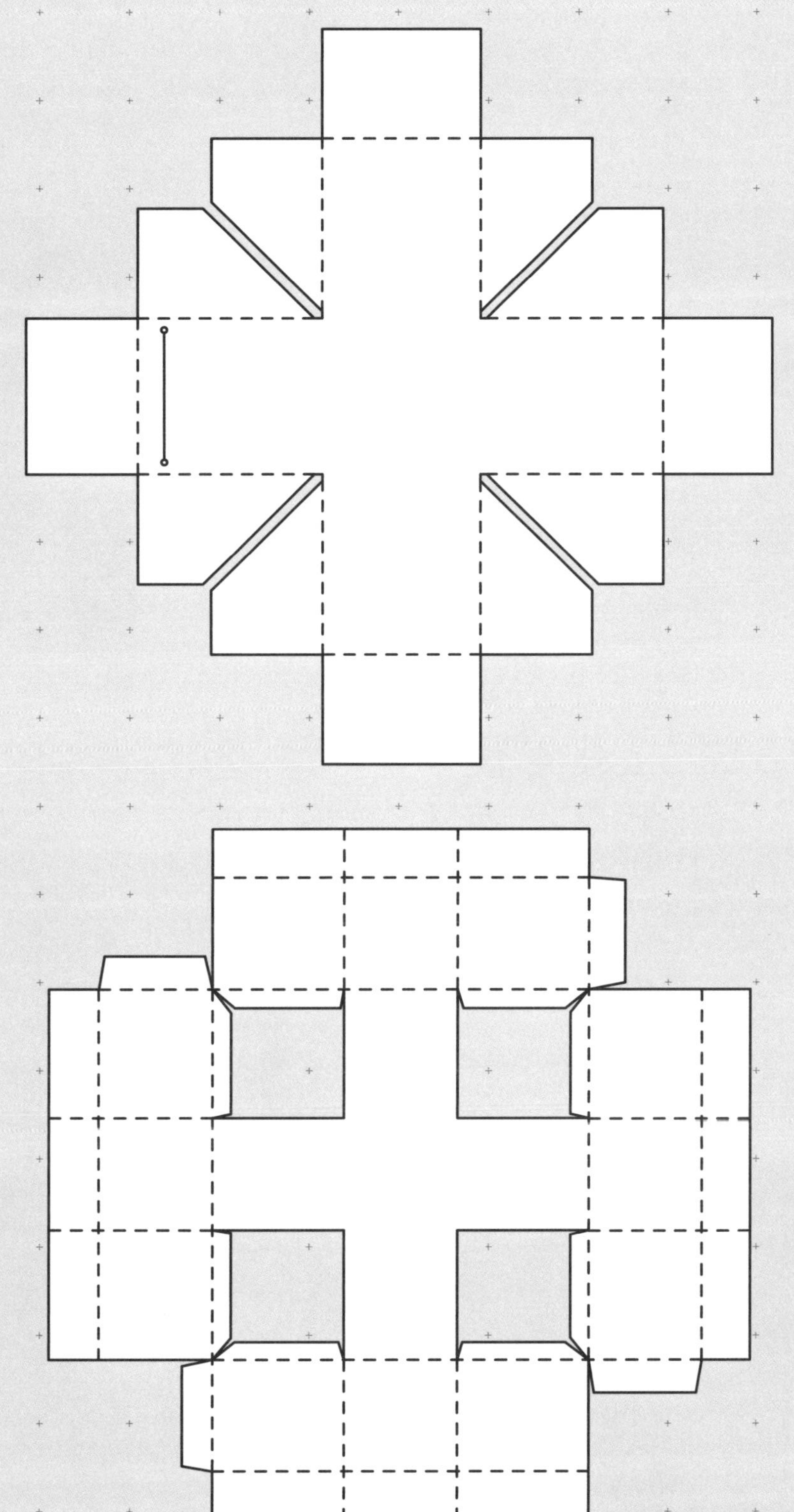

GORGET

Design **Natalia Wysocka**

A Gorget is a piece of armor that protects the throat or the wimple worn by the women in the medieval period. The package was created to be as protective and decorative as the gorget.

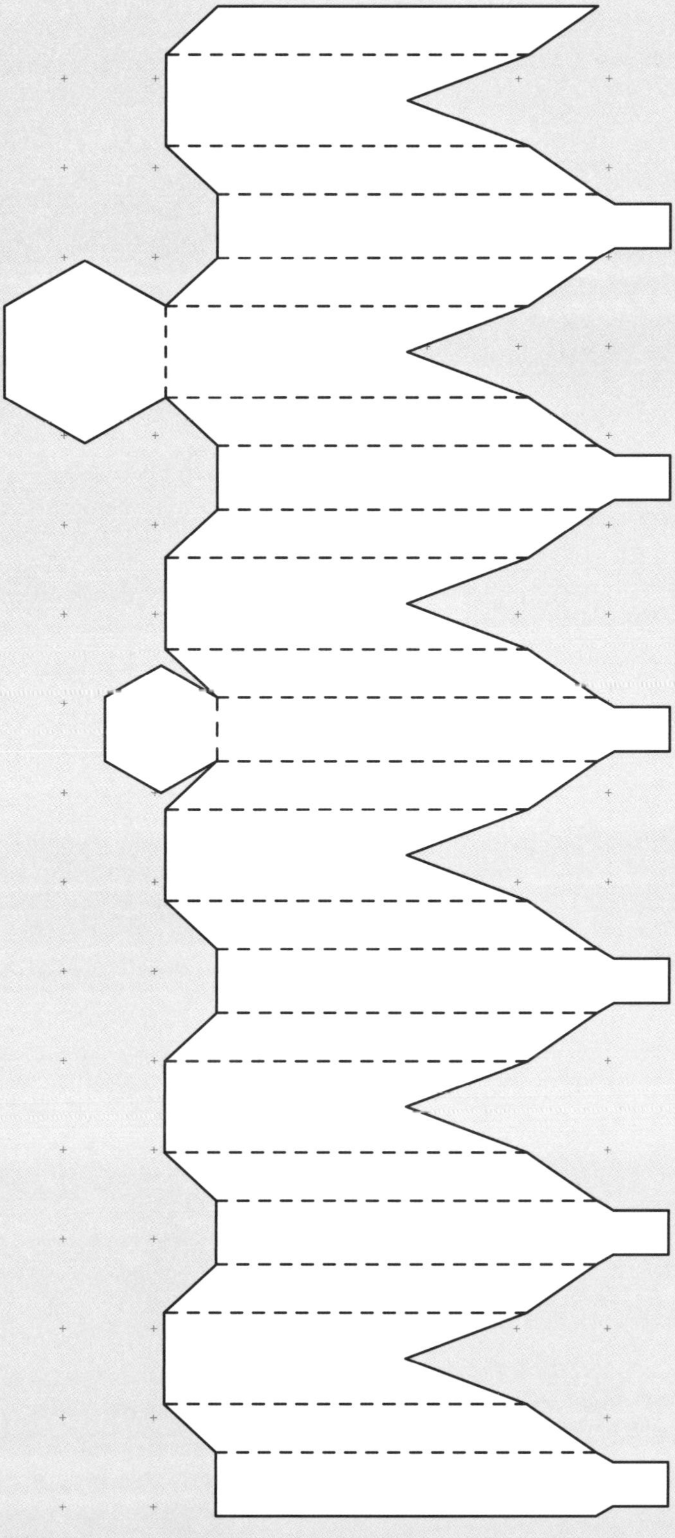

DESSERT PACKAGING TEEPEE

Design **Karolína Fardová**

This packaging is for a fluffy Czech dessert Indiánek (Little Indian). It is made of one-piece recyclable paper, yet the structure is highly protective.

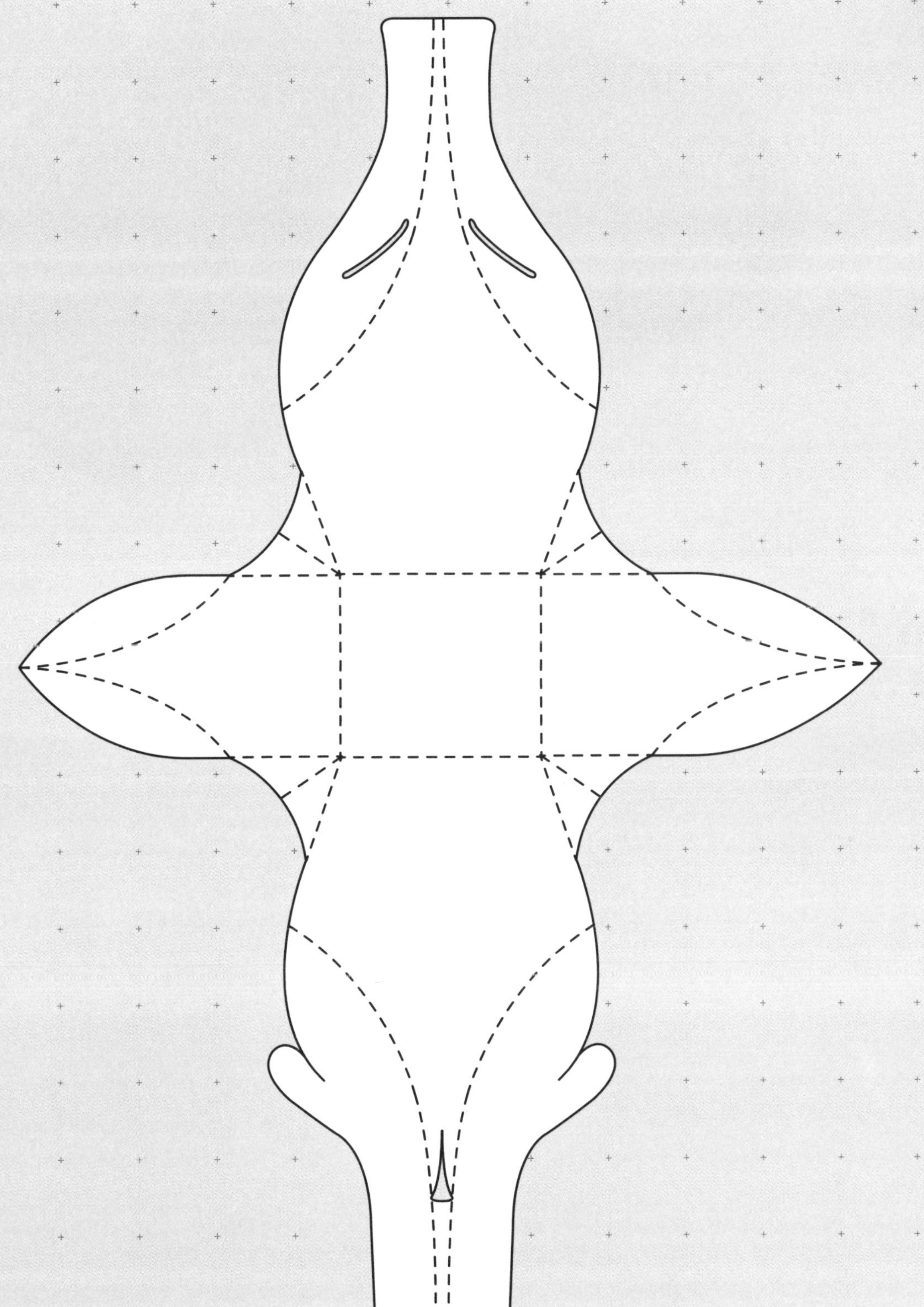

DOMOV

Design Rudolf Vychovalý

This simple folding box was designed as a surprising birthday and anniversary present. Domov means "home" and is a traditional Slovak folk symbolism. The way of serving alcohol in glass jars and in a house-shaped box is to generate a home-made touch.

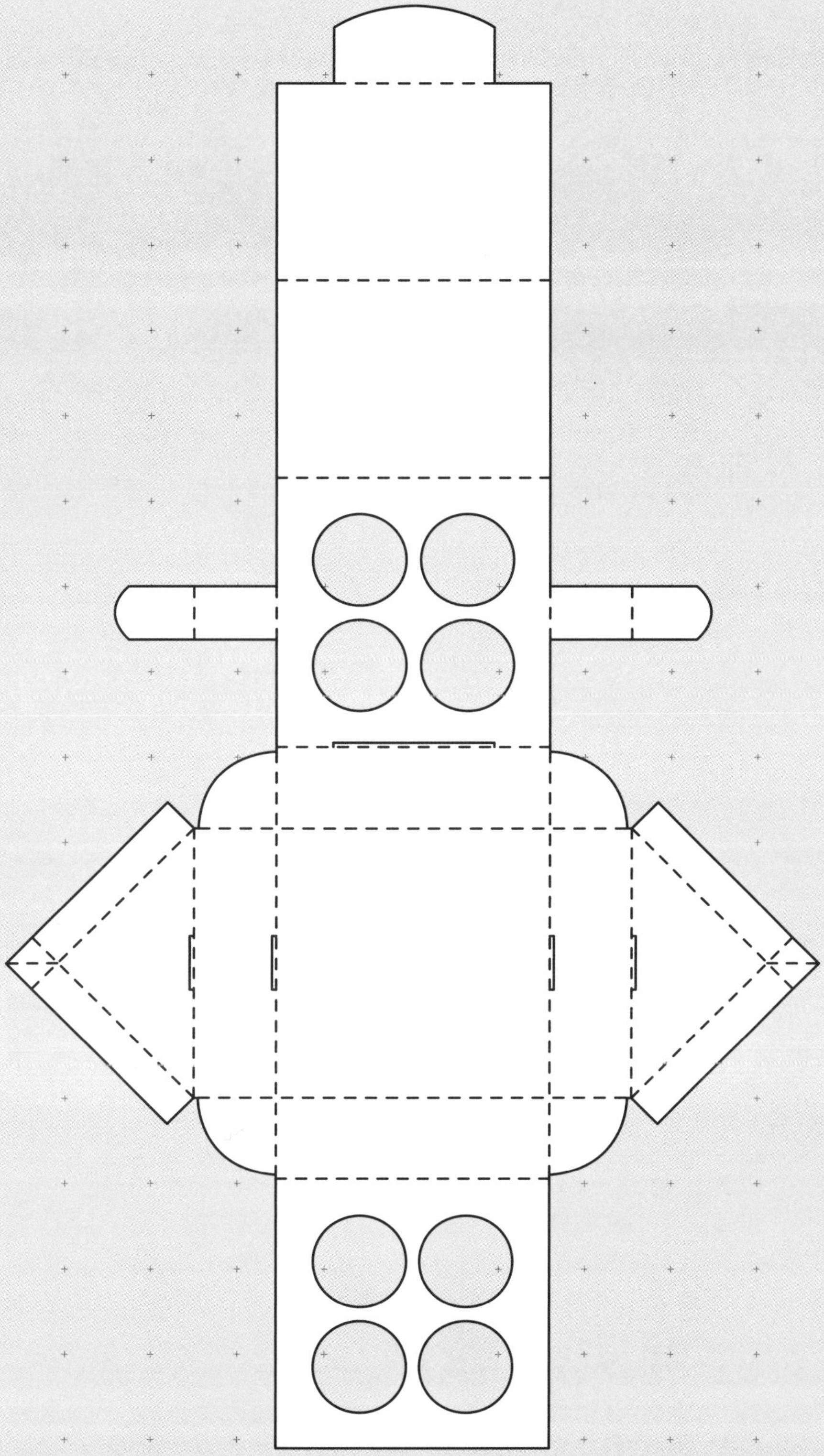

SONGJIANG TEA

Design **Huang, Yao-Tsung**

Incorporating the product's natural cultivation, the packaging design is based on the belief of Zen. It aims to give the consumers an extraordinary experience with a visual graphic of traditional Chinese landscape painting and the special lotus leaf unfolding structure.

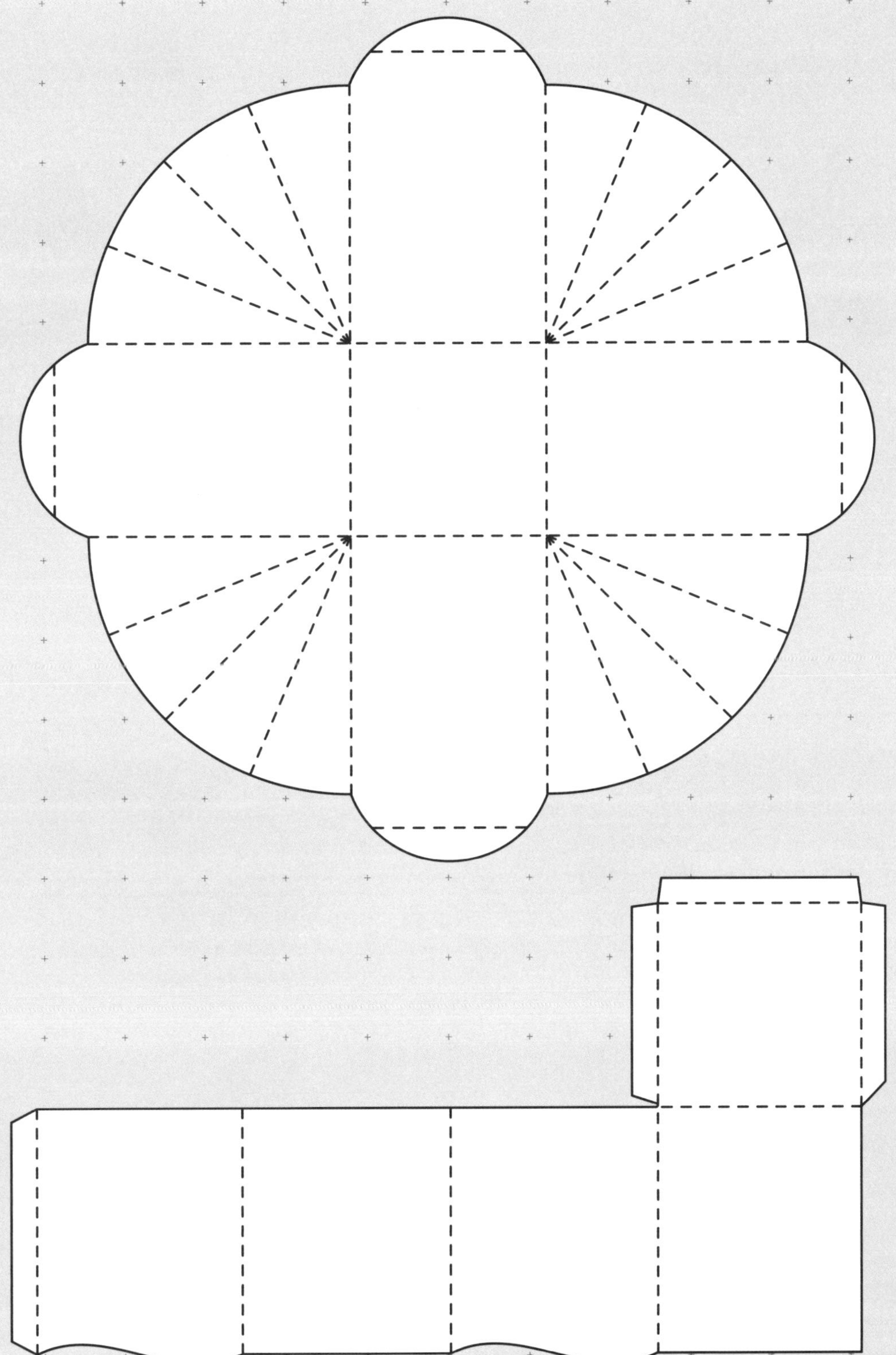

TISSUE BOX

Design **Natalia Wysocka**

This pyramid packaging consists of an outer box and an inside box which is divided into three containers for three different moist towelettes. The holes at the bottom of the containers allow easy access to the tissues.

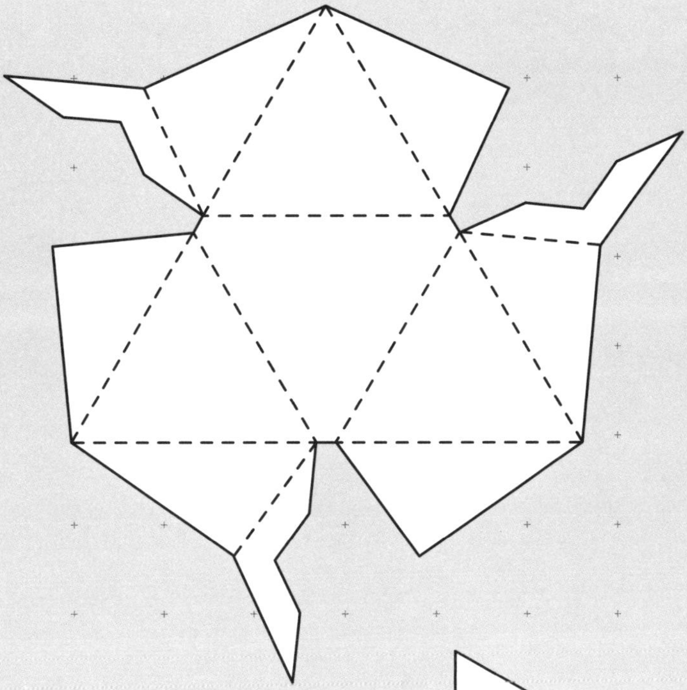

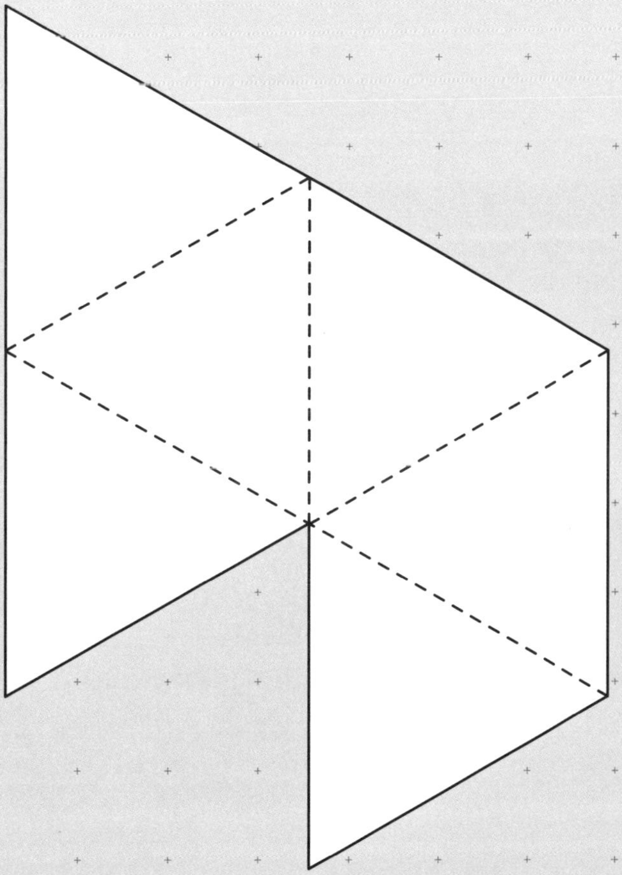

DINNER TIME

Design **Dan Ogren, Kaz Ishii**

This is refreshing package design that breaks the trend of the "Italian look" for a series of items that are associated with pasta dinners. Aesthetically, the designers wanted to capture the homemade feeling with clean, simple and purposeful design elements. All parts of the project are either screen-printed or vinyl.

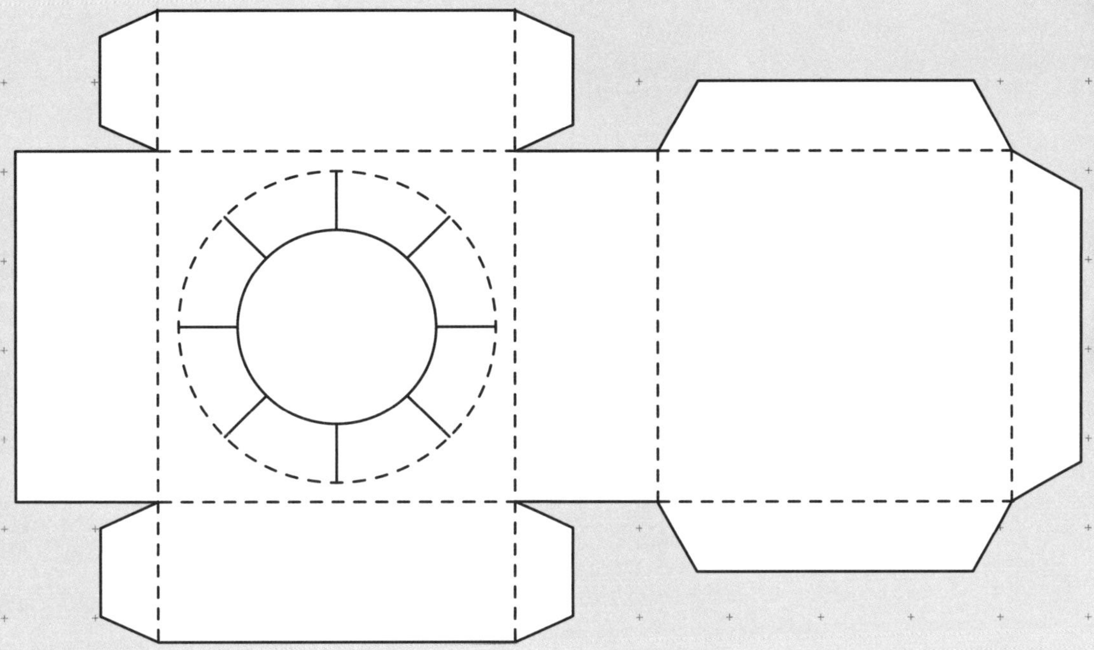

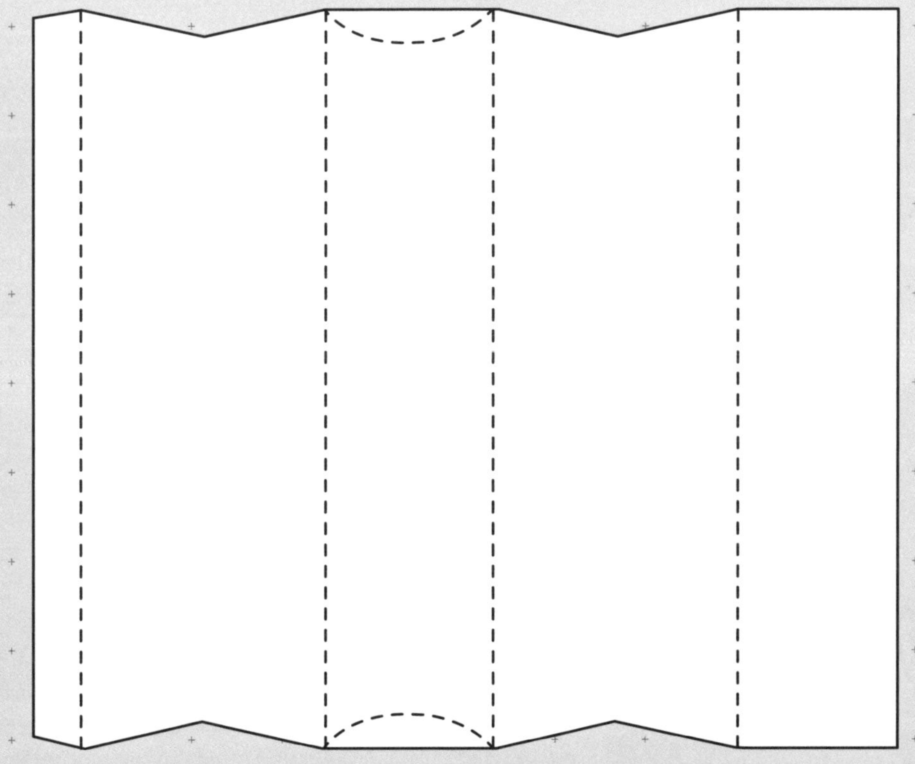

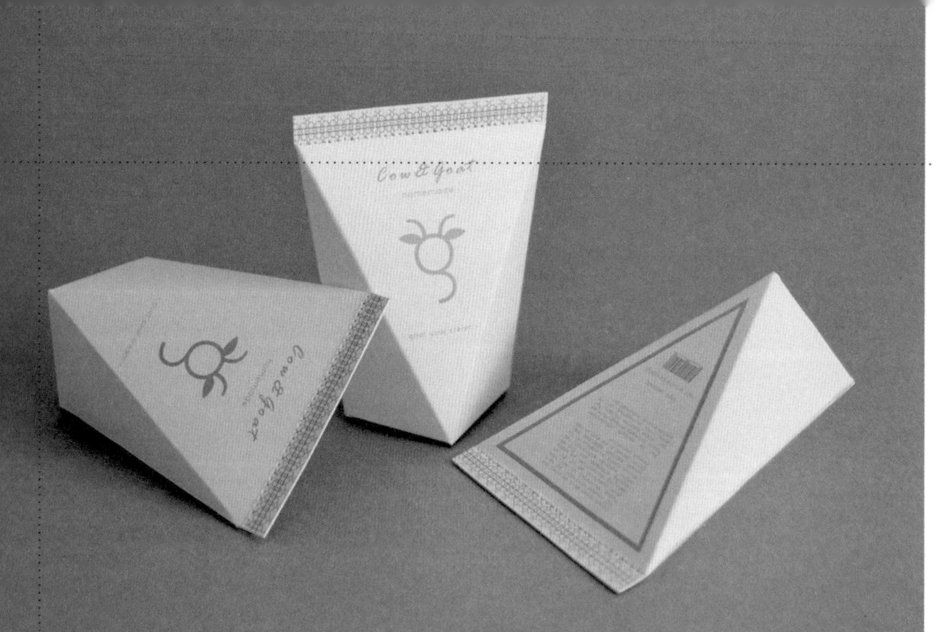

COW & GOAT HOMEMADE DAIRY PRODUCTS

Design **Anisja Alurović**

Geometry and simplicity is the basis of the design. The designer tried to create an "easy to use" and "easy to read" package that allows the product to impress at first sight. The surface of the box was kept clean for not upstaging the logotype and colour palette.

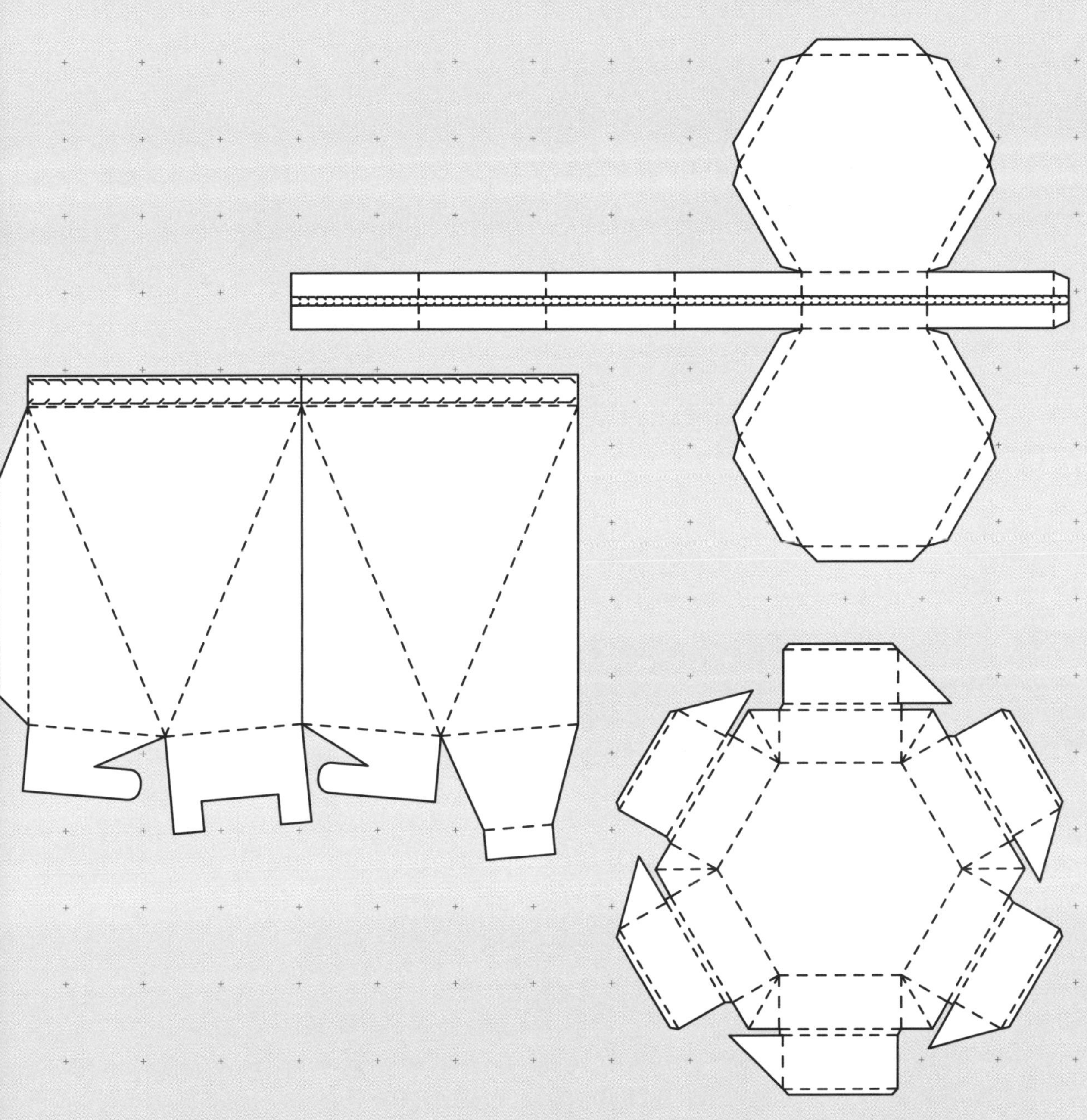

KARBON

Design **Anna Johansson, Nathalia Moggia, Rita Alton, Tove Alton, Linda**

The androgynous perfume had encouraged the designers to go beyond gender difference and look for the essence of all living things. The structure of this carbon-like box is simple and functional: it has a strong shelf impact, and it gives solid protection while minimizes material waste.

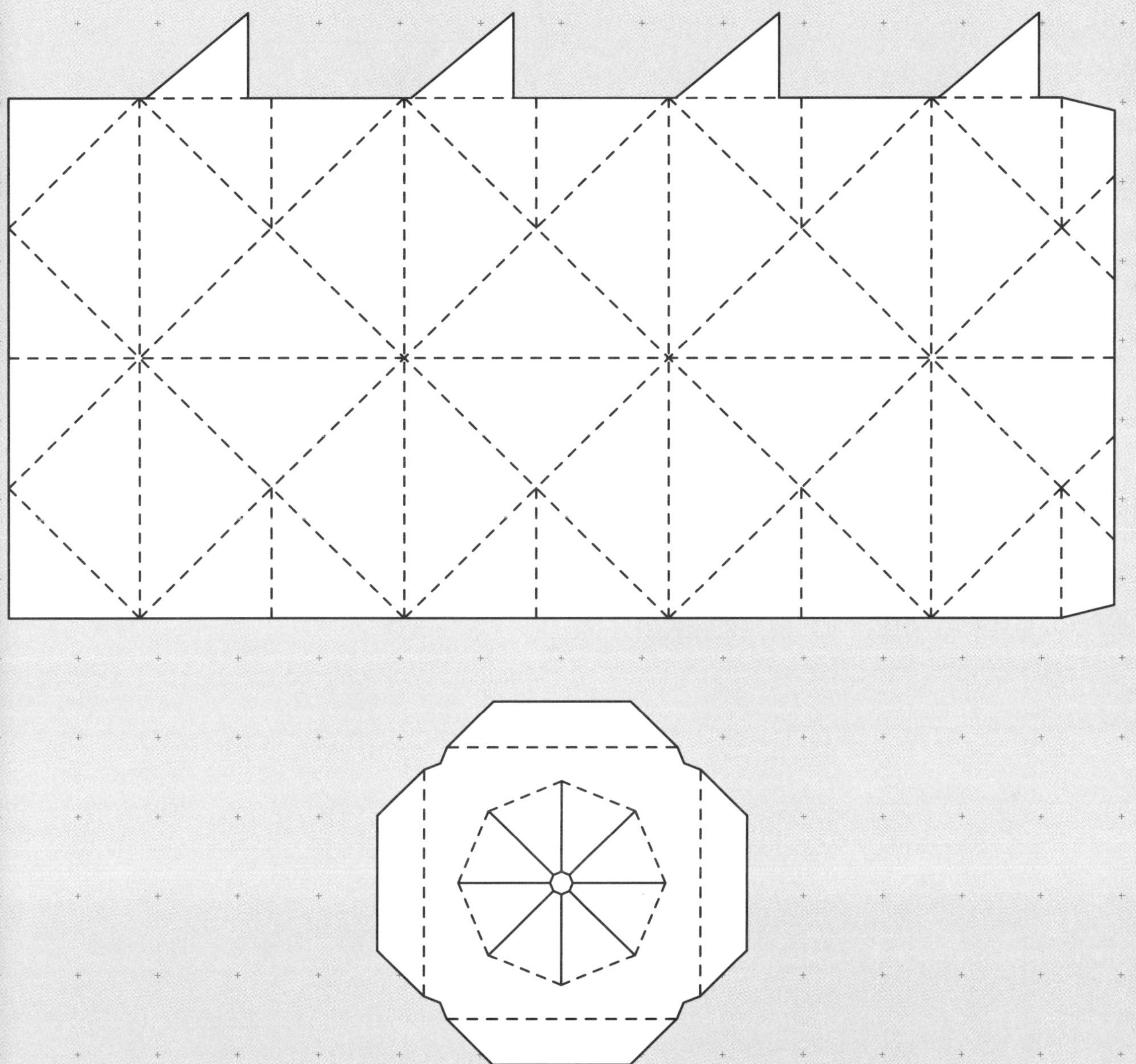

LOGOPLASTE MILK PACKAGING

Design Ilja Klemencov

This unusual milk carton communicates with customers in a friendly way. This is realized by the stamp effect in graphic design and the brand mascot—flying cow which embodies the positive nature of the brand.

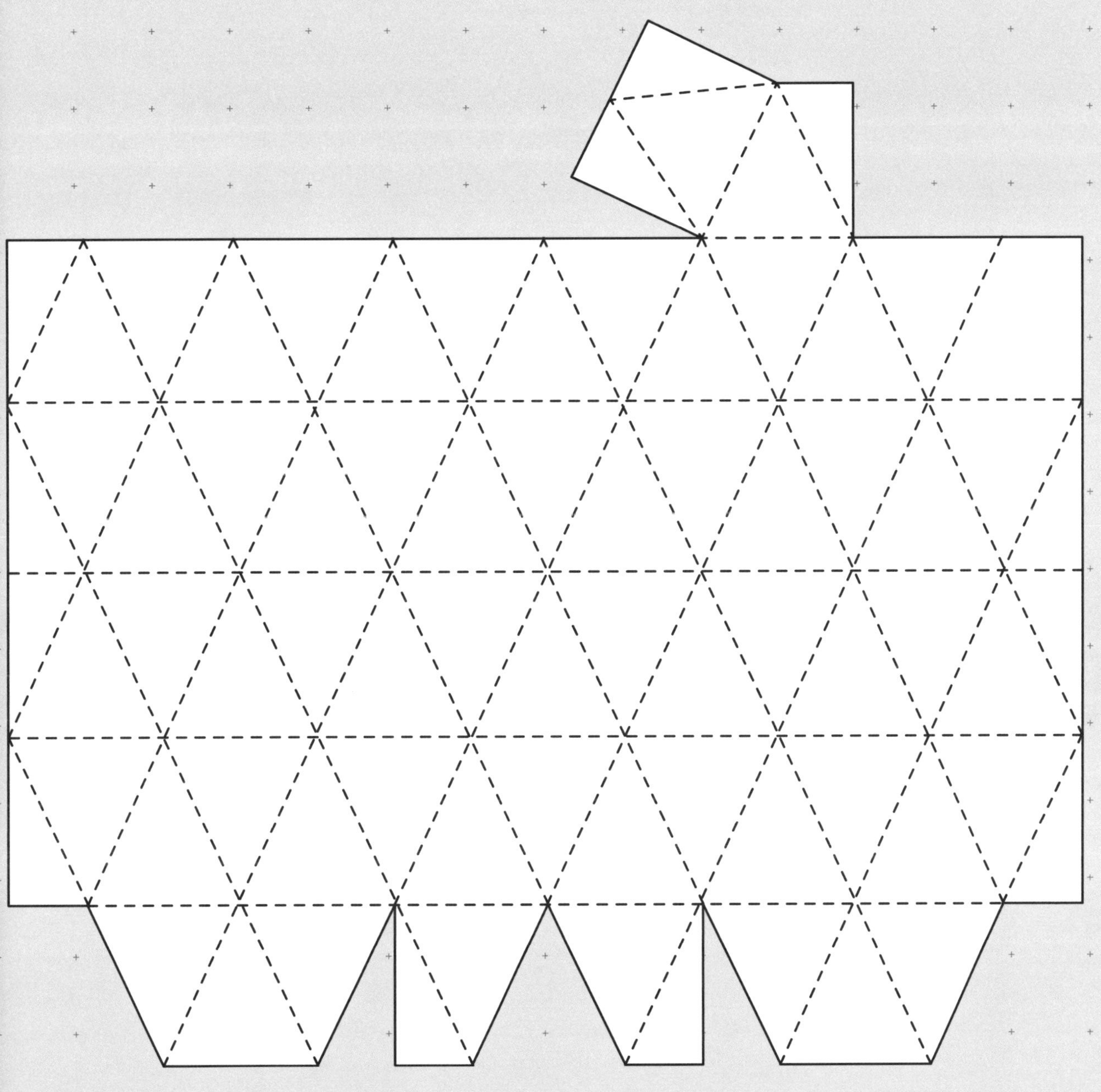

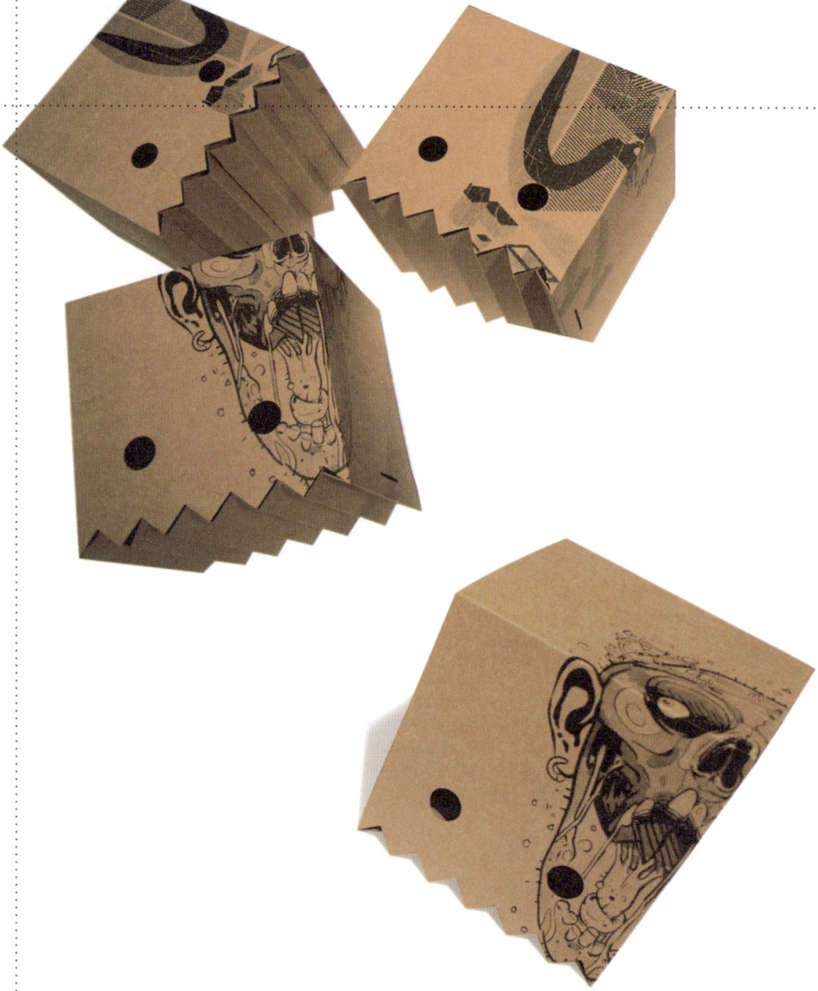

HEROKID MAGIC BOX

Design **Andreu Zaragoza**

The concept of this packaging design was to create a box that could be a T-shirt packet as well as a decorative and promotional element. The Herokid logo served as the inspiration to design this packet in corrugated cardboard that could be assembled without adhesive.

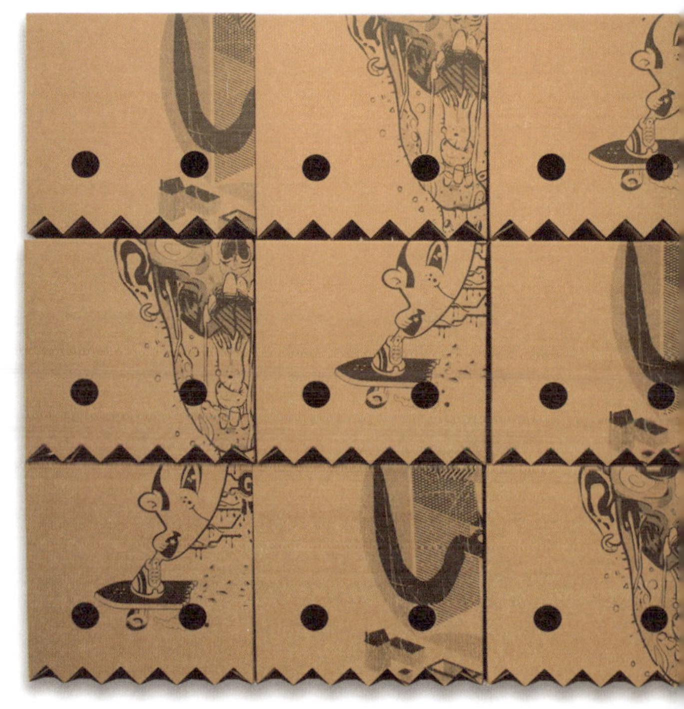

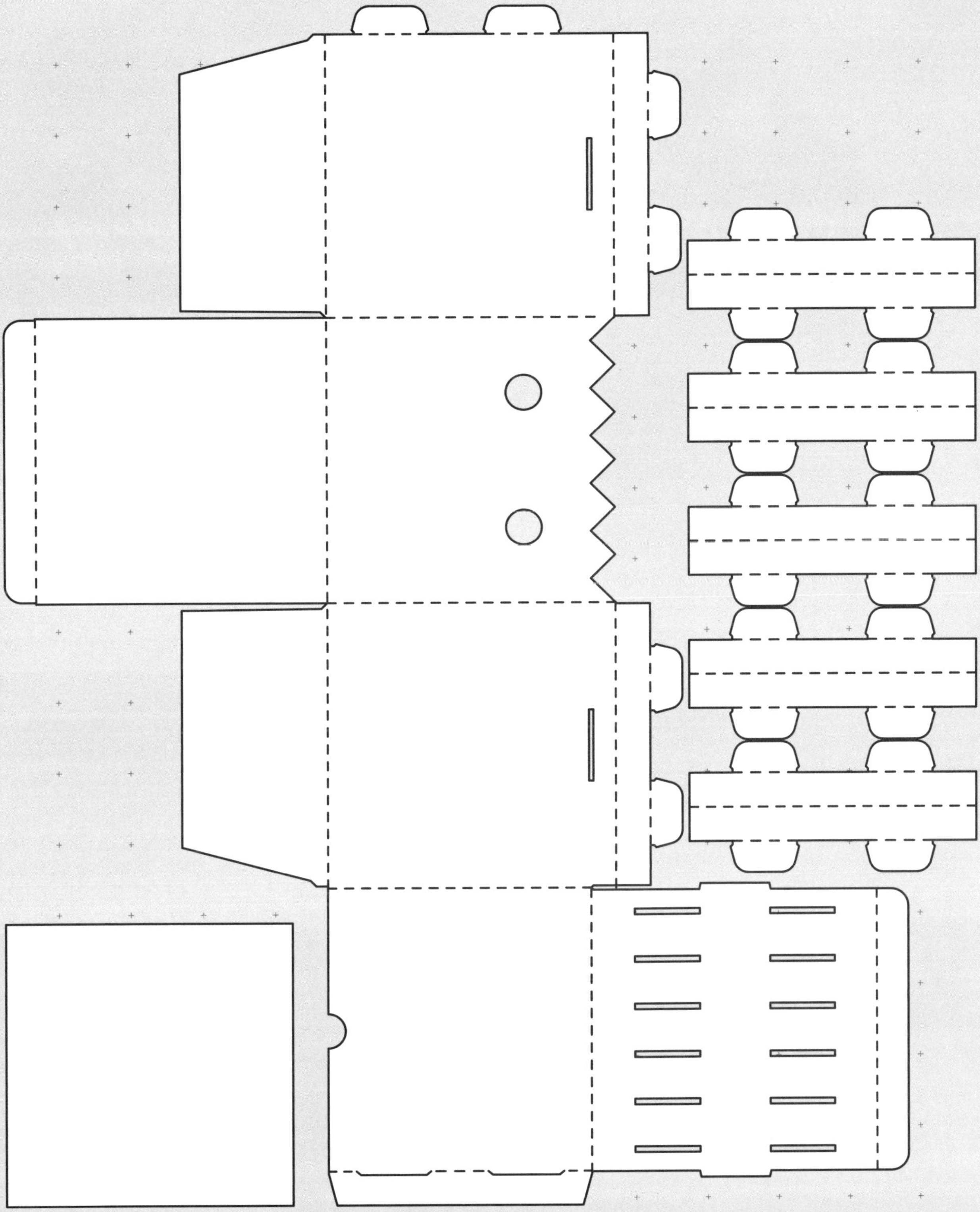

CHEESE PACKAGING

Design Ailice Samadi

Die-cutting holes in the surface of standard packet can be a cost effective way of producing a dramatic visual result. In this case, it has created an instantly recognizable representation of Swiss cheese. Swiss cheese has a distinctive appearance, as the blocks of cheese are riddled with holes known as "eyes", a distinguishing feature which has come to be the graphic shorthand for all cheeses.

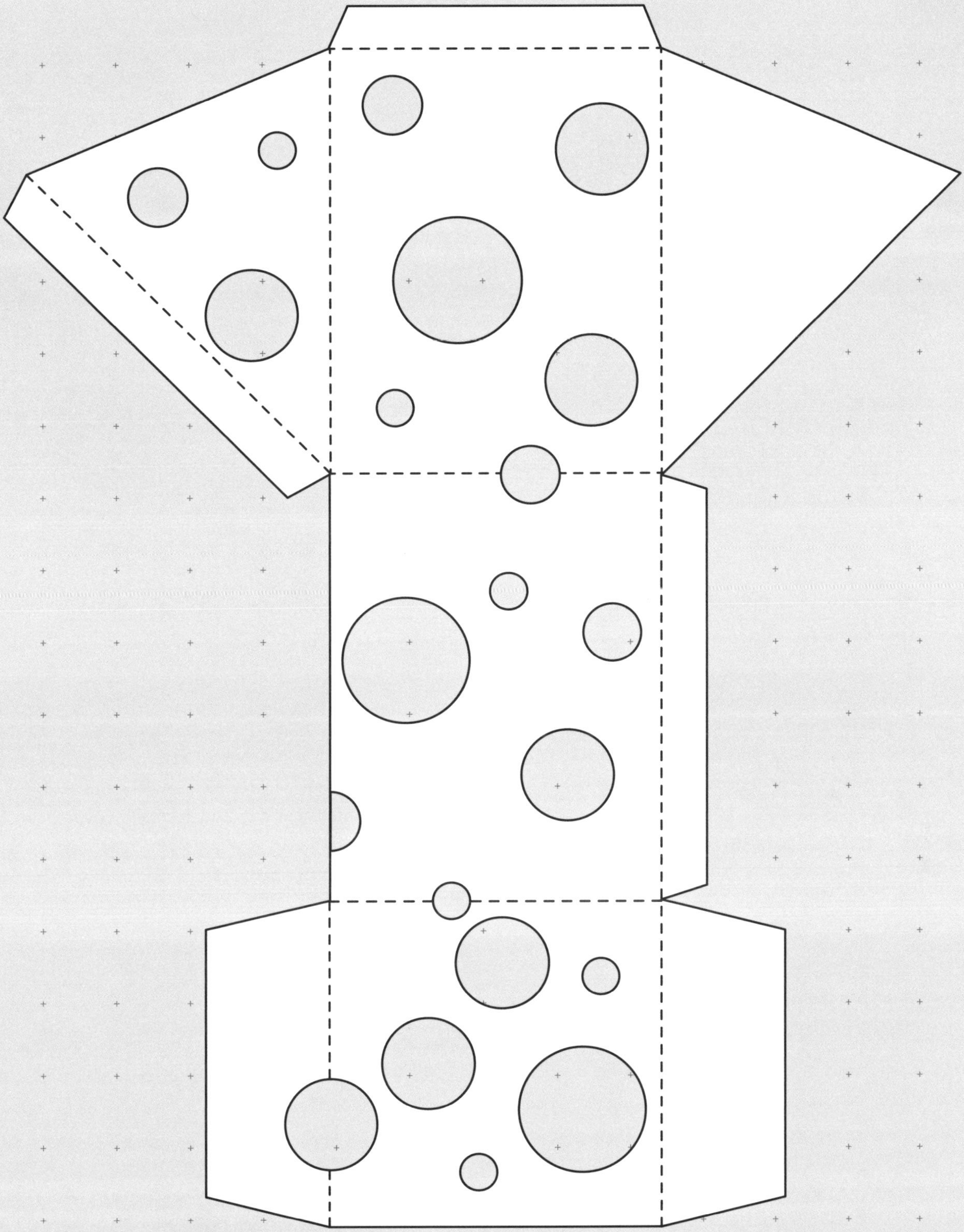

DESKTOP CLOCK

Design **Chris Anderson**

The clock mechanism is sold separately from the cardboard main body of the clock. The clock body is made from 100% recycled cardboard, making it an environmentally friendly piece of design. The concept behind it is that the packaging becomes the product with the help of the "how to build your desktop clock" instructions sheet provided. The easy to follow steps take a matter of minutes and leave you with a unique desktop clock, which not only looks good, but is also a means of supporting sustainable design.

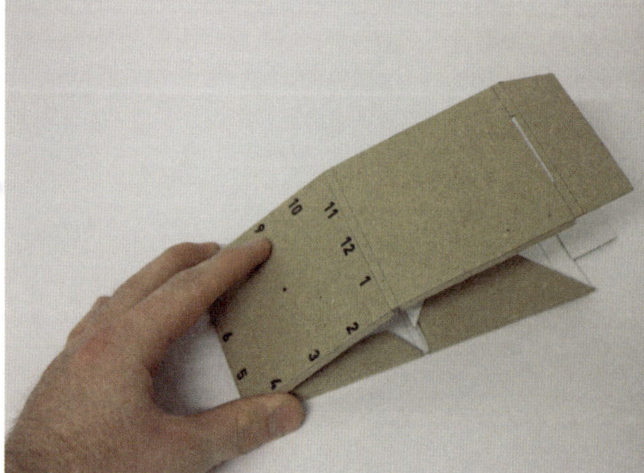

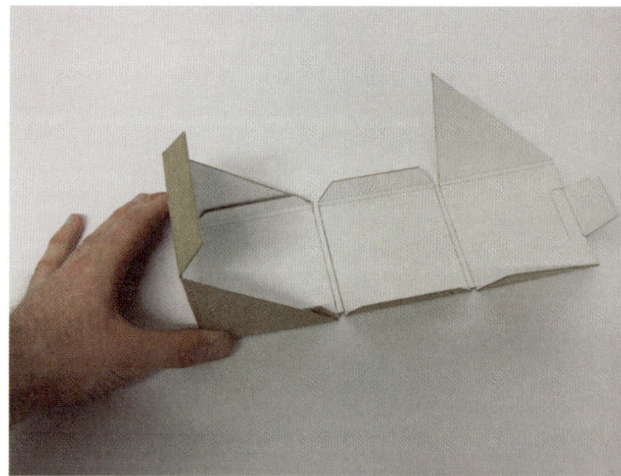

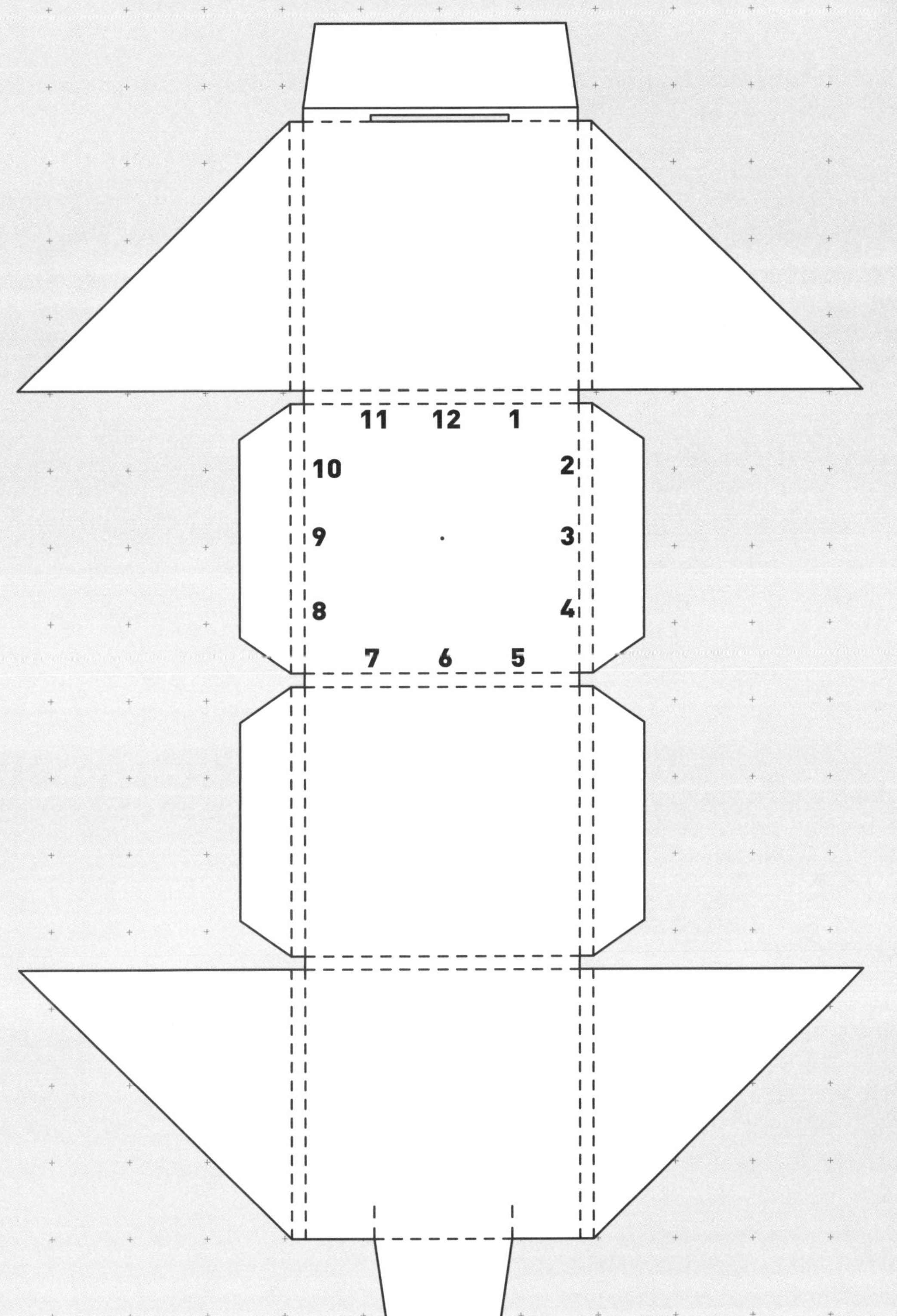
11
12
1
10
2
9
3
8
4
7
6
5

LAMP

Design **Chris Anderson**

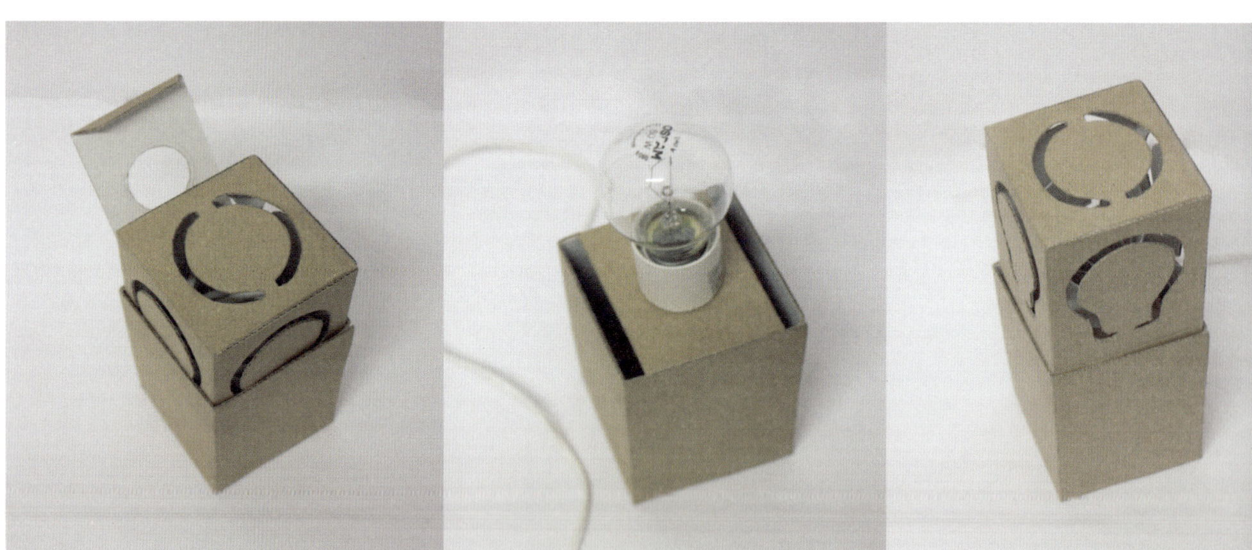

The idea behind the Lamp is to enforce the concept of "packaging as the product". It reduces unwanted material by eliminating the outer packaging. It therefore constitutes a very unique piece of packaging design. All that is required for constructing the Lamp is contained inside, including an instructions sheet on "how to build your lamp". This lamp not only helps protect the environment by using only 100% recycled cardboard, but also holds its own in the field of unique and sustainable product and packaging design.

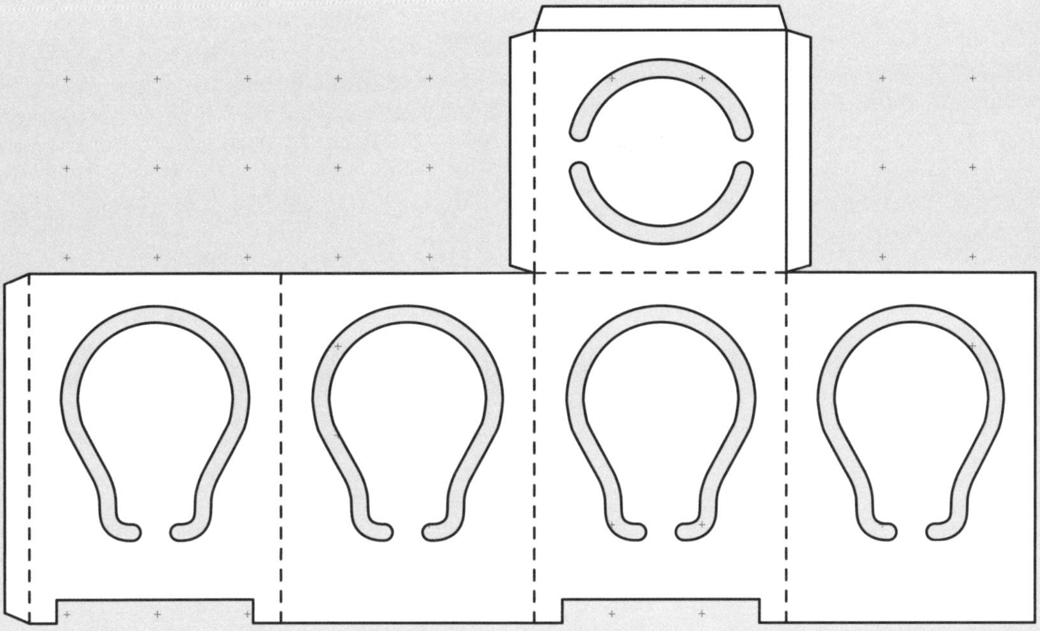

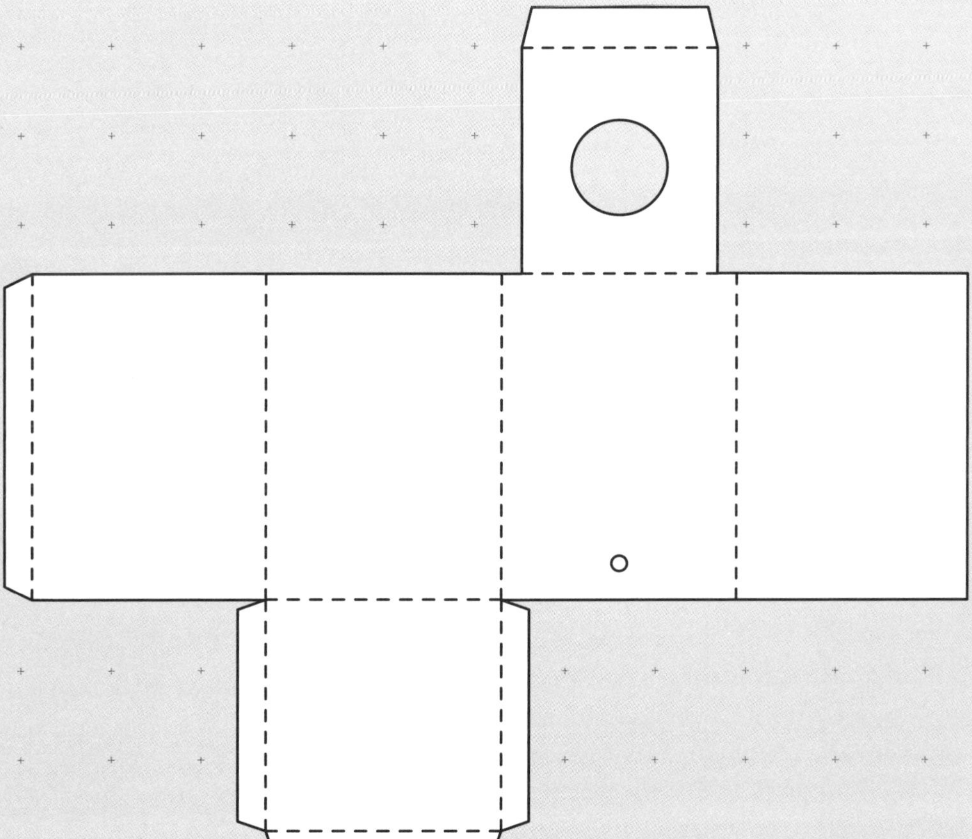

COMA WINE

Design Andreu Zaragoza

This is a packaging design for a very exclusive wine produced in Catalonia by a group of young winemakers who take pride in producing a high quality product irrespective of its commercial viability. The design employs black cardboard with the bold graphic of the label marked in white.

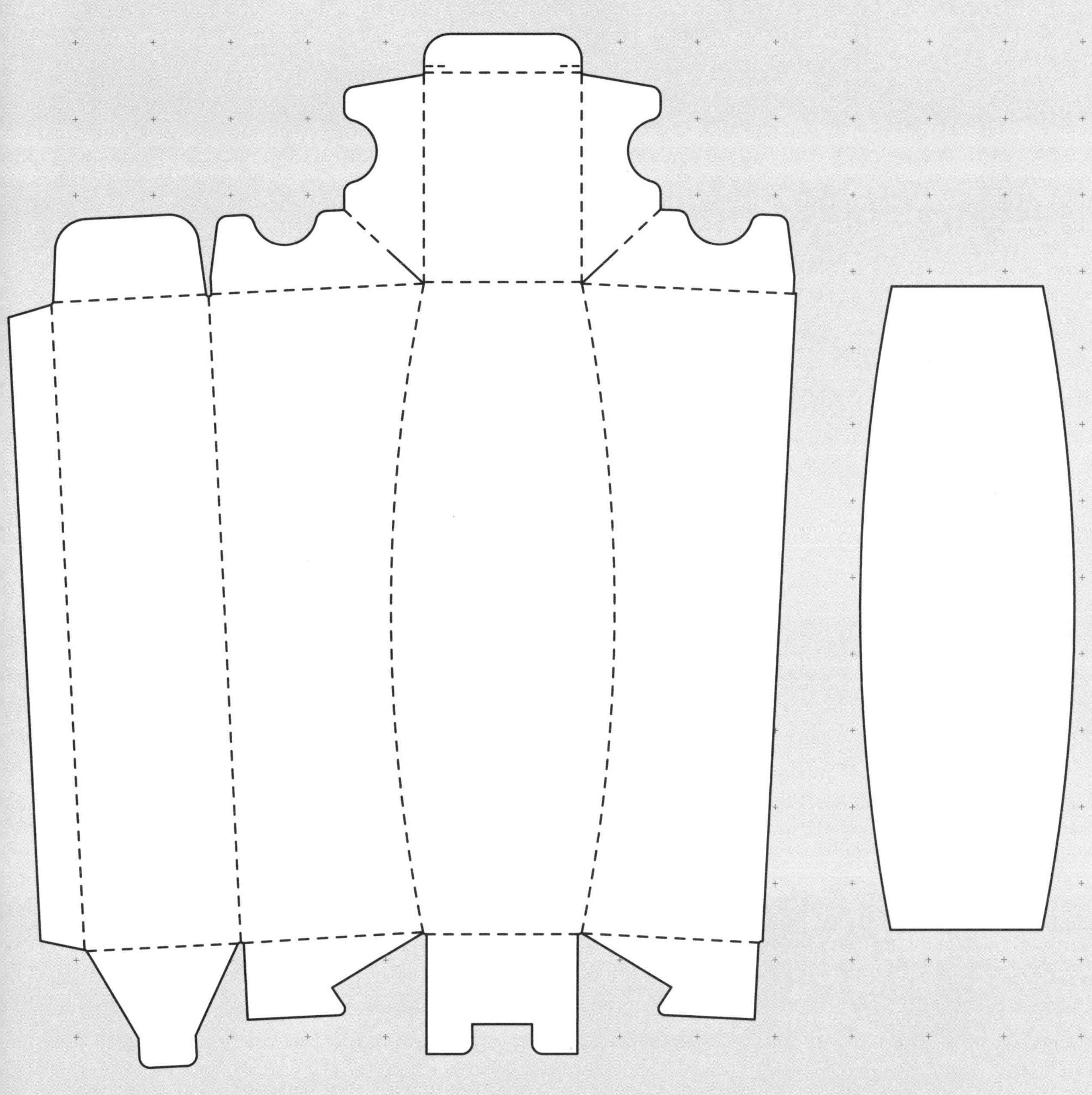

MEO

Design Chi Hey Lee

The design of the Meo egg packaging is aimed at encouraging children to eat more eggs. The packaging line has six different characters: Hungry BBQ, Crying Chili, Wild Ranch, Sexy Honey, Baby Island, and Salty Pepper. The names refer to sauces, with the idea that the children can choose their favourite sauce to accompany their hard-boiled egg and play with the cute characters while they are eating it.

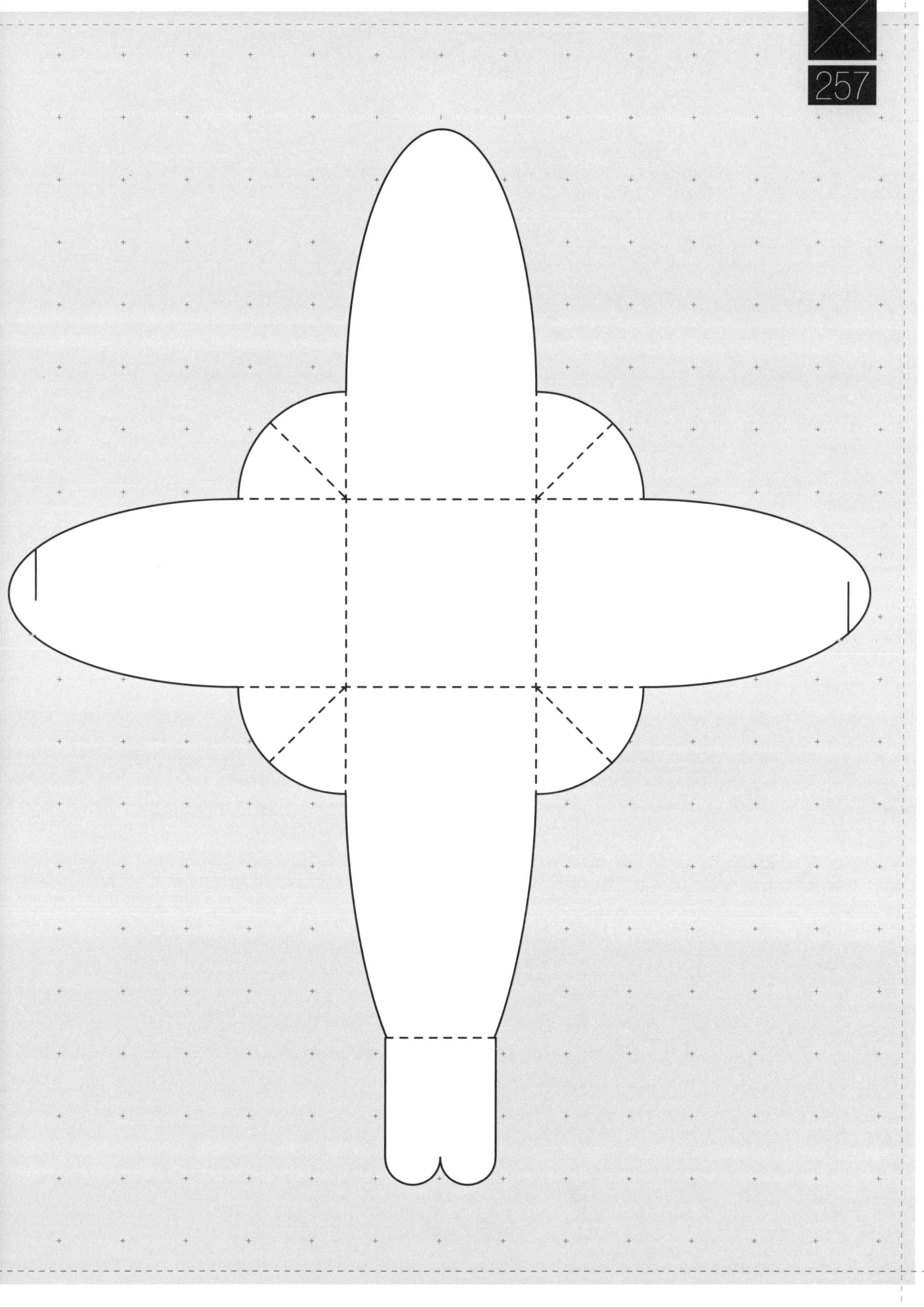

WE ARE GOING TO TIE THE KNOT

Design **Chris Trivizas**

In Greek, the same word means both "to hang" and "to get married". When the father of the bride says "I will hang them", he means that he will bind the couple in the holy bond of marriage. This linguistic oddity inspired a humorous wedding invitation that includes a rope and instructions on how to make a slip knot.

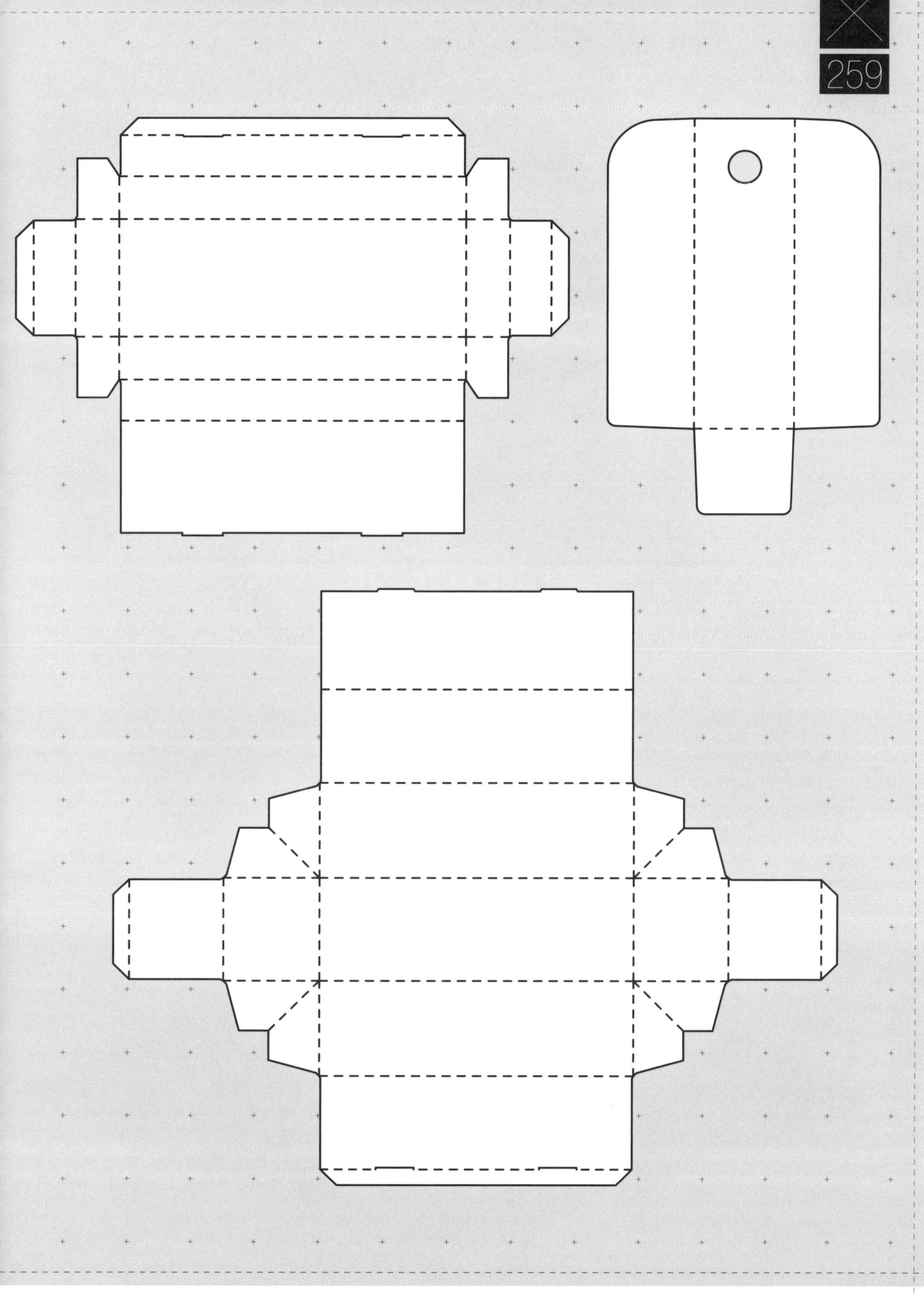

PRECIOUS PACKAGING

Design **Tristan Ostrowski**

The design not just a protective container, but one which would present its contents in this way so as to increase the user's perceived value of the egg. In this case, the egg box was redesigned to make it reveal the eggs one at a time as the user unfurls the net. This generates a stronger emotional response to each of the eggs, making them appear more precious to the consumer than if they were grouped together. For minimal cost and ease of manufacture, the net itself is constructed from a single piece of card which mechanically tabs together, avoiding the need for glue and its associated process.

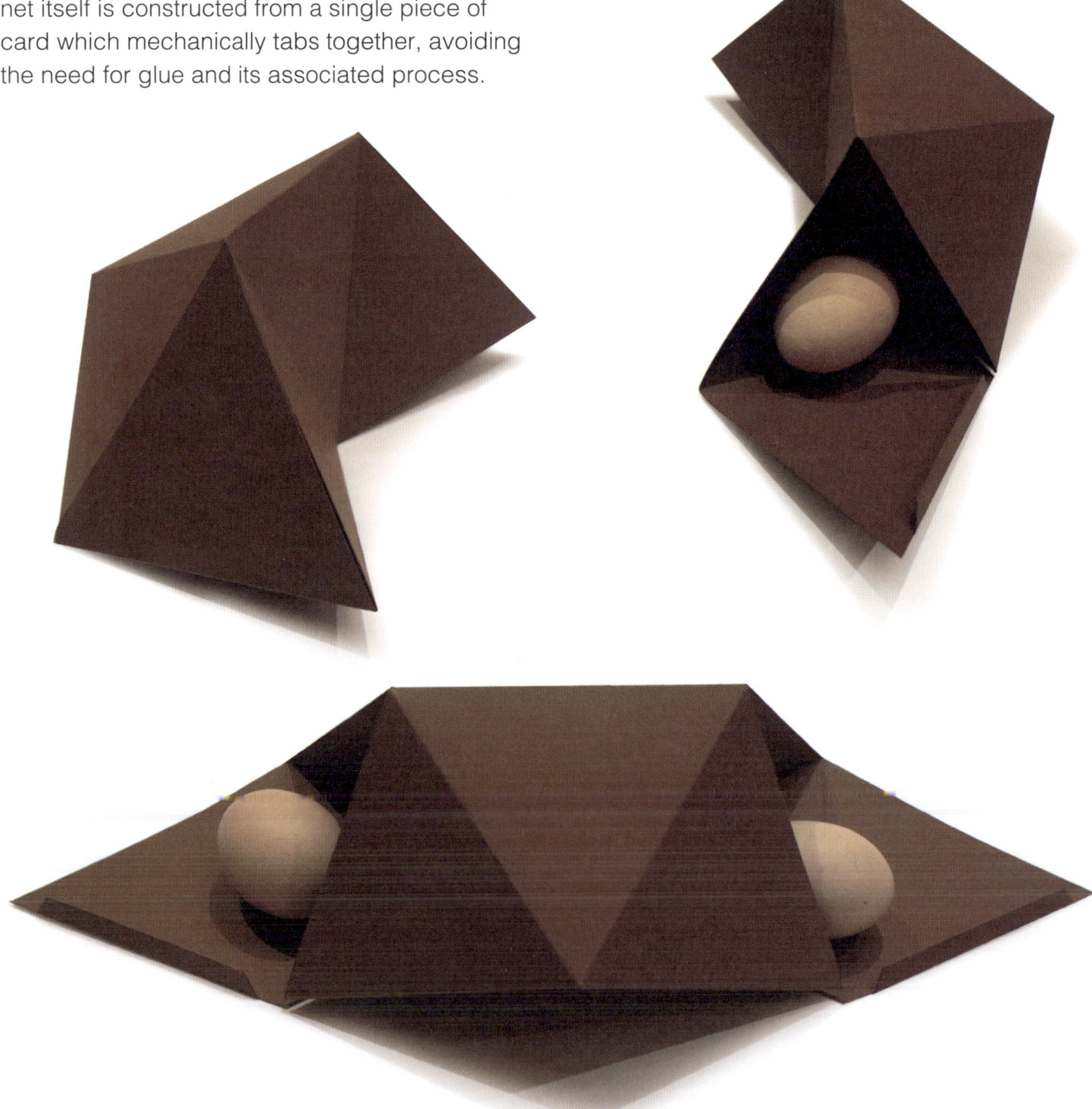

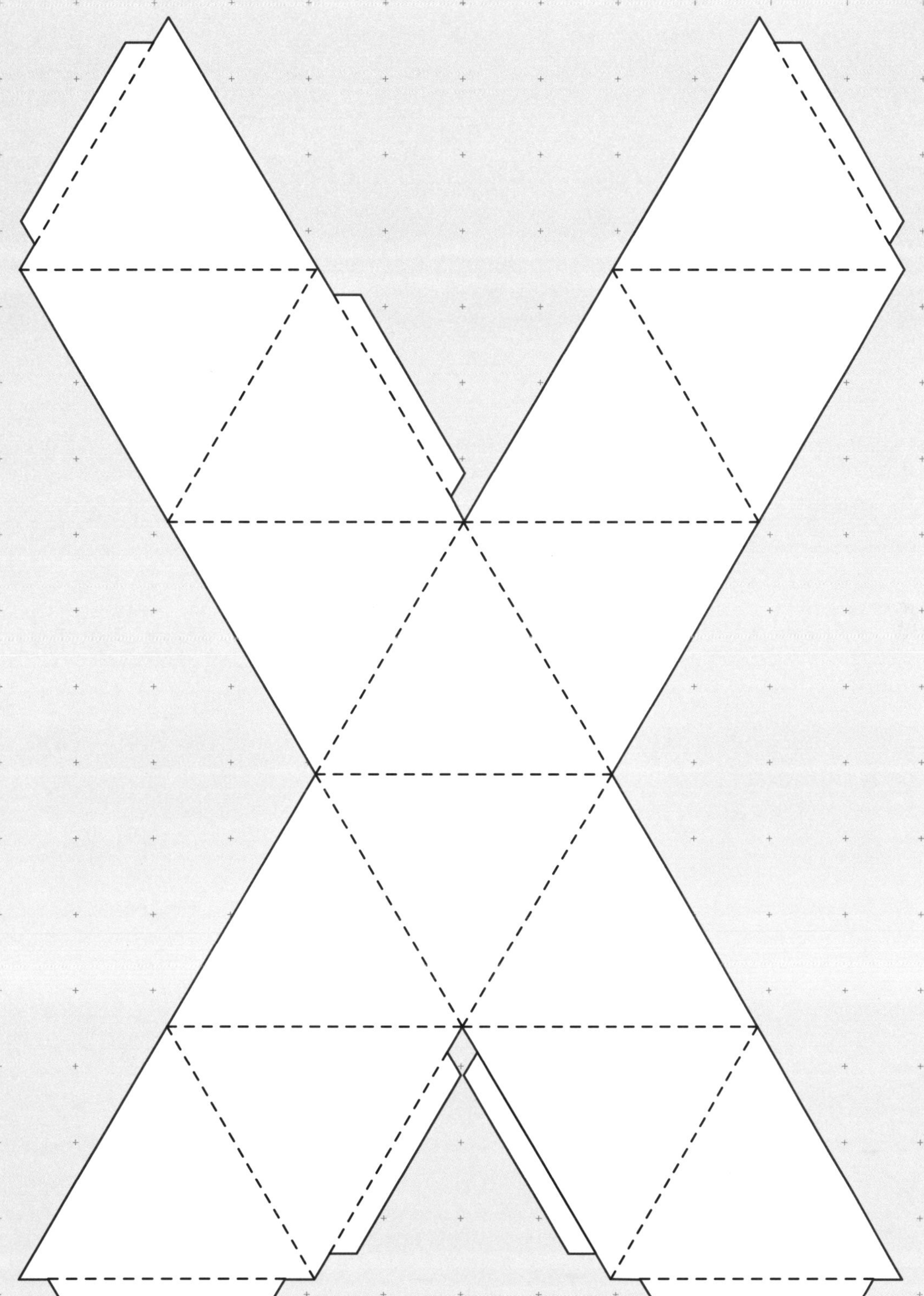

CHOZEN FLASH-FROZEN CHOCOLATES

Design Janet Feldman, Amanda Dennelly

Life is like a box of chocolates with Chozen's flash-frozen chocolates by Cadbury. This sweet treat is wrapped in elegant packaging that resembles a folded snowflake.

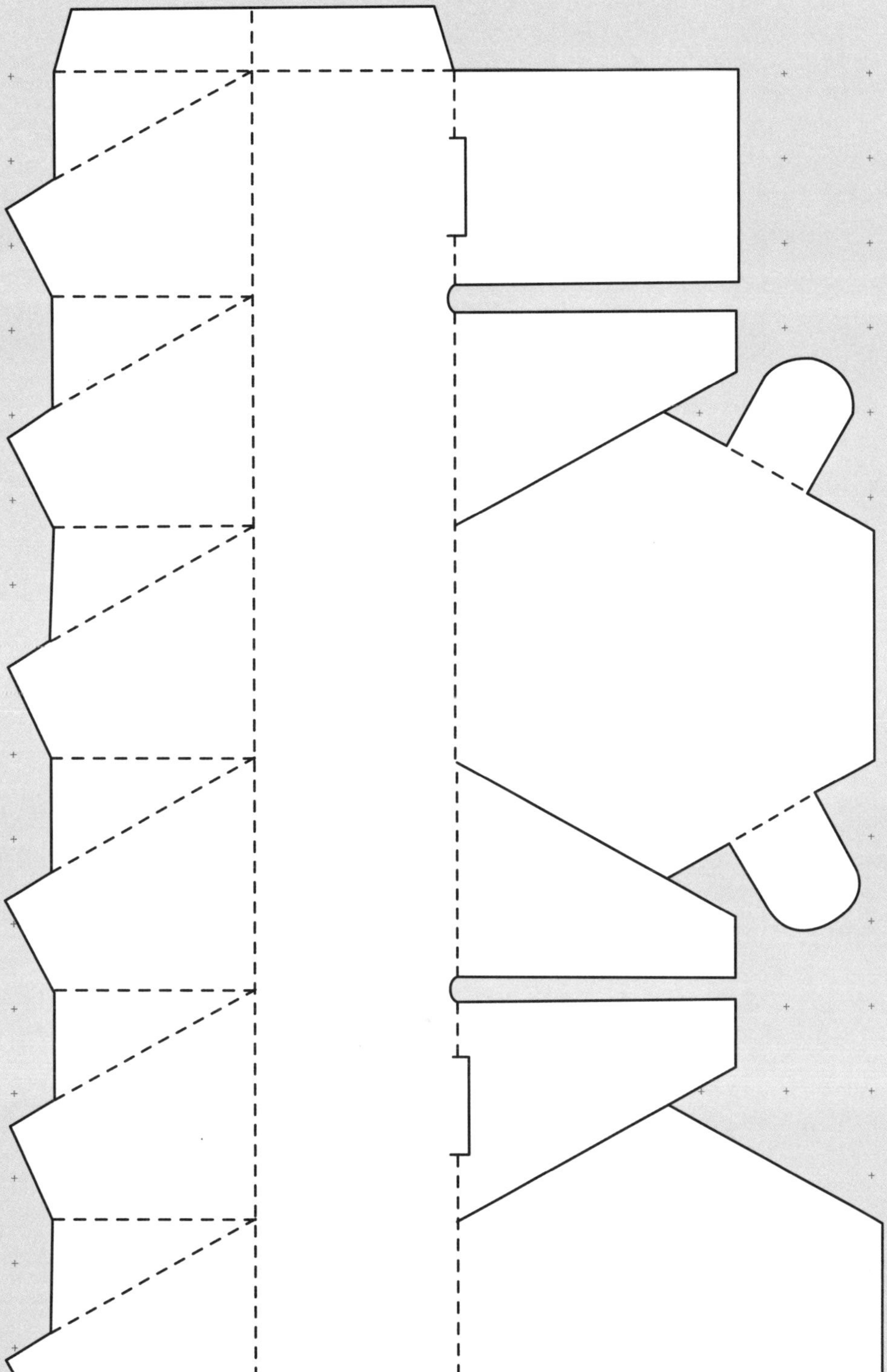

HAPPY FACTORY SEWING KIT

Design **Juliana Ker**

The Happy Factory Sewing Kit is an industry information pack and incorporates the Happy Factory brand identity with unique packaging design. The kit is designed in the shape of a factory and contains elements that could be found in a sewing kit. Each item in the kit reinforces the brand identity through consistent use of the signature aesthetics, imagery and colour palette.

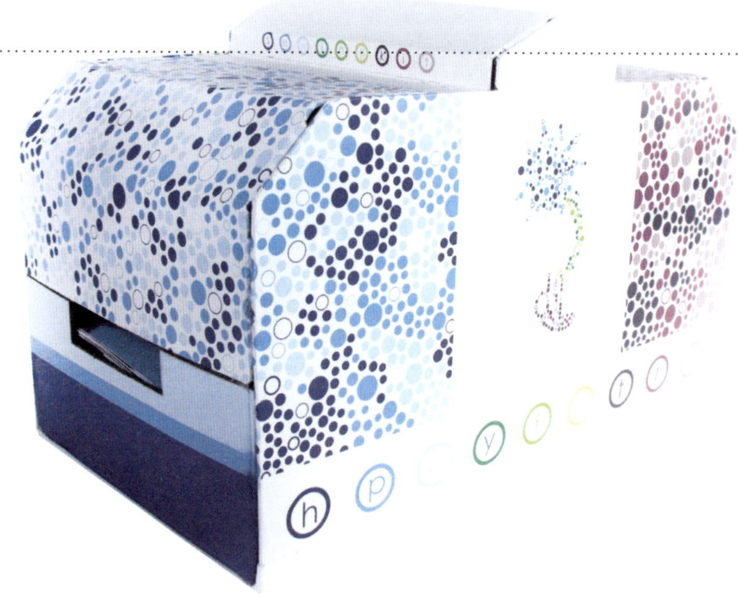

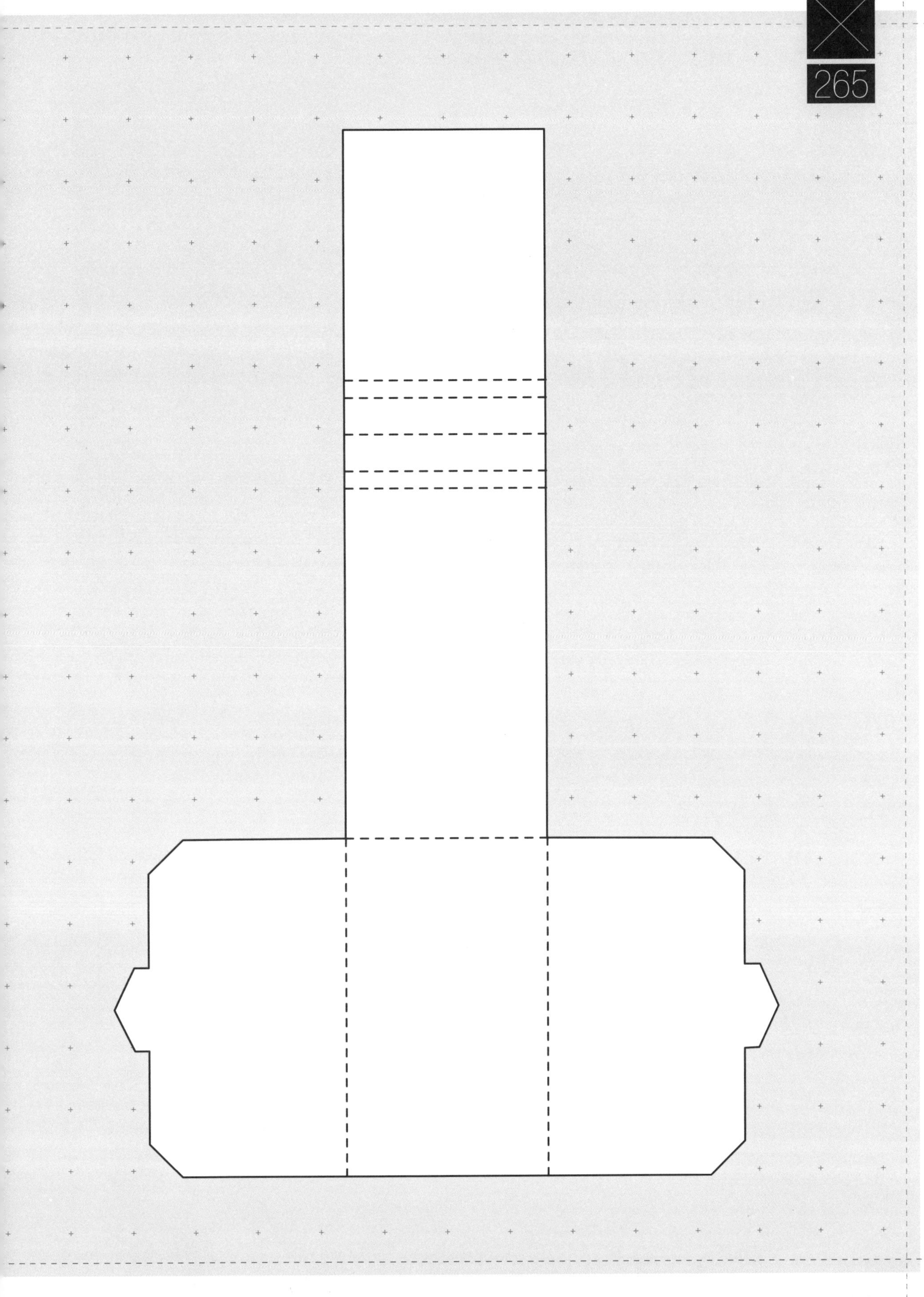

LOVE & HATE LIGHT BULB PACK

Design Juan Regueiro

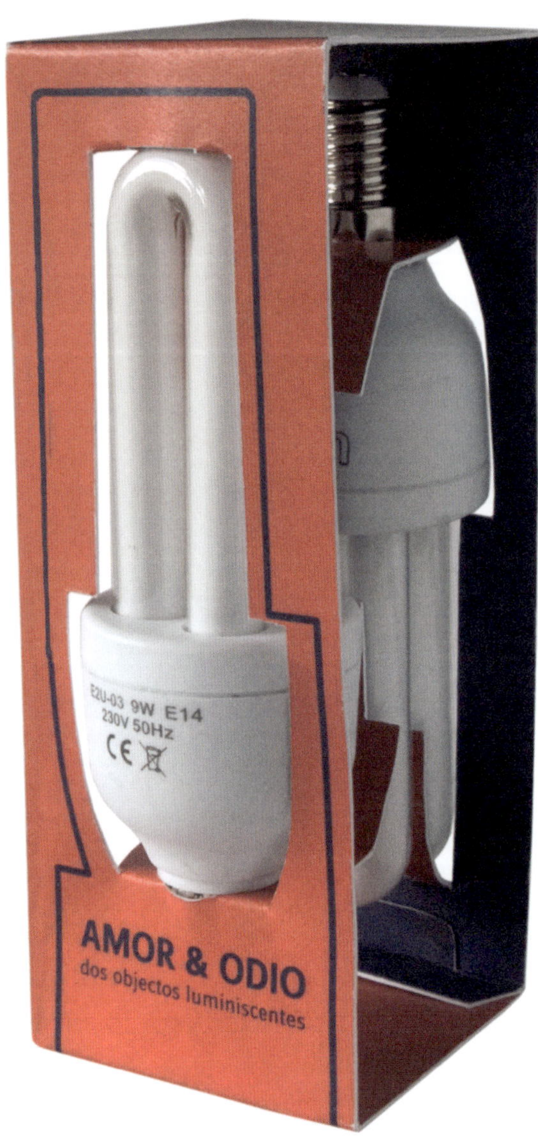

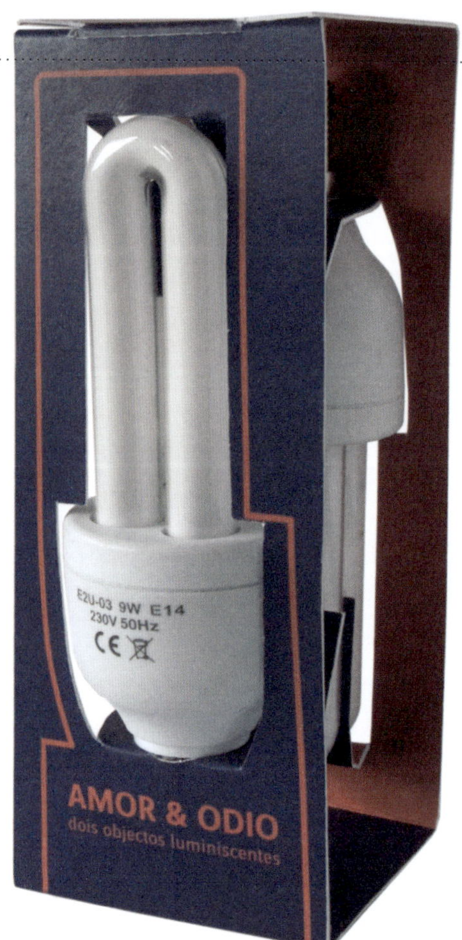

The game behind this design originated in the idea of a pack to hold two light bulbs based on the concept of "love" and "hate". The bulbs, while being held in the same pack, could not touch each other. A single band of cardboard forms the structure of the packaging and is printed with two contrasting colours that are reversed on each side to reflect the interrelation of opposites.

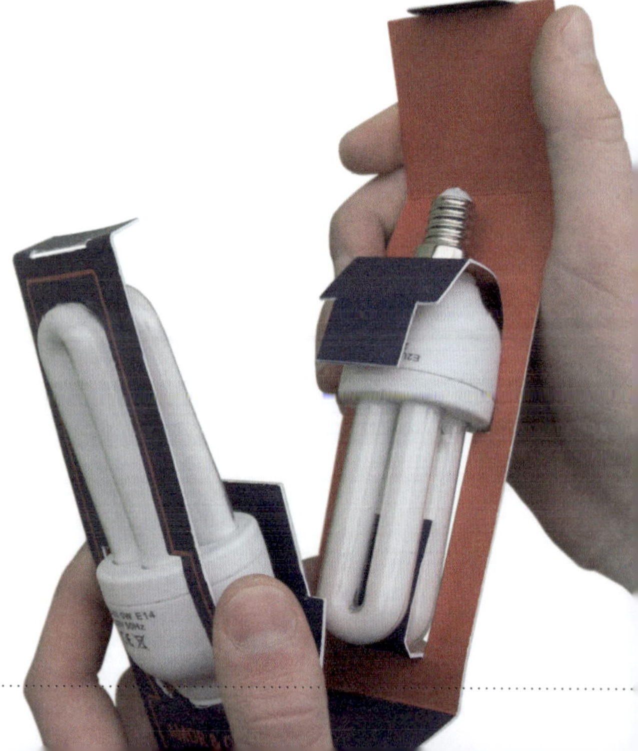

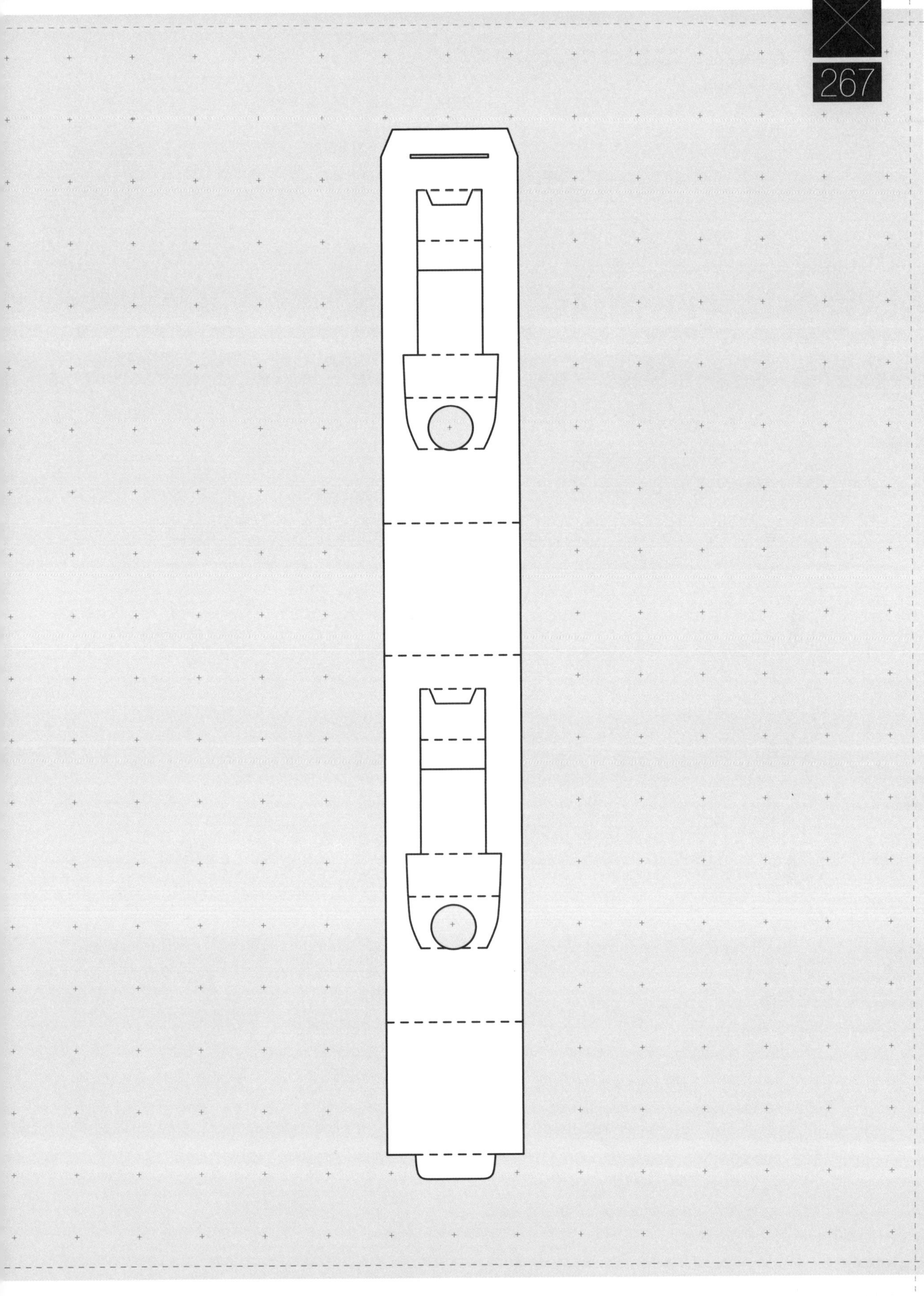

MILCHRING COLLECTING BOX

Design Gerlinde Gruber

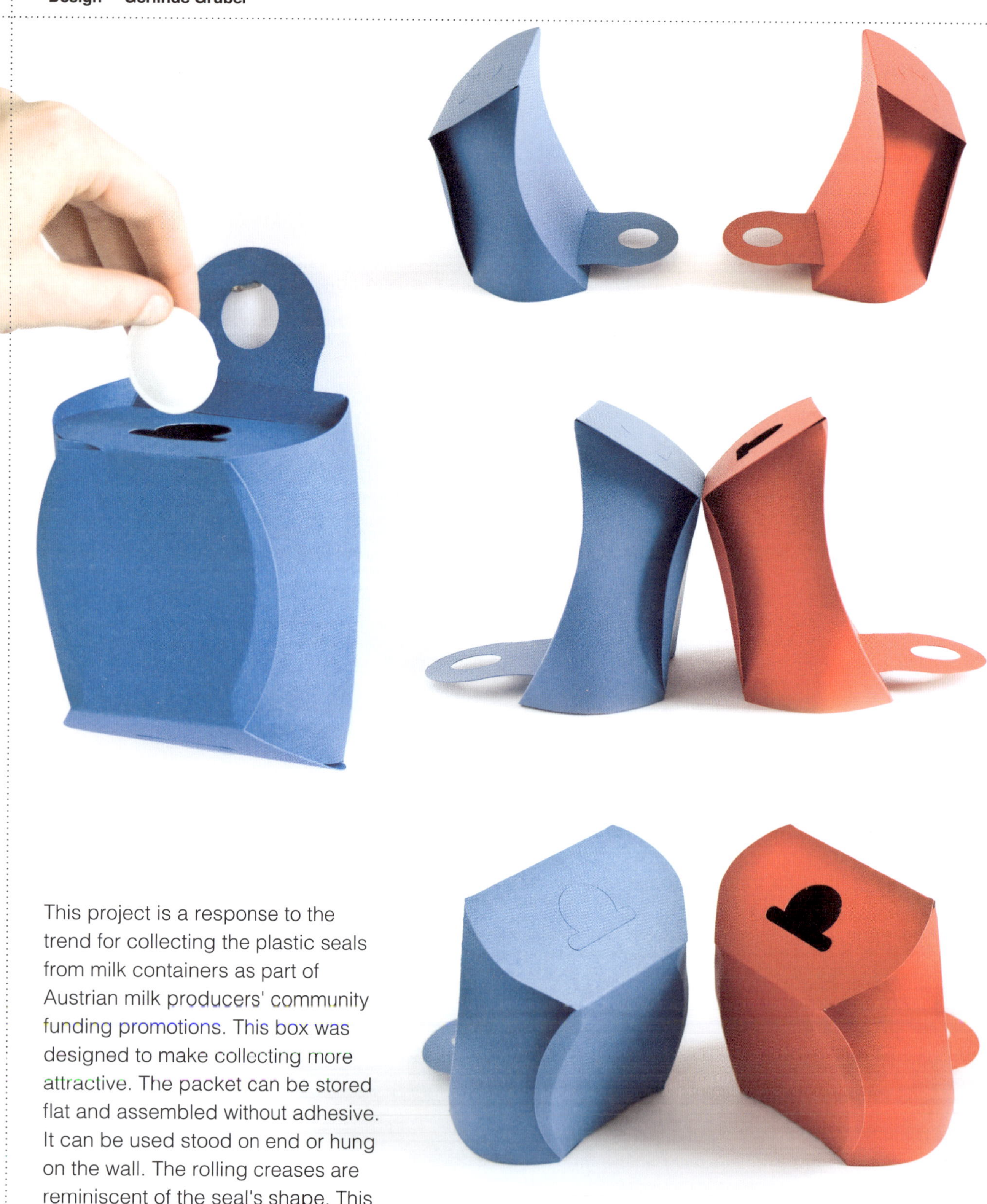

This project is a response to the trend for collecting the plastic seals from milk containers as part of Austrian milk producers' community funding promotions. This box was designed to make collecting more attractive. The packet can be stored flat and assembled without adhesive. It can be used stood on end or hung on the wall. The rolling creases are reminiscent of the seal's shape. This interesting and eye-catching box has a capacity of 70 pieces.

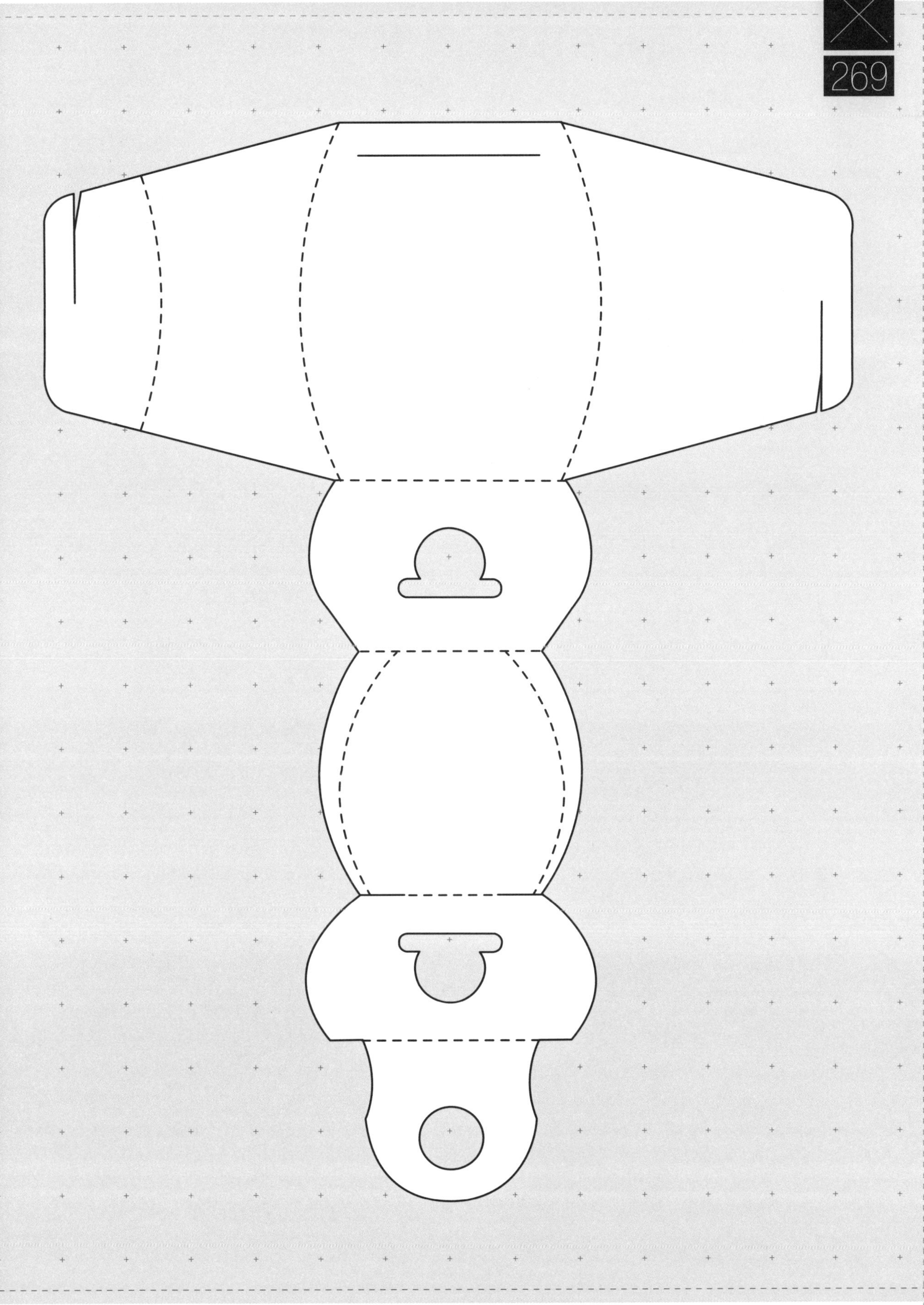

170 FAHRENHEIT TEA LEAVES

Design Karen Kum

The 170 Fahrenheit Tea Leaves range represents the tea traditions of three regions with a strong tea-drinking culture: China, Japan and England, and complements them with a fourth product called simply The Art of Elegancy. Chinese tea is represented by Dragon Well tea, Japanese by Nourishing Sencha tea, English by English Breakfast tea, and the climax of elegance by Red Amaranth Jasmine Art Tea. To convey the geographical provenance of each product, the graphic design of each packet includes references to the architecture and the history of the tea culture of each country.

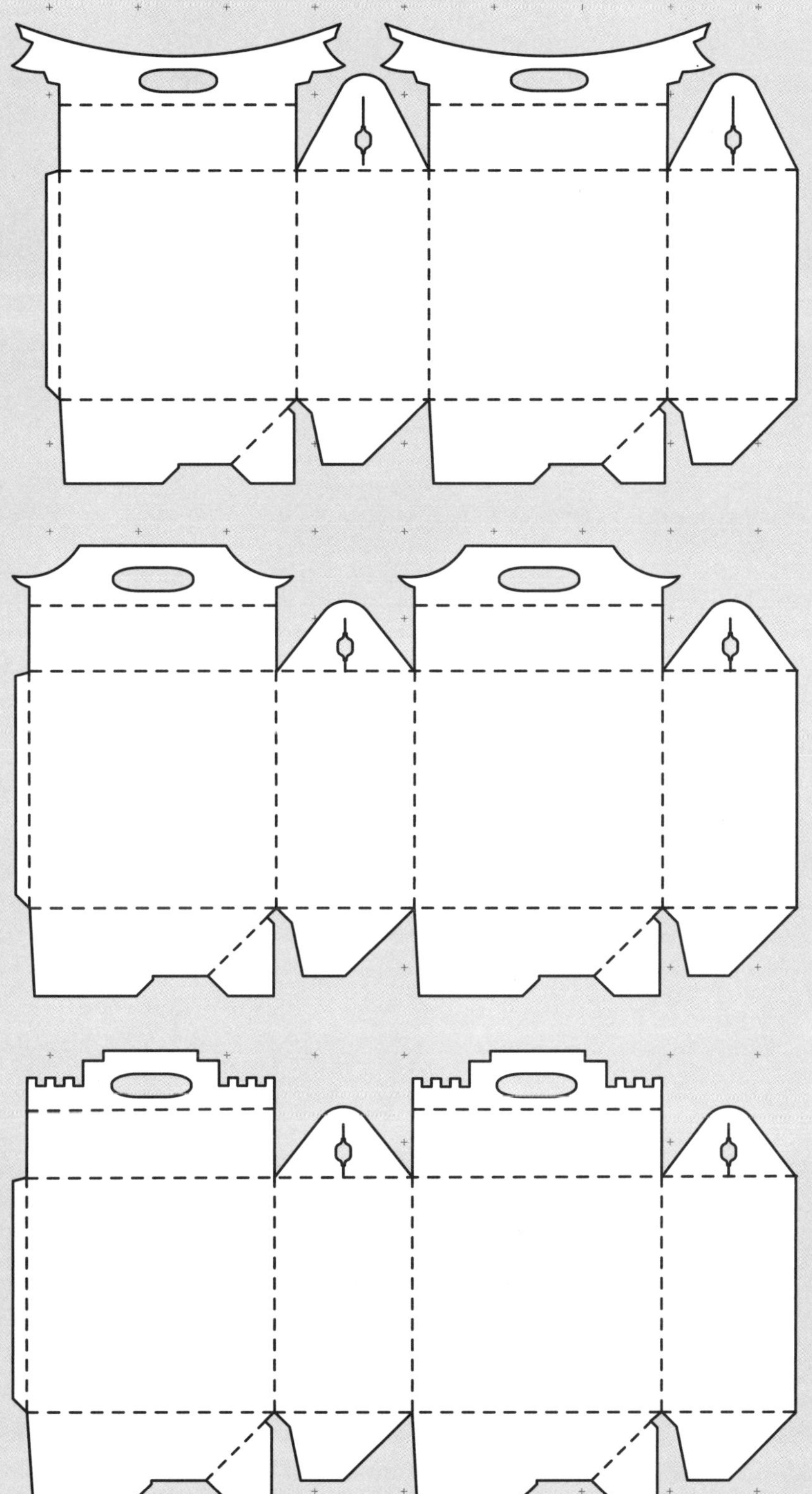

ESTECK 30STK

Design **Gerlinde Gruber**

This innovative toy is comprised of E-shaped plastic bricks, each of which has three cross cuts to allow them to interlock. There is an almost infinite range of configurations for combining the pieces. The custom made non-glued packaging holds 30 pieces of the bricks.

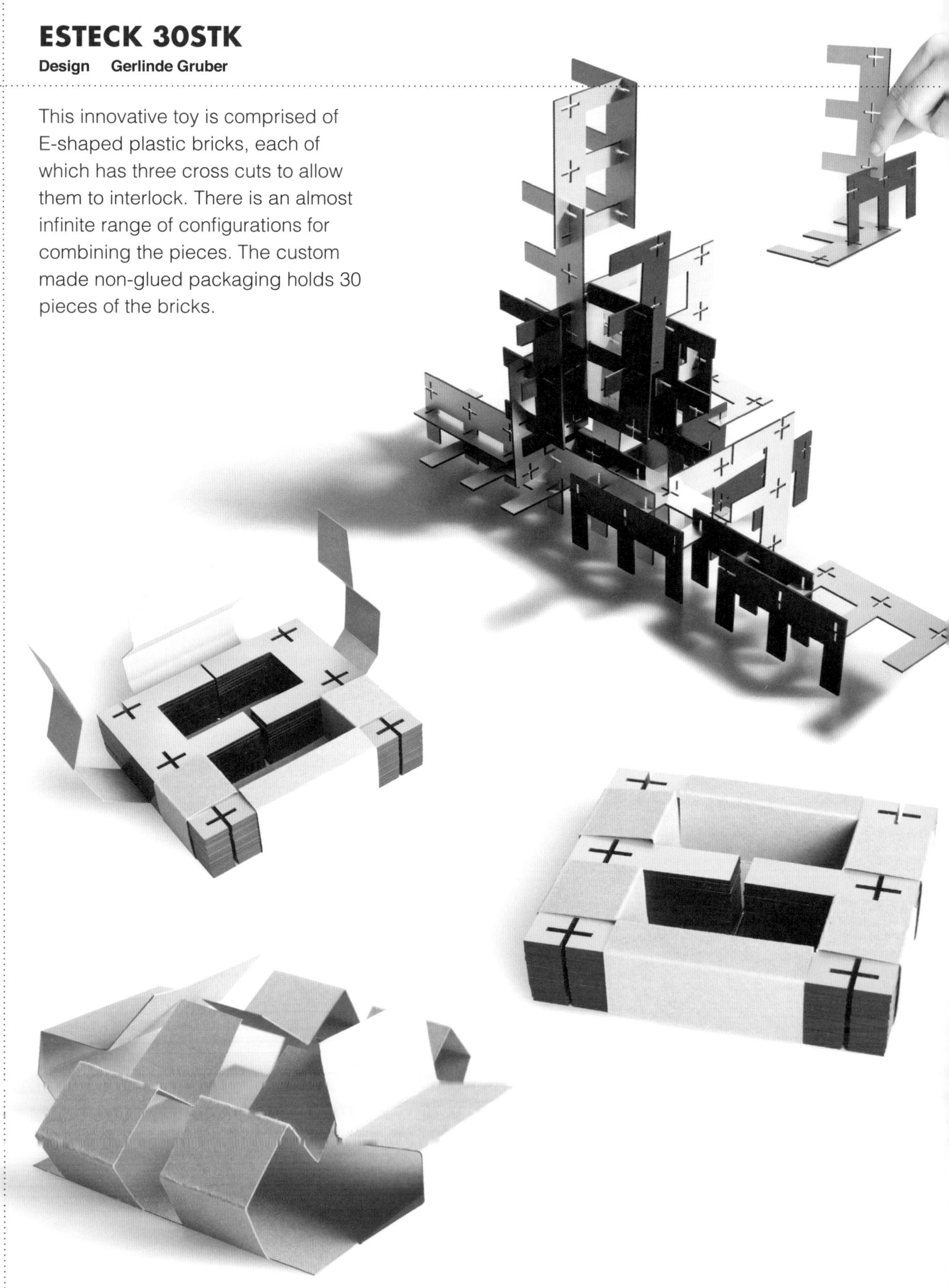

PACKET FOR A NATIONAL PRODUCT

Design **Lubica Kulomberová**

This shoe box is characterized by clean purposeful design on the inside and minimalistic graphic design on the outside. The shoes can be accessed from both ends of the box. On opening, the box takes the shape of two independent triangular storage segments. Each shoe is thus stored separated from the other and therefore better protected from damage. The materials used are recycled cardboard in combination with fresh, vibrantly coloured papers.

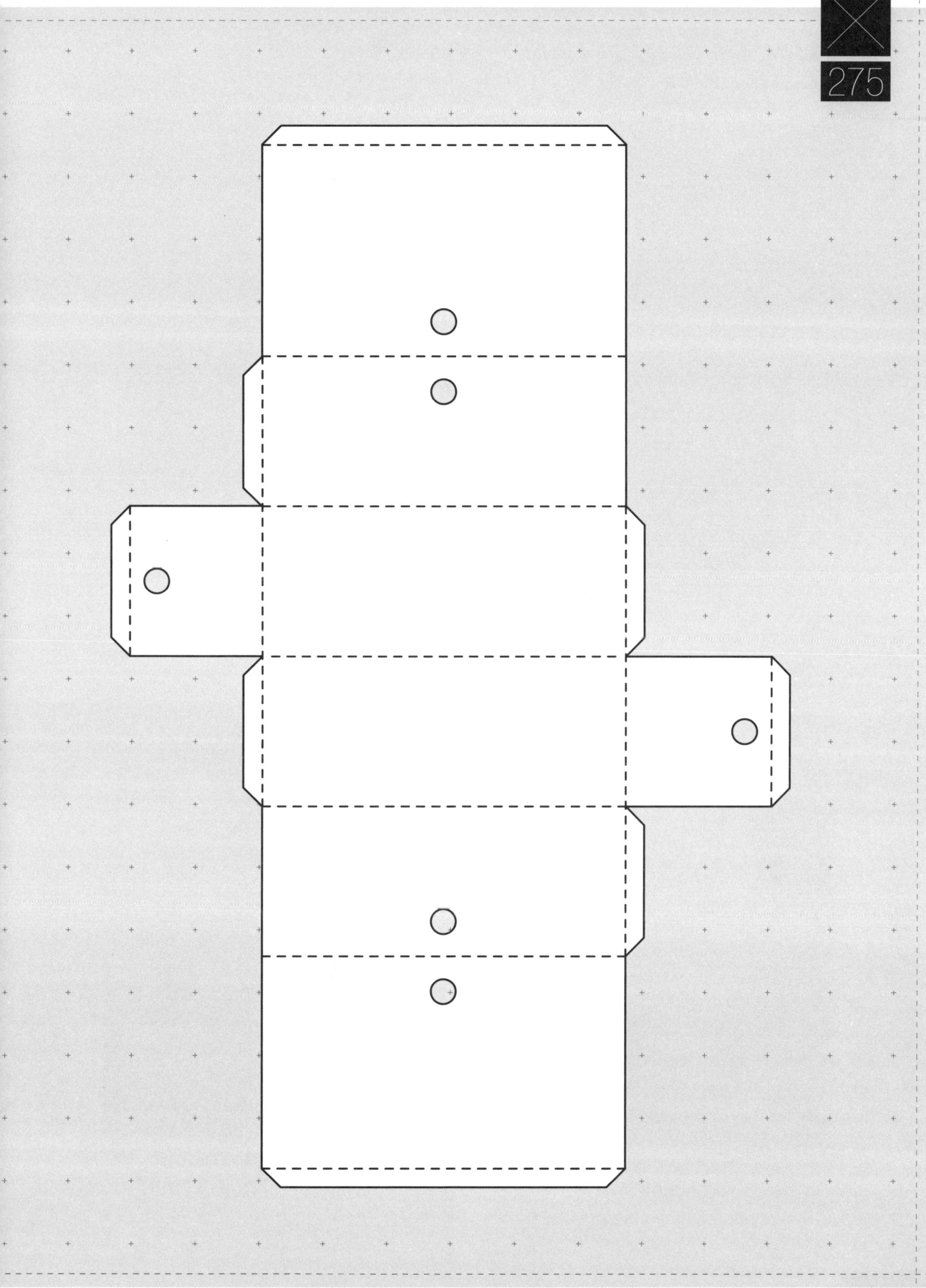

PUT A SOCK IN IT

Design Lisa Shocket

This design for sock packaging combines humor and cynicism.

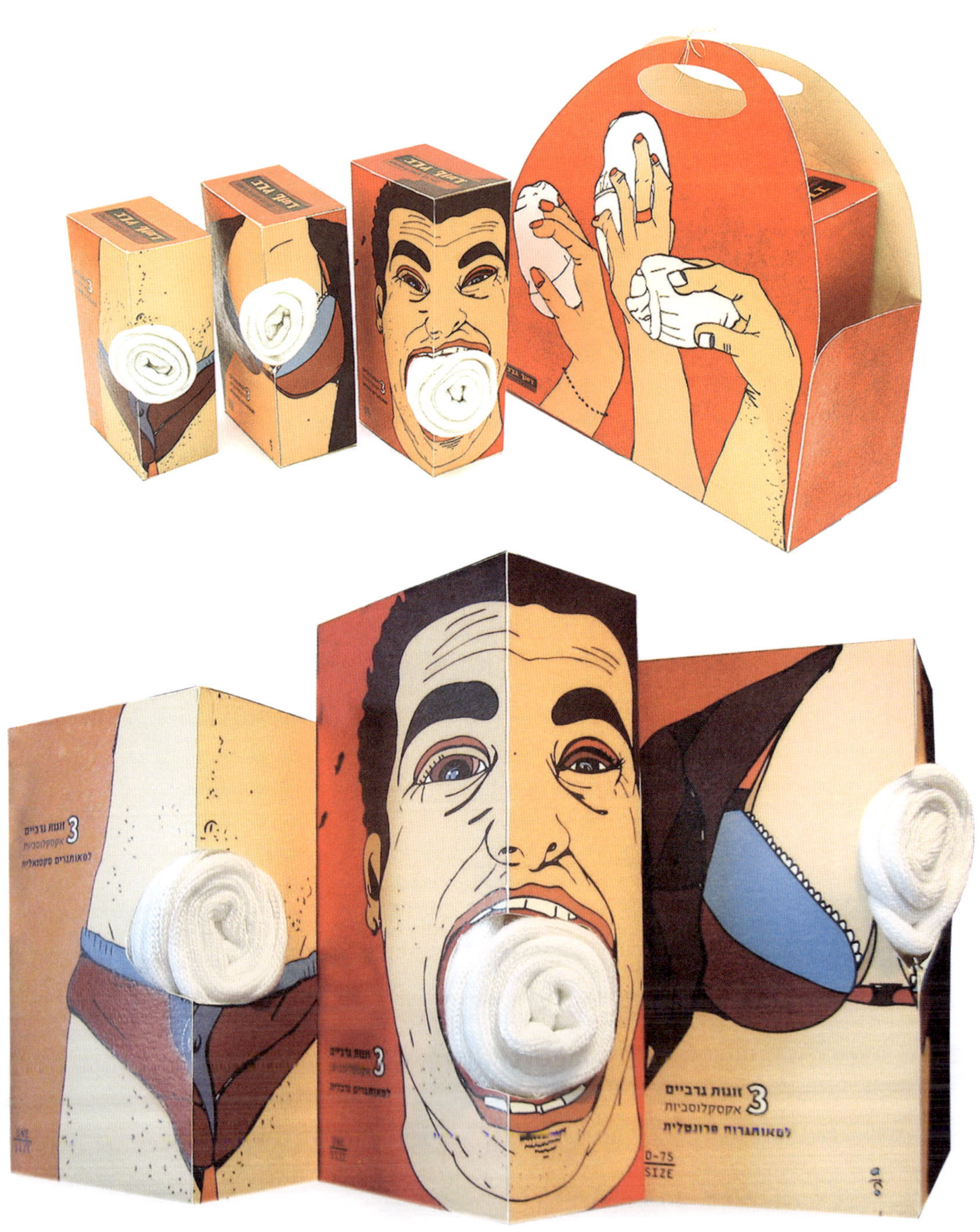

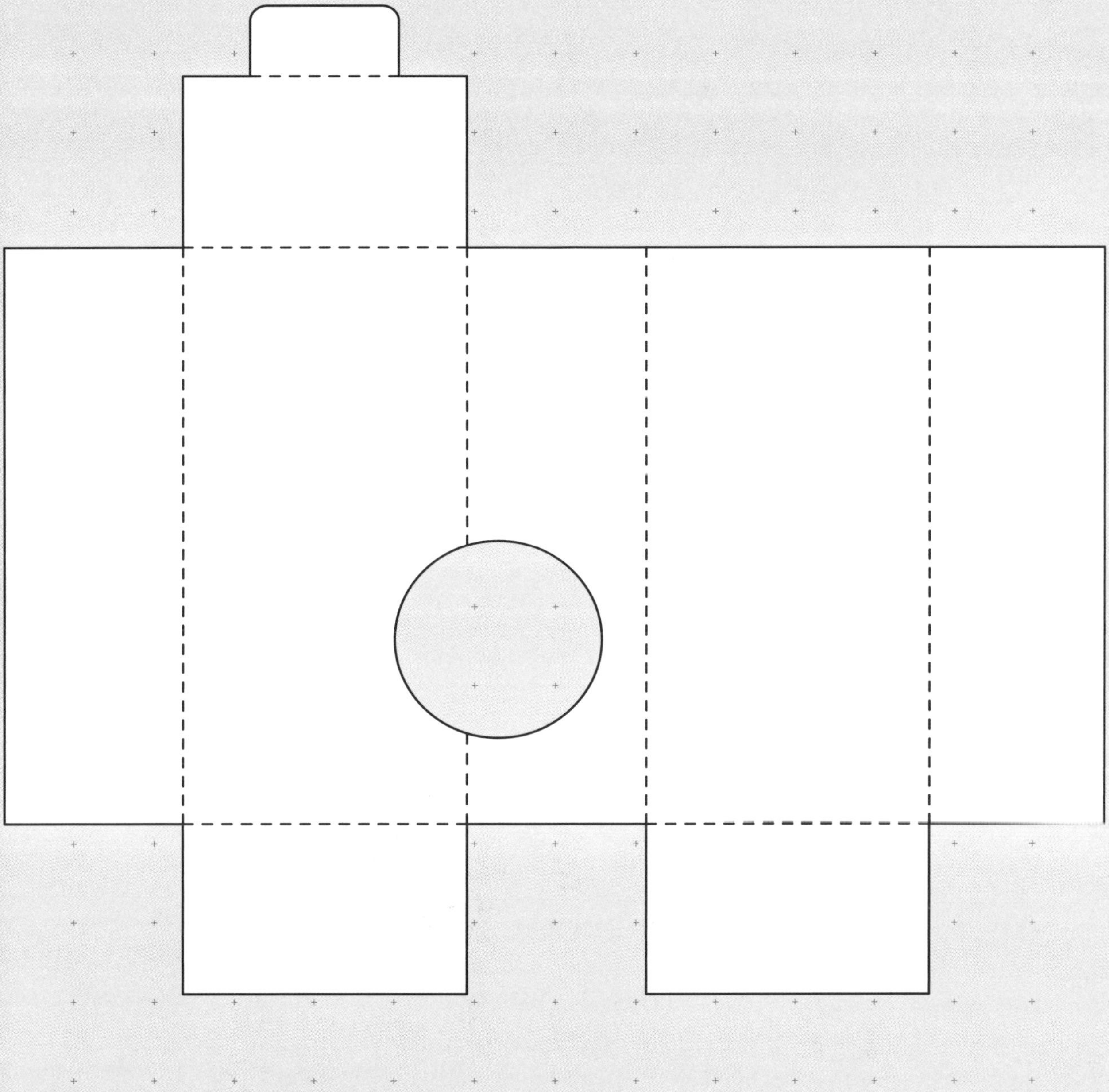

OTHELLO CHOCALATE PACKAGING

Design Lisa Shocket

This chocolate packaging design was inspired by Shakespeare's *Othello*. Each character in the play—Othello, Desdemona and Iago—is used to represent a differently flavoured product.

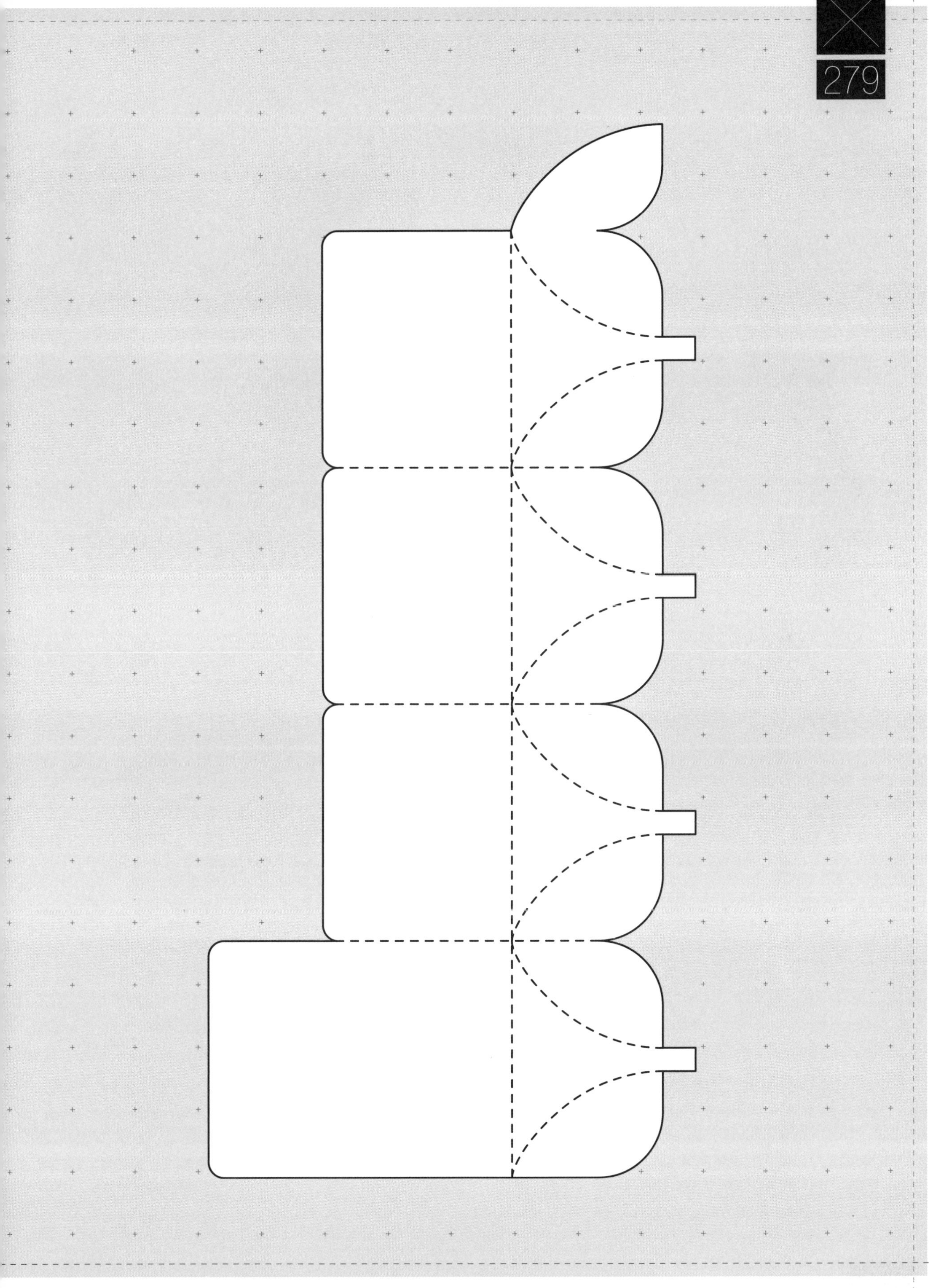

RANNOU METIVIER MACAROONS

Design **Lucie Lherault**

This packaging was created for the confectioner, Rannou Métivier. Their reputation is built on their famed macaroons which are made to their own fiercely guarded recipe. With this package the designer wanted to reflect the authenticity of the product and the mystery of its fabrication. The pattern of the box expresses the delicacy, excellence and expertise of Rannou Métivier.

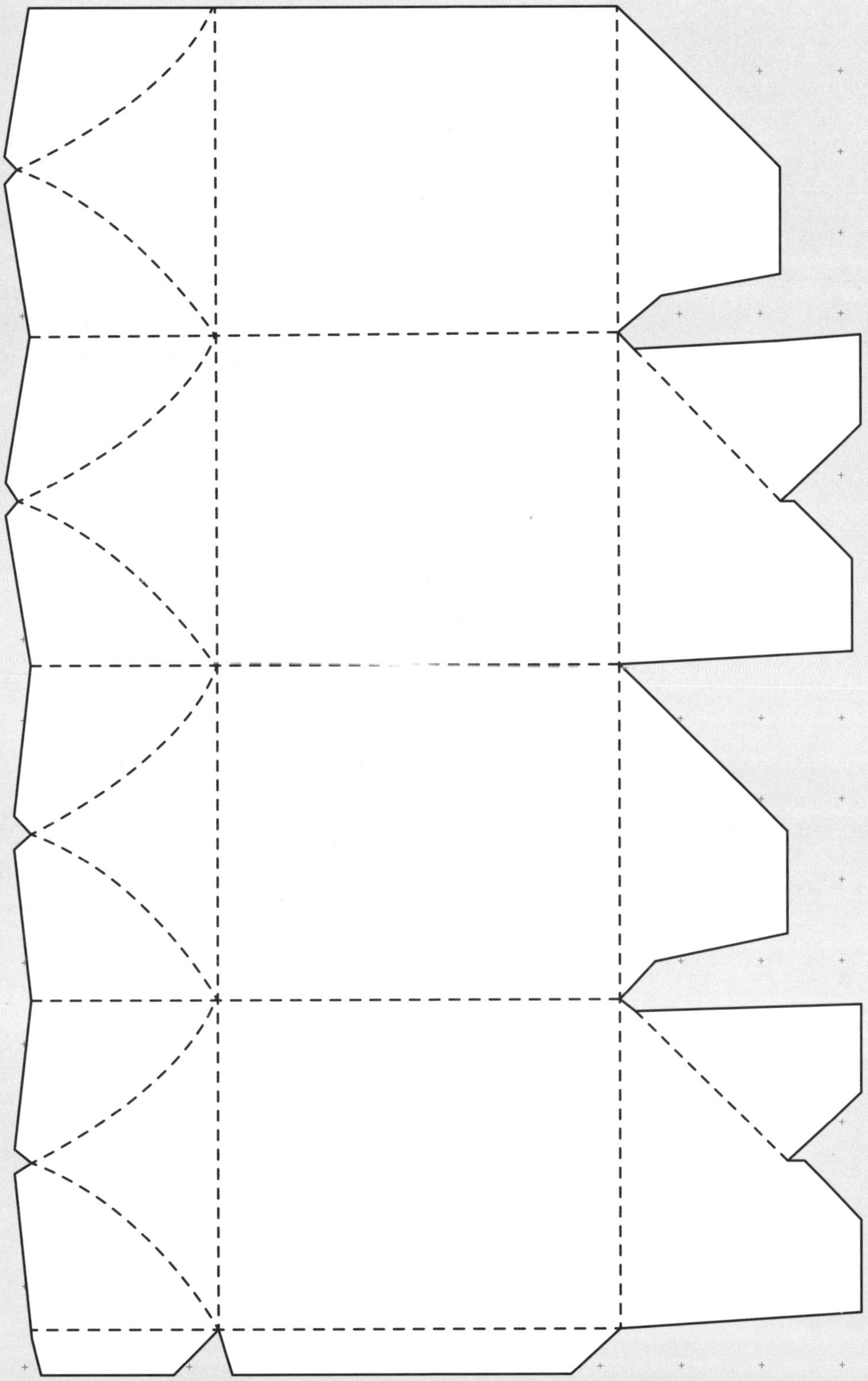

V-CUBE 2

Design **Andreas Kloroglou**

The unique shape of this packet was made by dividing a cube in half diagonally and combining the resultant triangular prism with a full cube. The most challenging part of the project was in the choice of materials. The limited budget effectively restricted the materials used to a folded PVC packet for the product and coardboard as the prism base. Another issue was adapting the same packet to hold two different dimensions of cubes. This was resolved by inserting a small inflated element to fill the empty areas and hold the smaller cube in place.

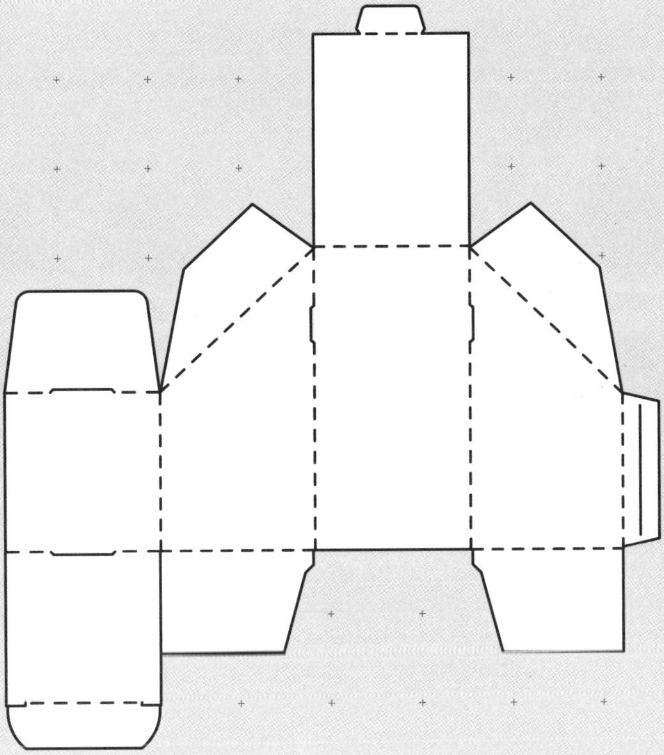

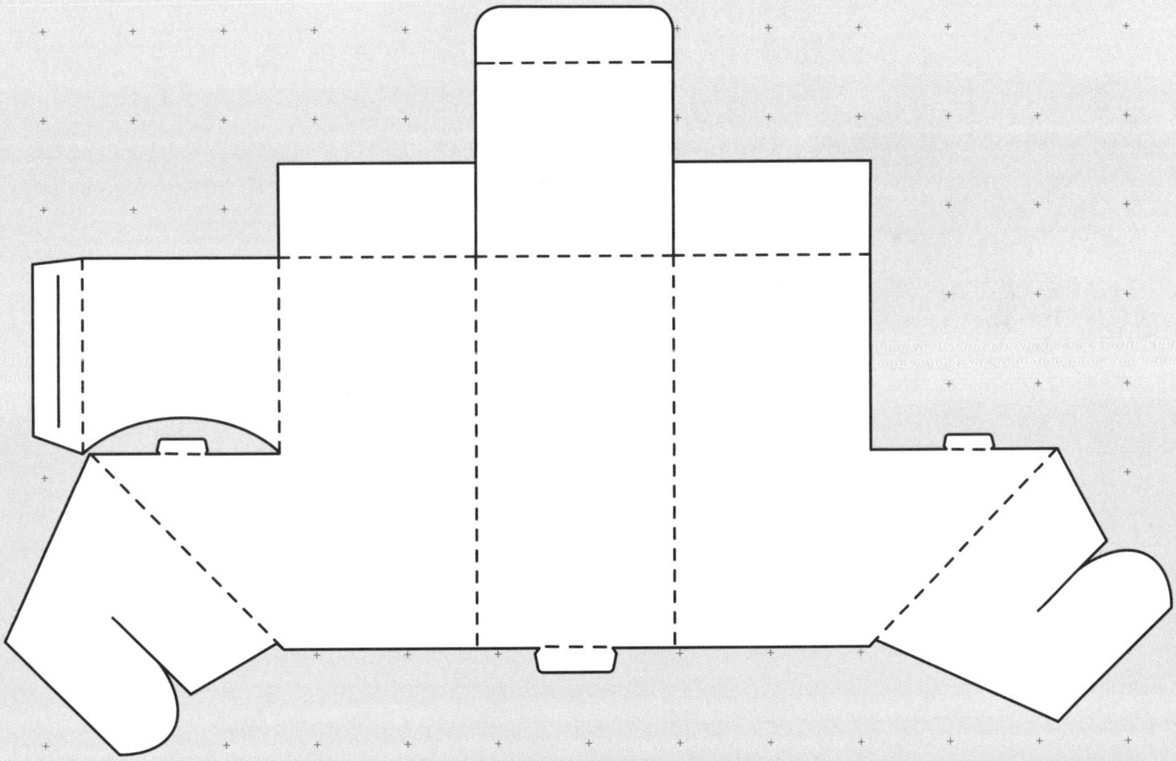

V-CUBE FLAG SERIES

Design **Andreas Kioroglou**

The package uses a combination of unglued paper and PET plastic. The packaging form is quite aggressive, giving the impression that the cube is suspended in the air and has the advantage of easy stacking. The most challenging part of the project was the cardboard base of the packaging. It could not be glued mechanically, so had to be made with a fold sequence and lock tabs. The plastic cover of the product had to be glued by hand so lock tabs were necessary to ensure absolute product visibility. The final solution looks great from all sides. The inflated PET part, consisting of two "V" letters, makes the product stand in the air.

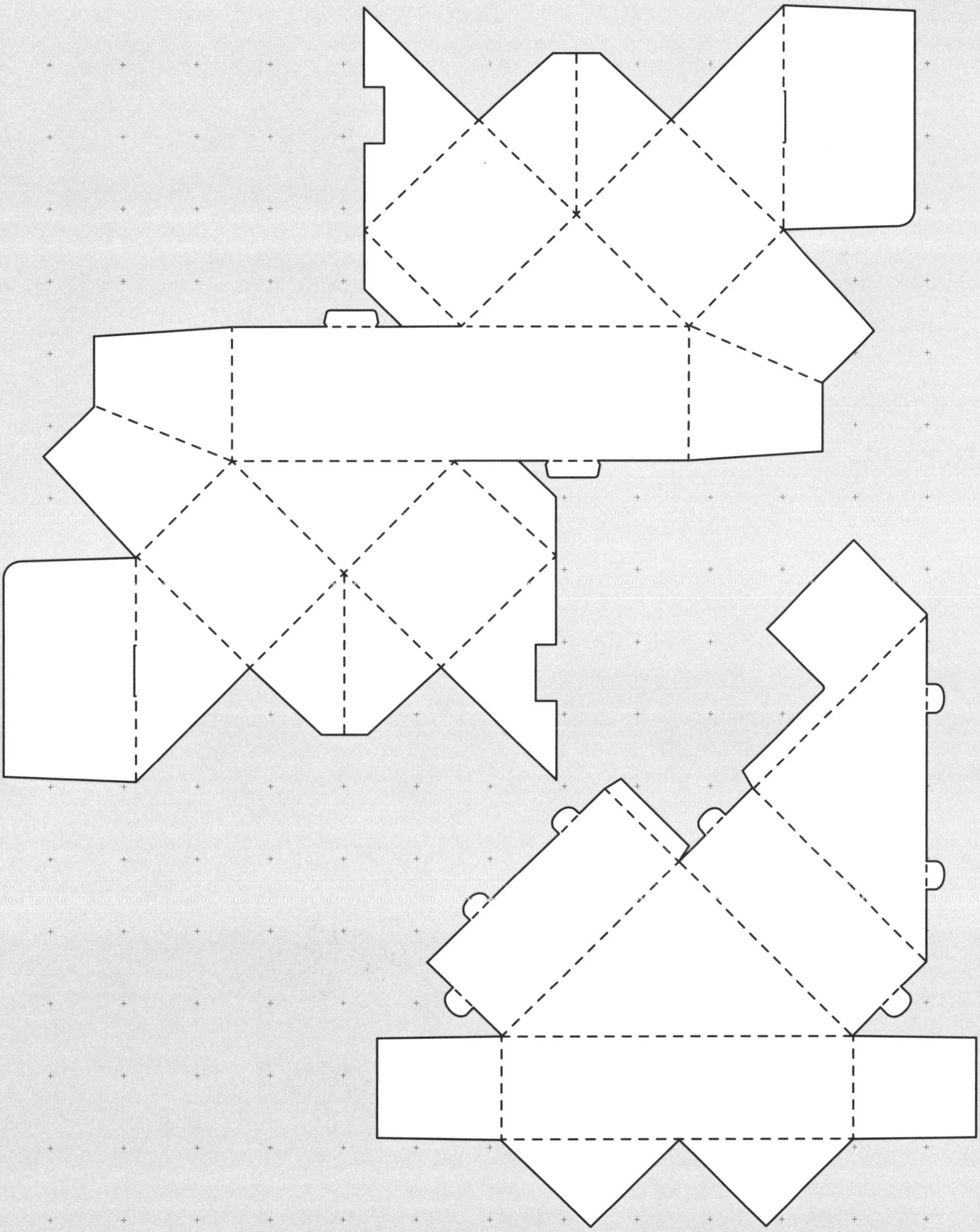

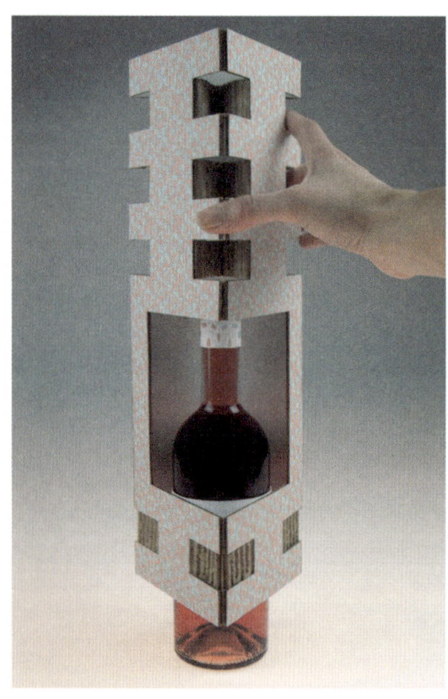

BURST

Design　Melissa Ginsiorsky

This promotional wine packaging utilizes a unique cardboard form, geometric patterning, and creative copywriting in order to spark the interest of the consumer.

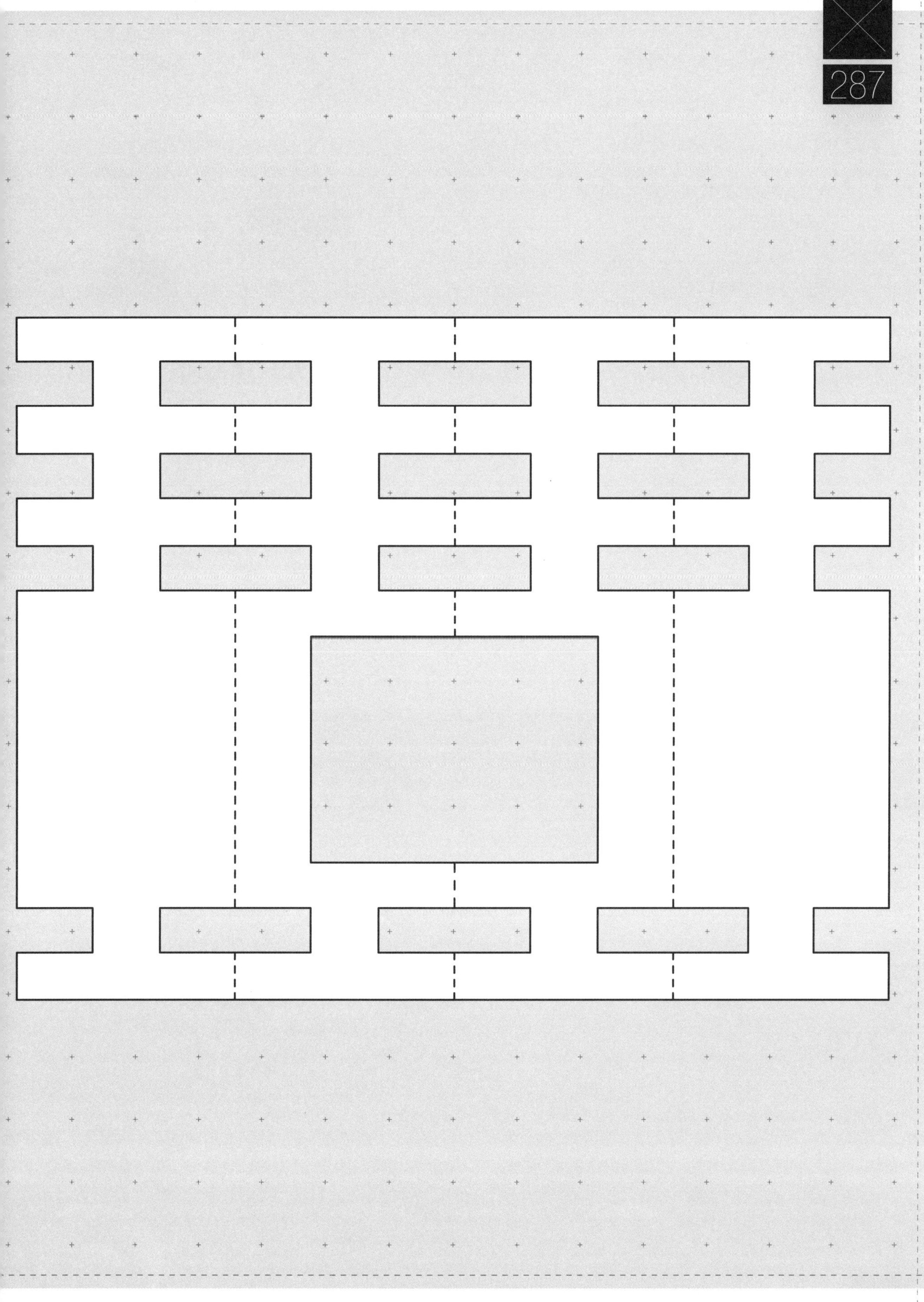

LEGA-LEGA T-SHIRT

Design **Igor Penovic**

The new collection of Lega-lega T-shirts called for a new packaging design. Mit design Studio designed a packaging that communicate the freshness and originality of the brand through form, not just graphics. The form associated with a milk carton is both descriptive and practical. It's not glued shut so you can use it for storing something else once the T-shirt has been removed.

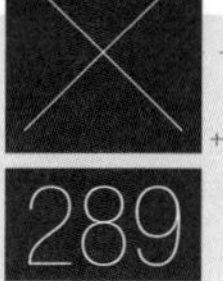

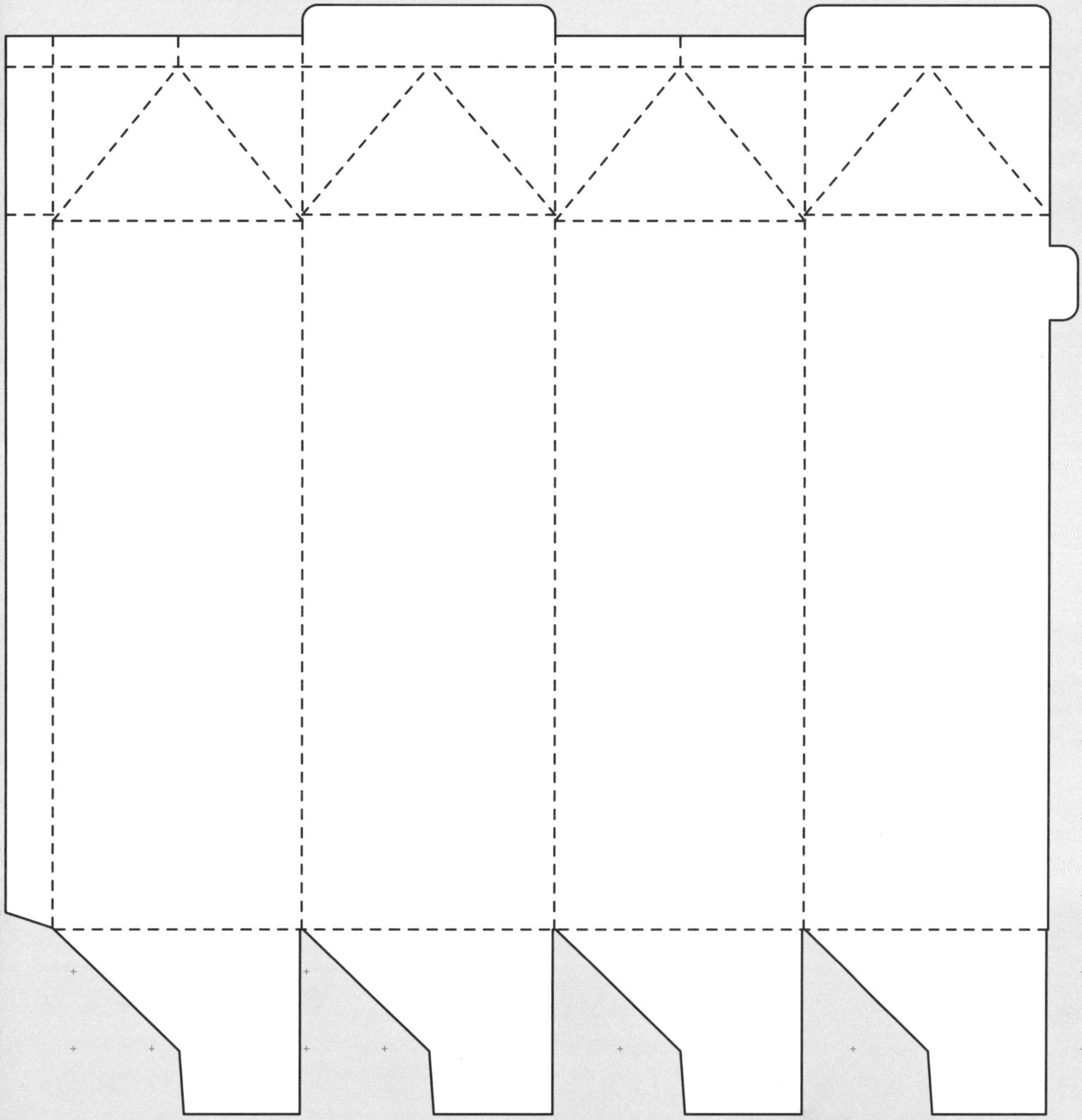

FREETALK ONLINE ECOPACK

Design **Marisol Escorza Hormazábal**

This project comprised the design of an inner package for online sales of the Freetalk TV camera by Samsung. There were many factors to be considered in the packaging design: keeping the product protected, optimizing materials and dimensions and using recycled materials. The Online Ecopack is made with recycled materials that are 100% recyclable: recycled cardboard that is eco-friendly, strong and light. The graphics are printed with soy ink that is environmentally friendly and available in bright colours. The inner package was developed considering the packing process as well as the displaying of product.

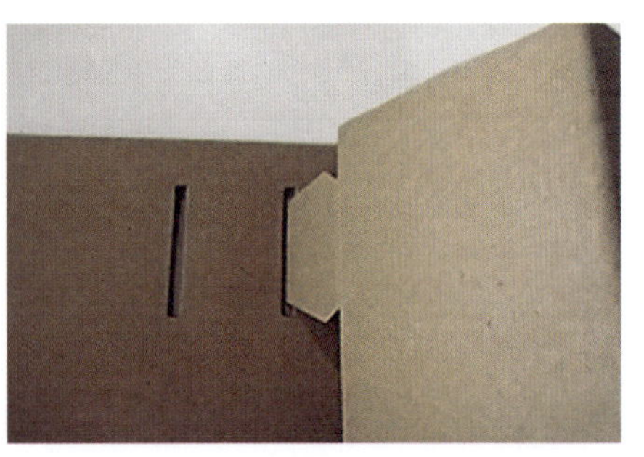

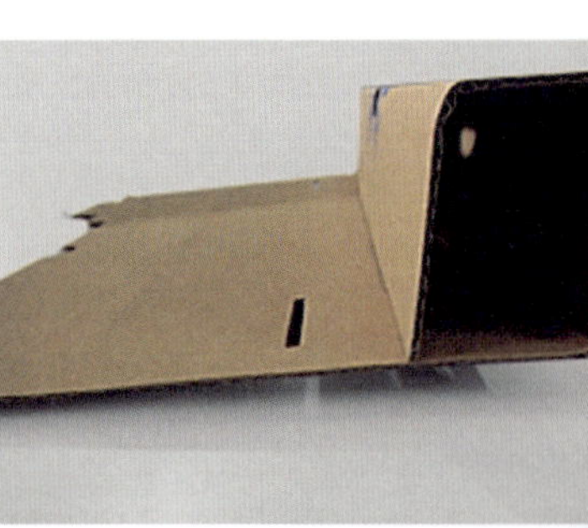

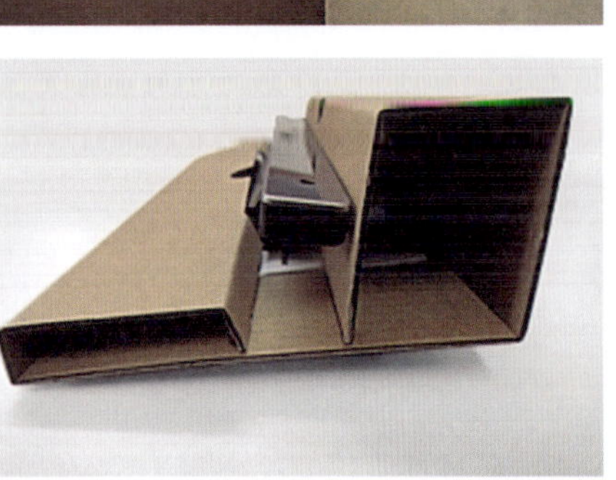

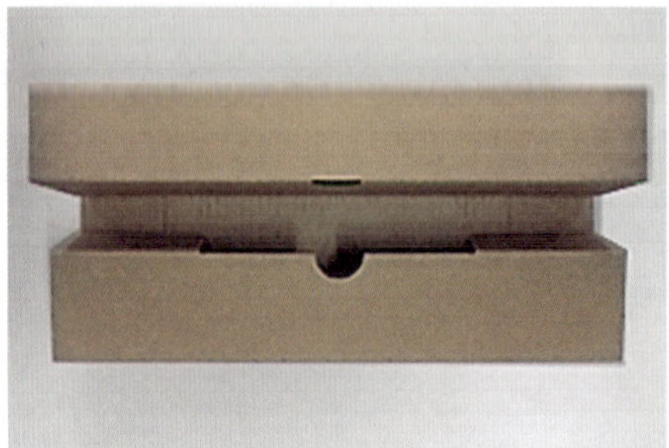

NO COCINO MAS TAKE-AWAY

Design **Marisol Escorza Hormazábal, Carolina Caycedo Villada**

"No Cocino Más" is a take-away offering homemade food. The concept can be translated as "I don't feel like cooking let's get a take-away". The project was around a croquette package design that would make transportation and consumption easier.

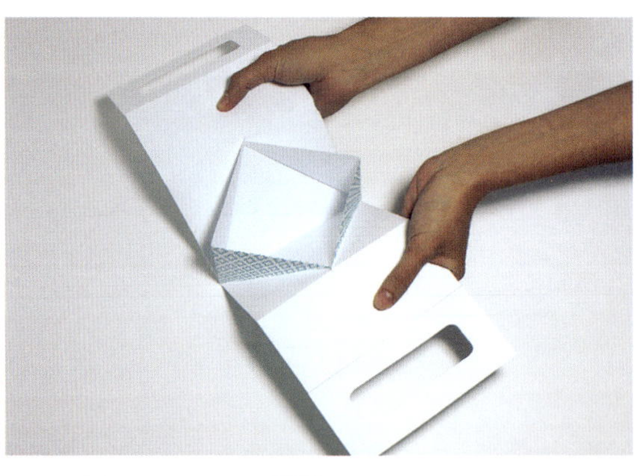

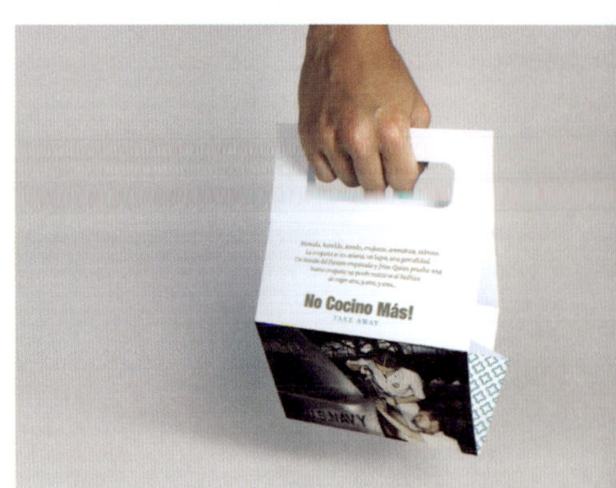

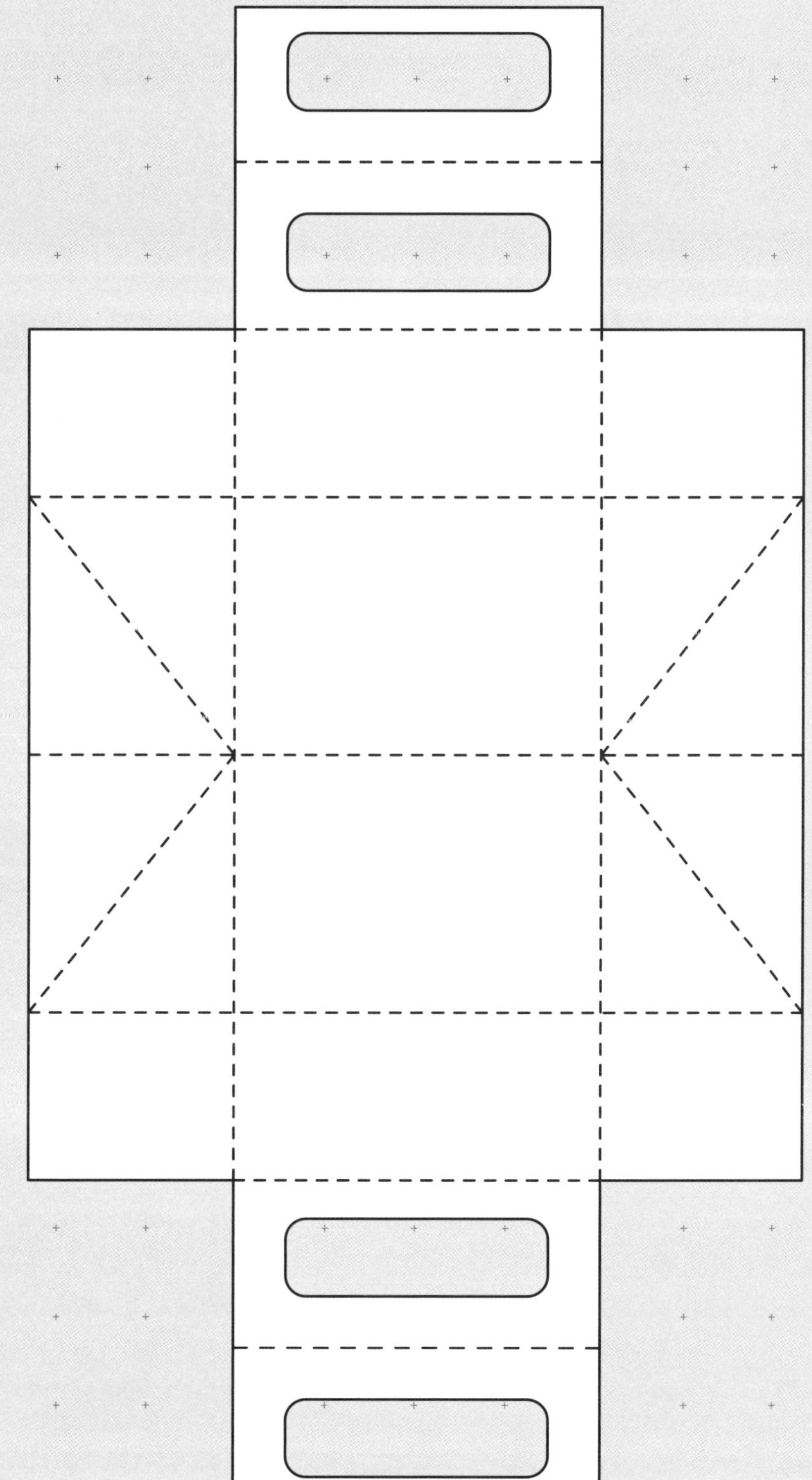

CHERRY BLOSSOM MODULAR BOXES

Design **Andreea Mocanu**

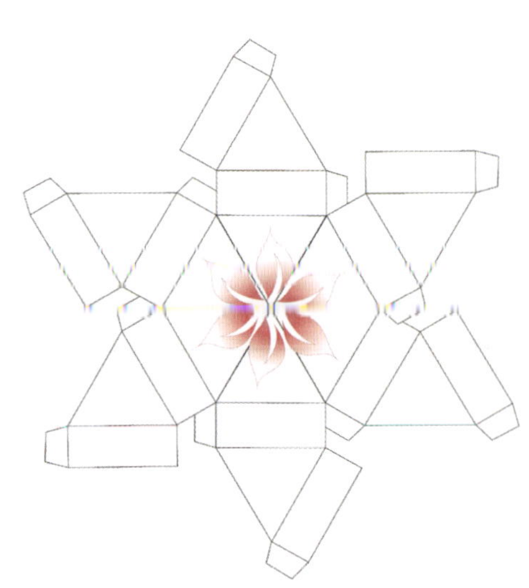

These delicate triangular Kleenex boxes were inspired by the traditional Japanese art of packaging. Once grouped, the small boxes create an elegant cherry blossom motif.

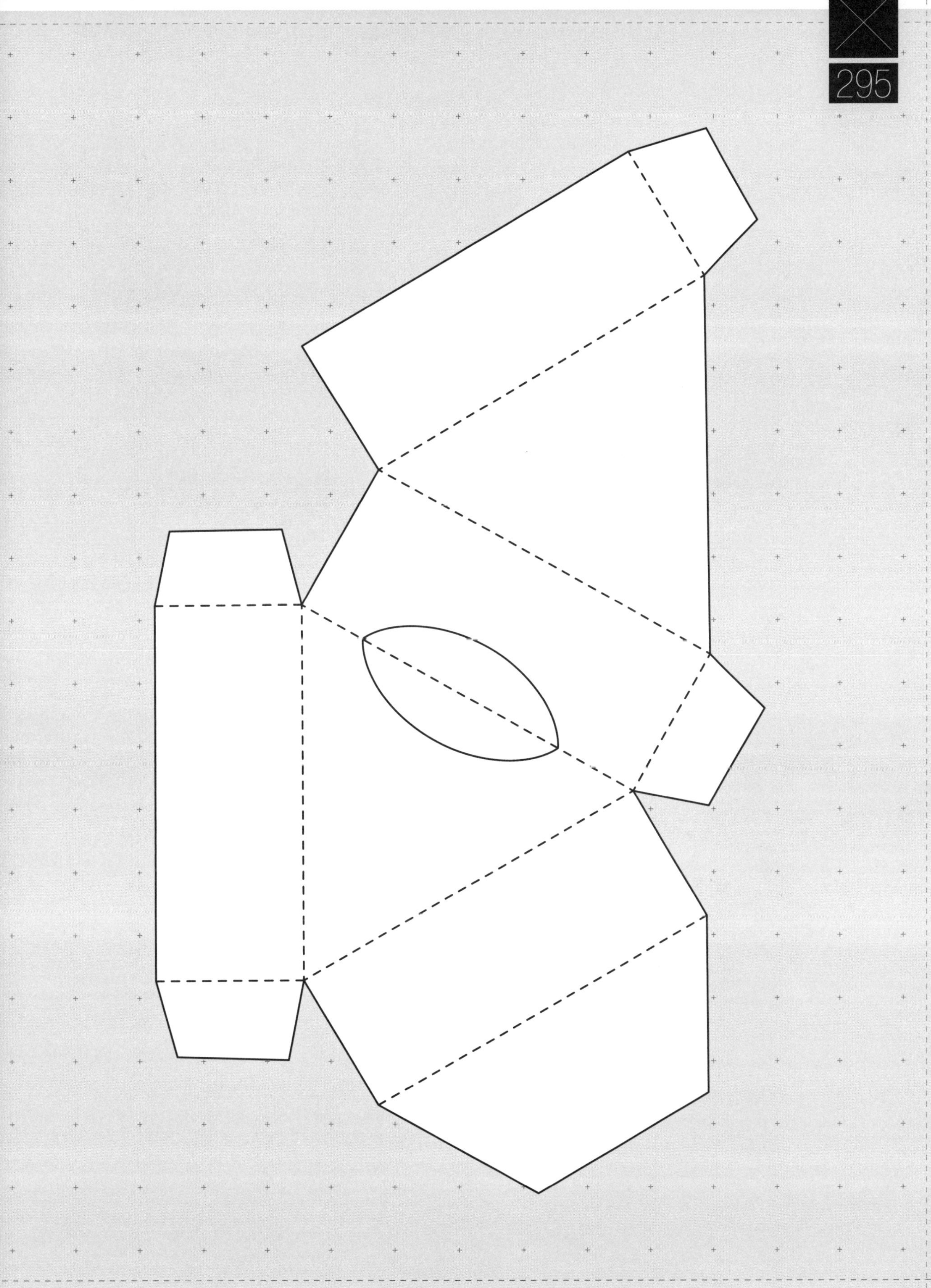

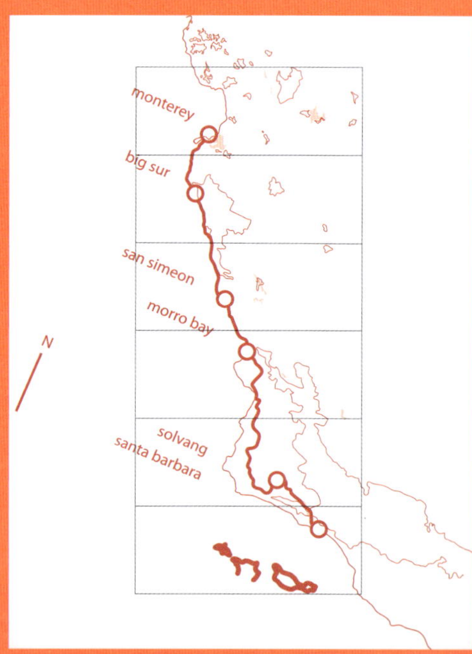

AAA TRIPKIT

Design **Olivia Paden**

TRIPKIT, which is targeted at elementary school-agedchildren, is playful, analog, modular, and social: it is a product aimed at getting the whole family involved in the learning process. The design took visual cues from the unfolding of a paper map, along with a rounded, child-friendly graphic presence. It was printed with offset lithography using spot PMS colours and soy based inks.

GLADE SCENTED OIL CANDLE

Design **Charissa Rais, Guia Camille Gali**

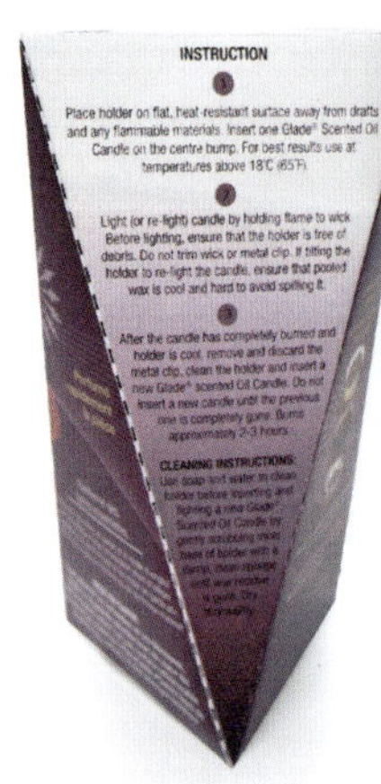

Eliminating the need for an additional plastic insert reduces company costs and supports sustainable initiatives. The redesigned triangular anti-prism includes a panel that folds inward as a candleholder, thus reducing the package to one substrate. It also reflects the oil candle's unique shape, generating a strong presence at retail.

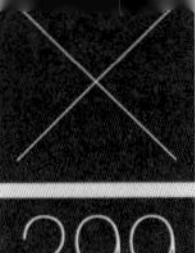

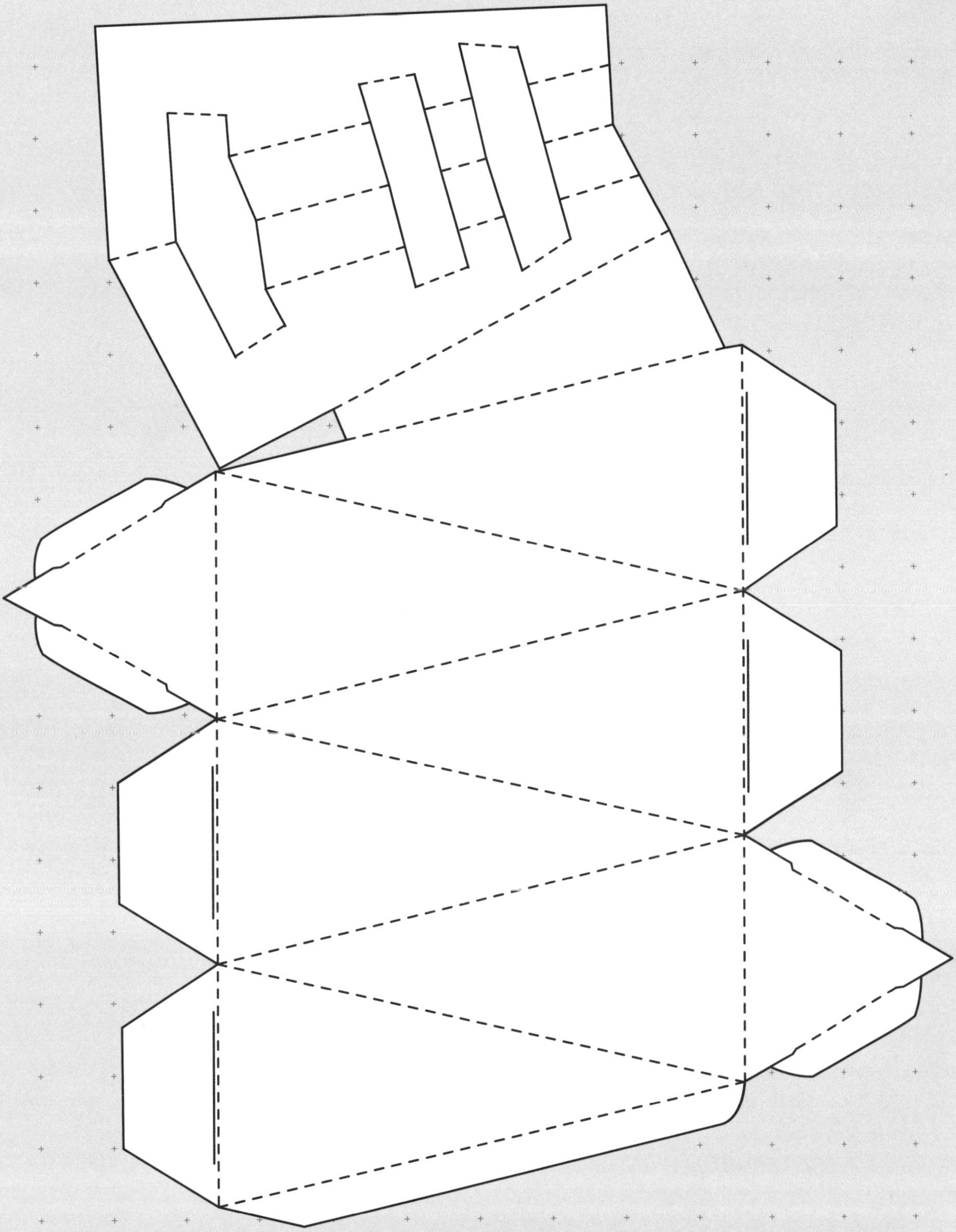

AWAKENING OF THE SENSES

Design **Anna Afinogenova, Irina Krucheva**

Coffee packaging for the Interpack Exhibition. The die-line was provided by the German packaging manufacturer, STI. The set includes 3 items: a coffee aroma pack, a dispenser for coffee-pods and a paper bag to carry 3 coffee cups.

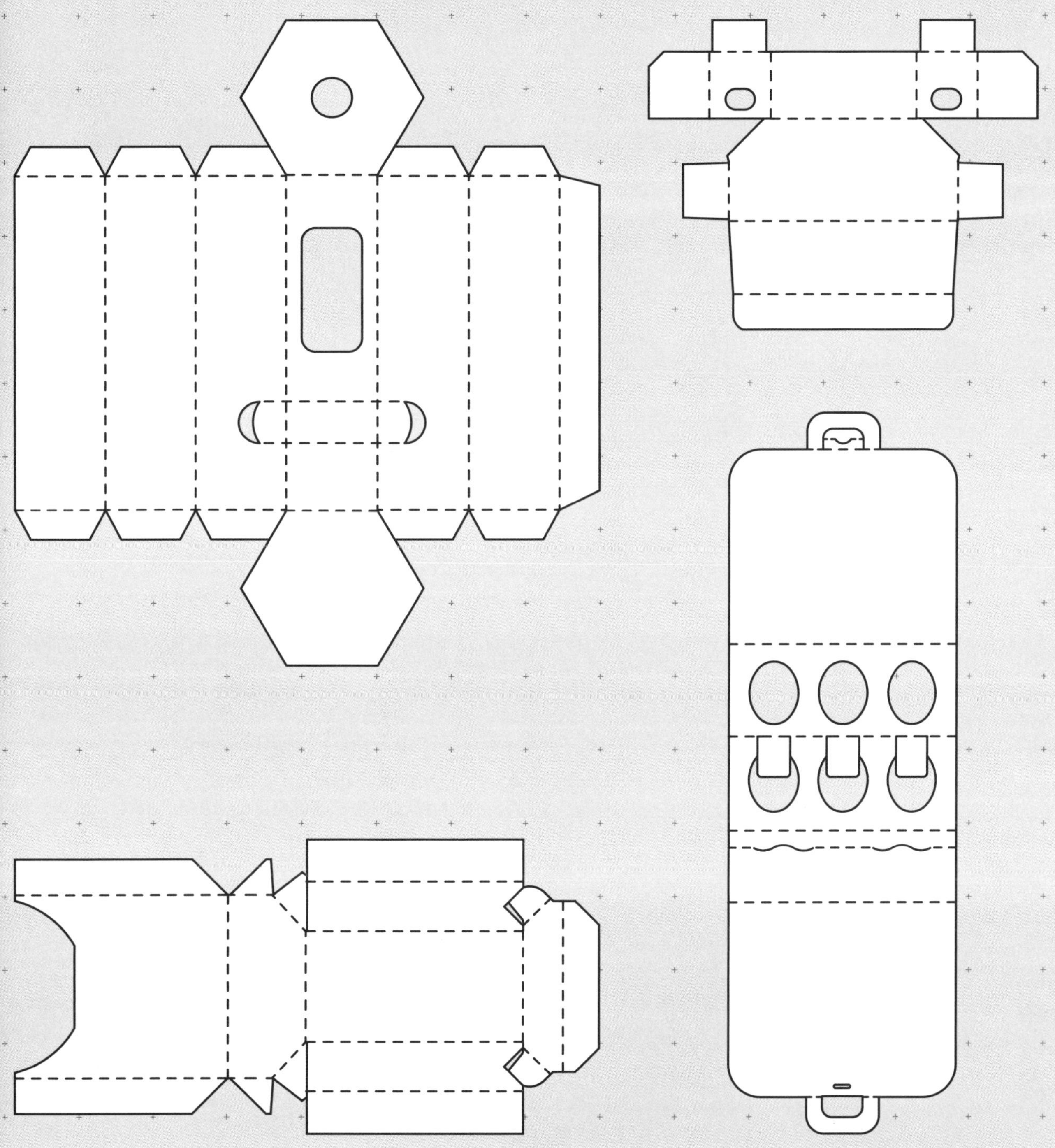

MERRIMINT CANDY CO. TRUFFLES

Design **Rachel Soeder**

Merrimint Candy Co. is a conceptual project which includes the branding, infographic recipe and packaging design. The design is clean and refreshing, just like the taste of their candies with the rejuvenating taste of mint.

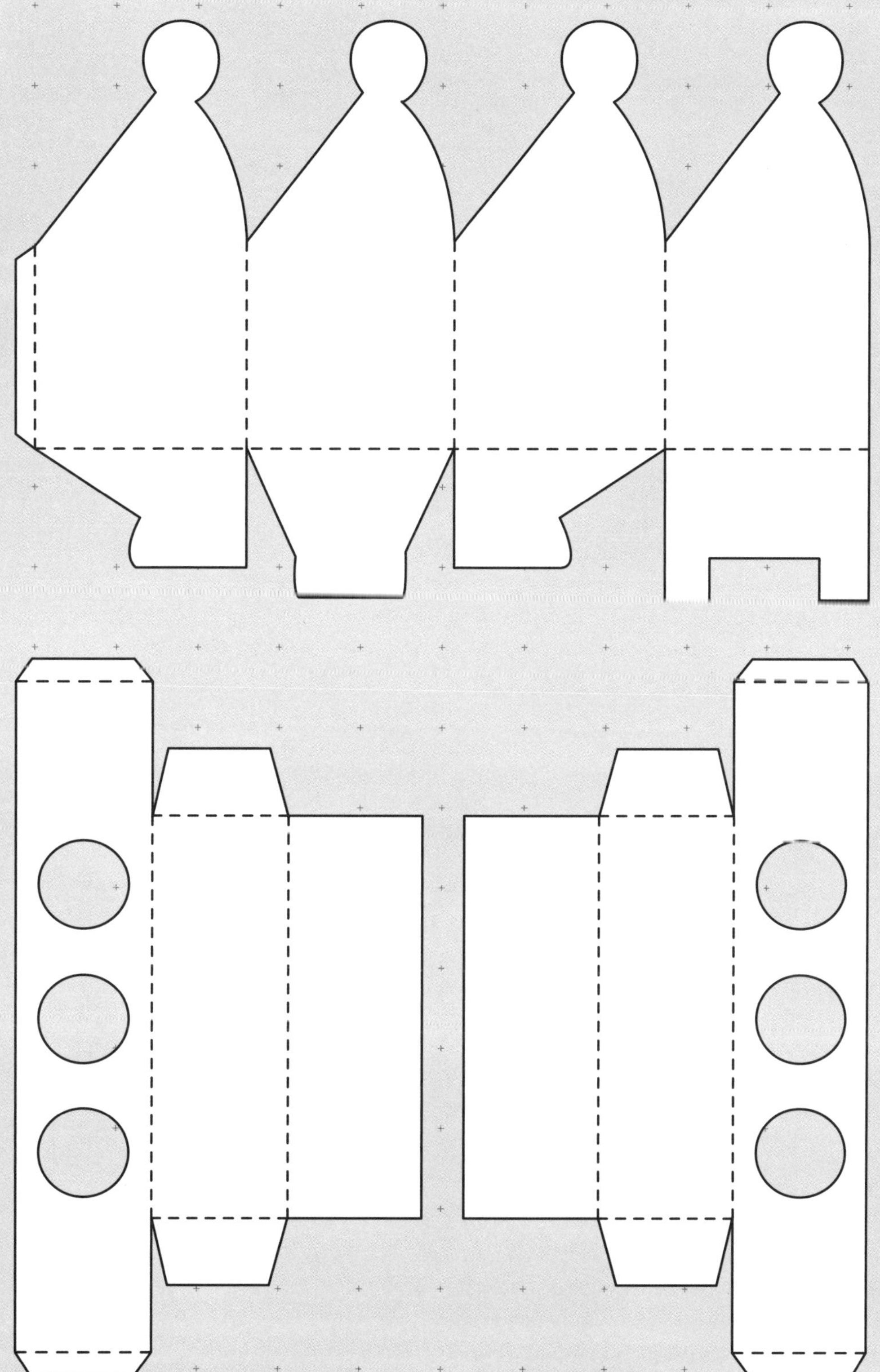

STEMIE BICYCLE STEM PAD

Design **Cameron Snelgar**

On most bikes the stems protrude towards the rider. They're a painful thing to hit. Stemie is designed to cover stem joints, cushioning them for potential impacts. The packaging needed to communicate what the product does. Hence, designers decided to mimic the basic configuration of a stem riser and stem on a bicycle by cutting a box diagonally to resemble a 90 degree corner (the basic shape of a bike stem). The packaging can be displayed standing, hanging or upright. As the product is durable and quite tactile, the designers mounted it on the outside of the box.

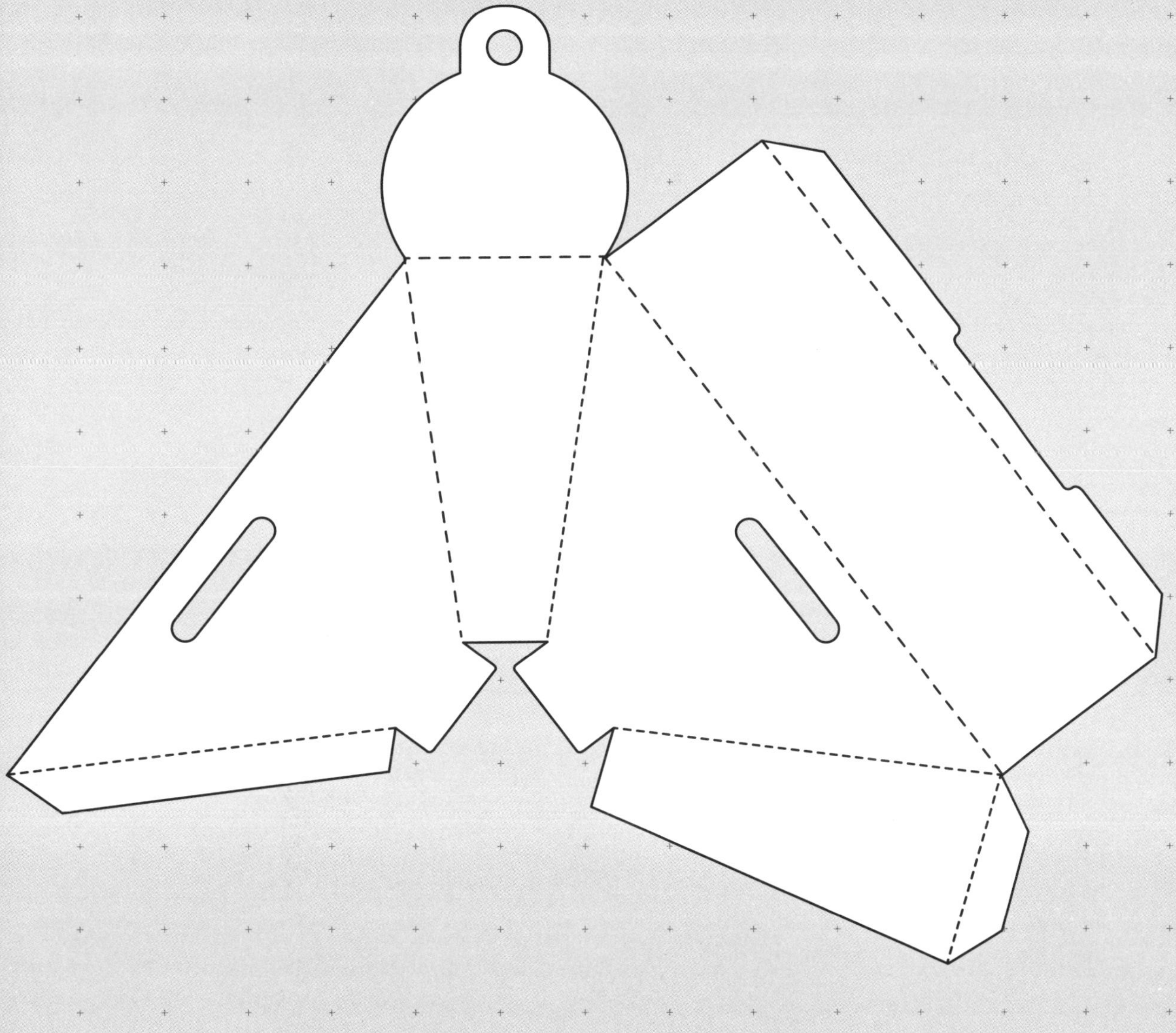

TASTE.

Design **Sam Stevens**

This is a new piece of food packaging encouraging "skill progression" in the kitchen environment for the aging non-dominant cook. Taste introduces a new step-by-step approach and encourages you to cook using convenience based ingredients. Once you have finished cooking, the carrier forms a planter in which you can grow small herbs that can be used later in your own cooking. This secondary use not only builds longevity into the packaging design, but also adds another layer of skill progression. A traditional and nostalgic visual language has been employed to make the user feel comfortable whilst cooking, encouraging them to form an emotional bond with the product.

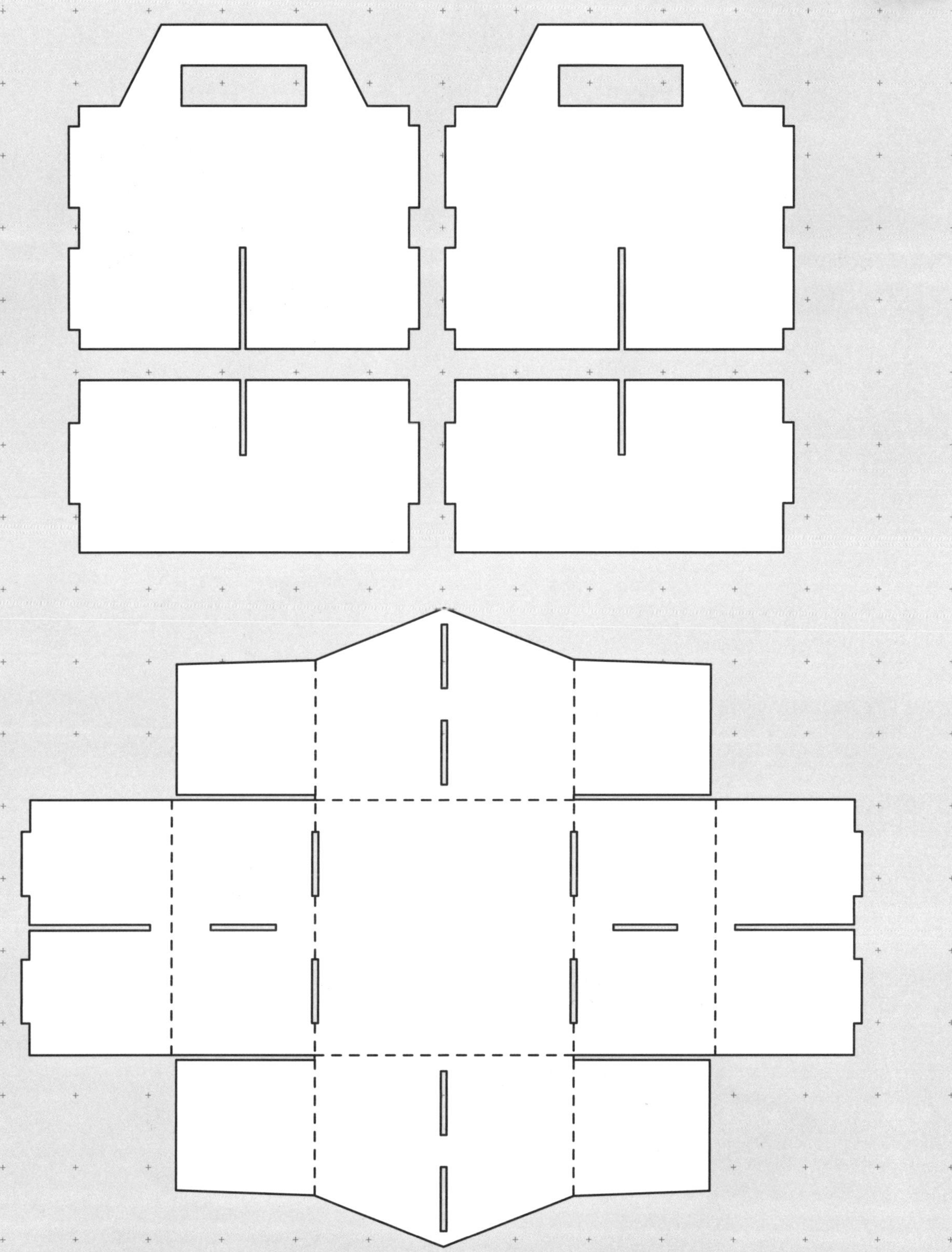

WAITROSE ITALIAN LUNCH RANGE

Design **Sarah Treanor**

The brief for this project was to design an organic lunch range for the retailer, Waitrose. The packaging is designed for convenient lunches on the go, with carrier handles and carefully sealed packets. All the packages are 100% recyclable. The graphic patterns featured throughout the packaging were inspired by the patterns of Italy, such as cobbled streets and ceramic tiles. The concepts behind the graphics of the packaging were embracing traditional Italian cuisine and the authenticity of the best and freshest ingredients.

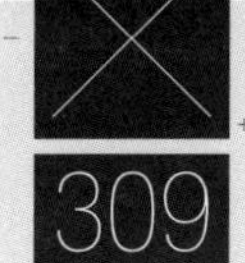

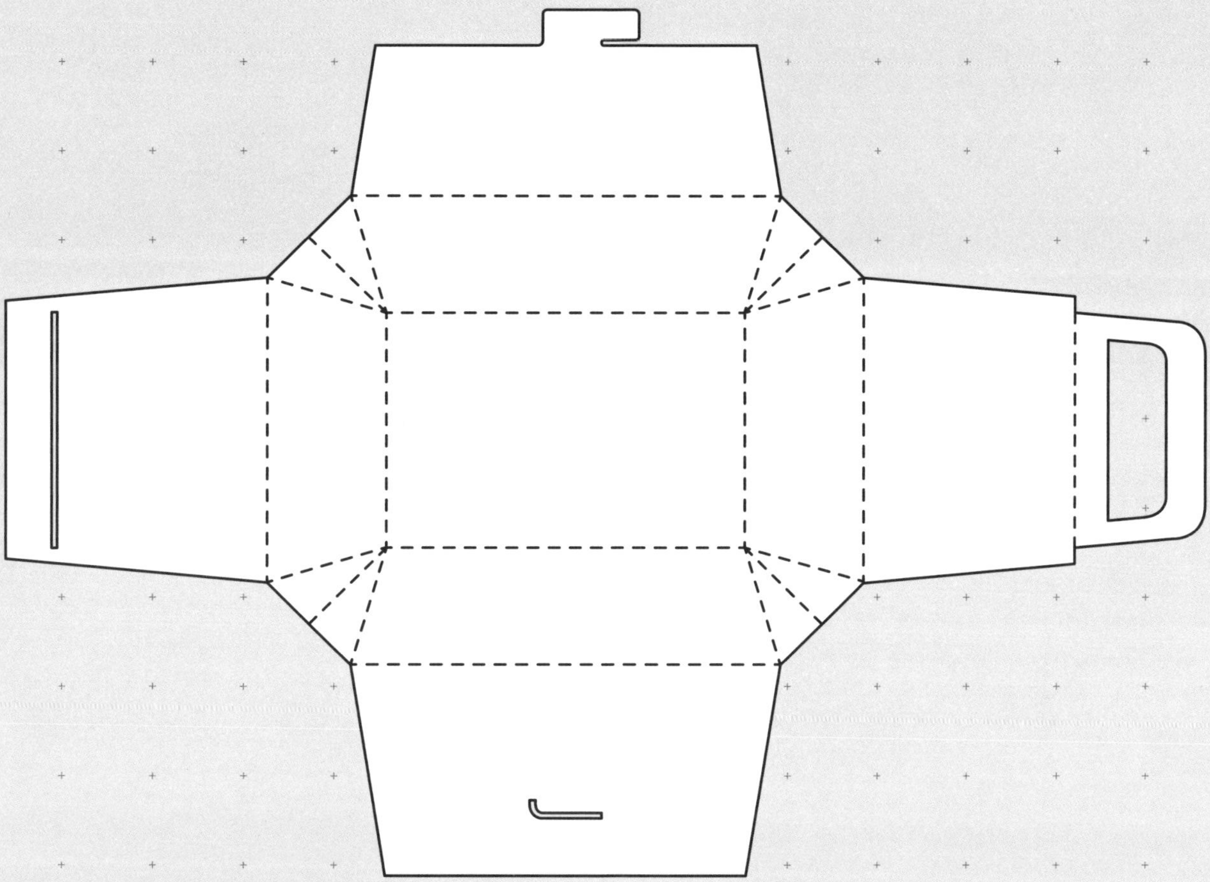

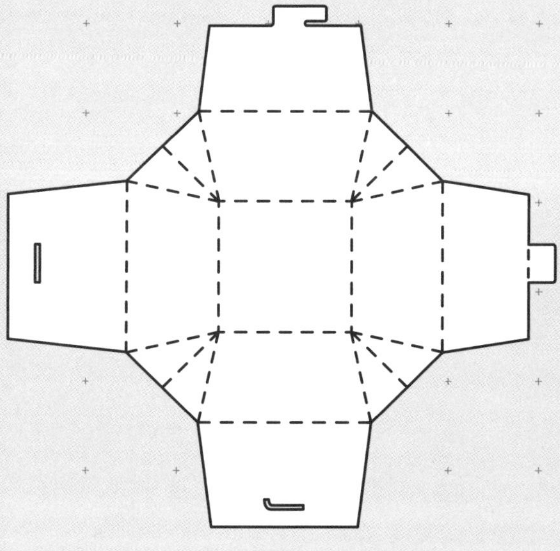

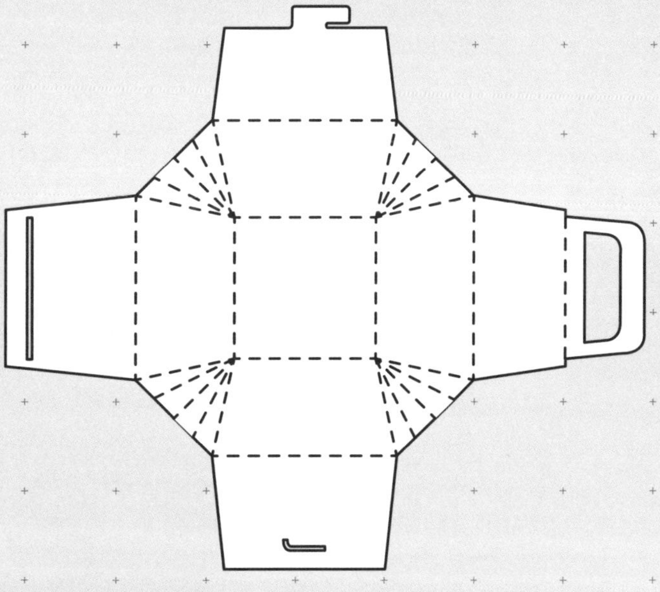

BOOSTERD BOX

Design Veljko Golubovic, Dusan Cezek

Booster energy drink from Serbia's Nectar comes in a new 4-pack design backed by an integrated campaign and featuring the character Boosterd. Boosterd Box is a simple transport cardboard Box, so production is easy and inexpensive. The simple design with limited colours is attractive and inexpensive.

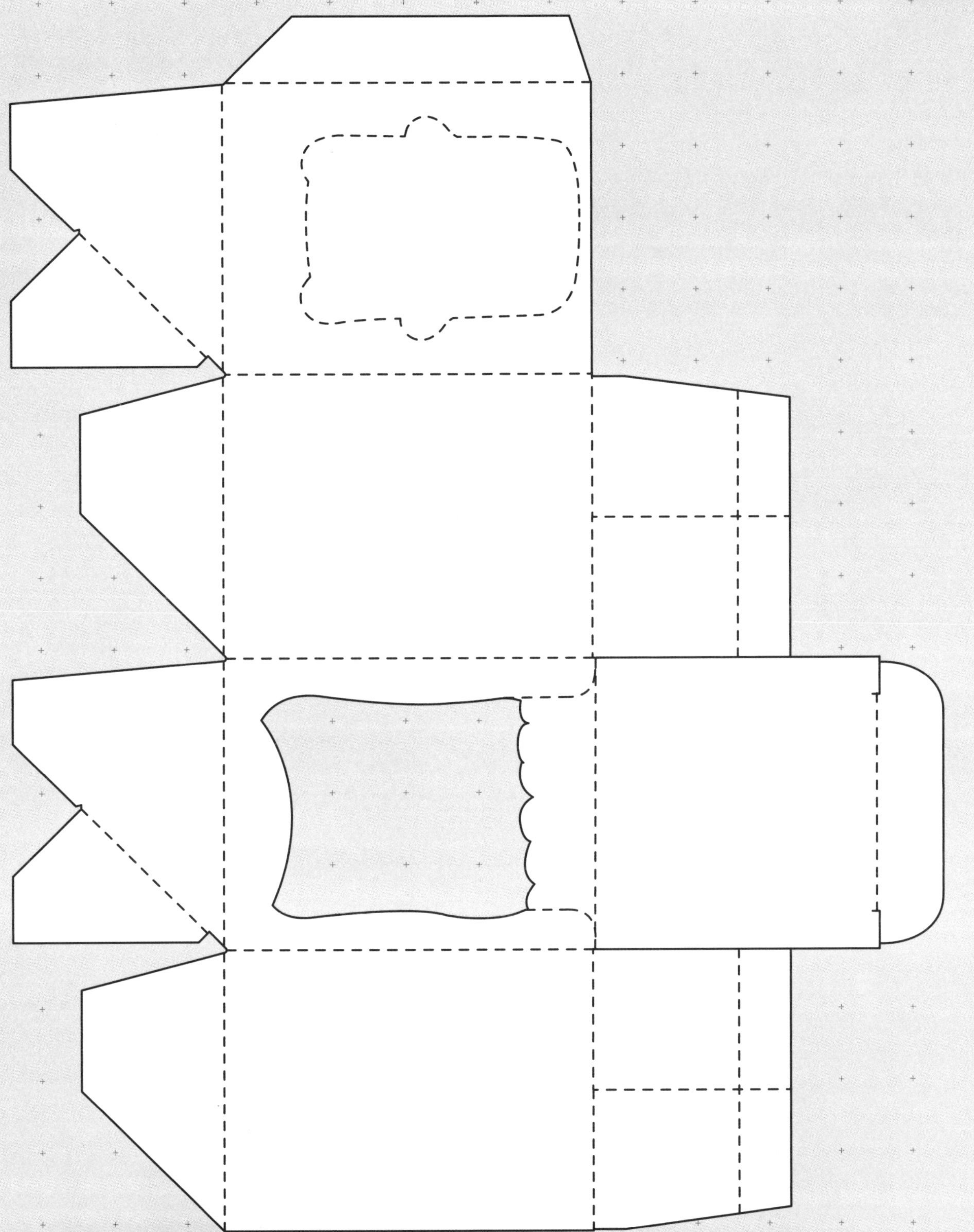

APPLE PACKAGING

Design **Katia Mikov**

This apple packaging was designed for displaying Israeli products at fruit and vegetable markets abroad. The concept for this design came from the shape of an eaten apple and the play between matter and void. The structure and size of the packet mimics the apple shape and each face is designed differently to allow dynamic display.

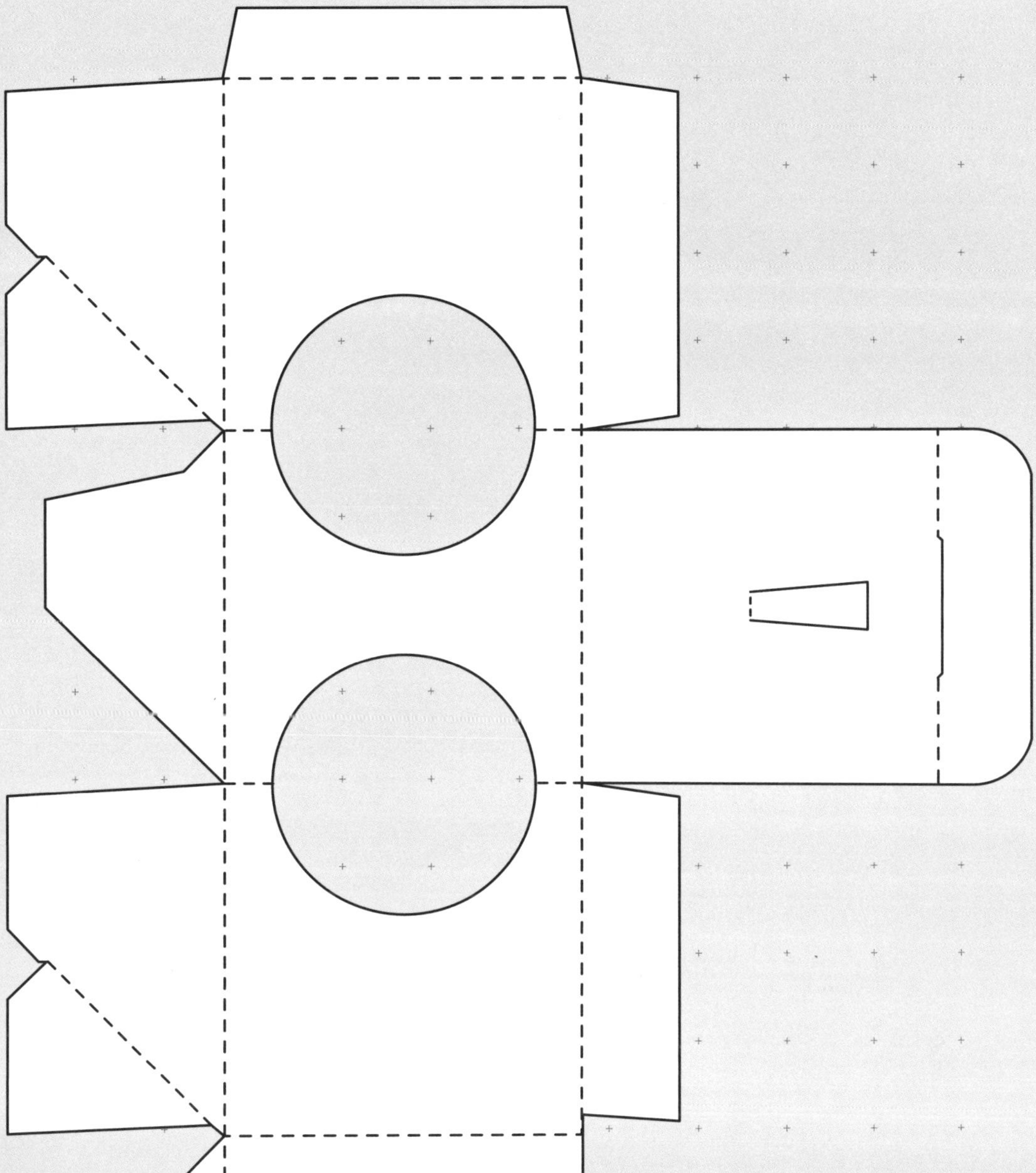

BITE ME CHOCOLATE

Design **Vasily Kassab**

The BITE ME brand was developed based on the concept of eating healthy portions of chocolate. The packaging reflects the percentage of cocoa in the product—the greater the percentage of cocoa to milk and other ingredients, the larger the chocolate bar and vice versa. The packaging uses colour to differentiate the different cocoa contents—70%, 80% and 90%—and the small gift chocolates. The packaging is 100% ink free, employing instead embossing, die cutting and laser engraving techniques to create a tactile play.

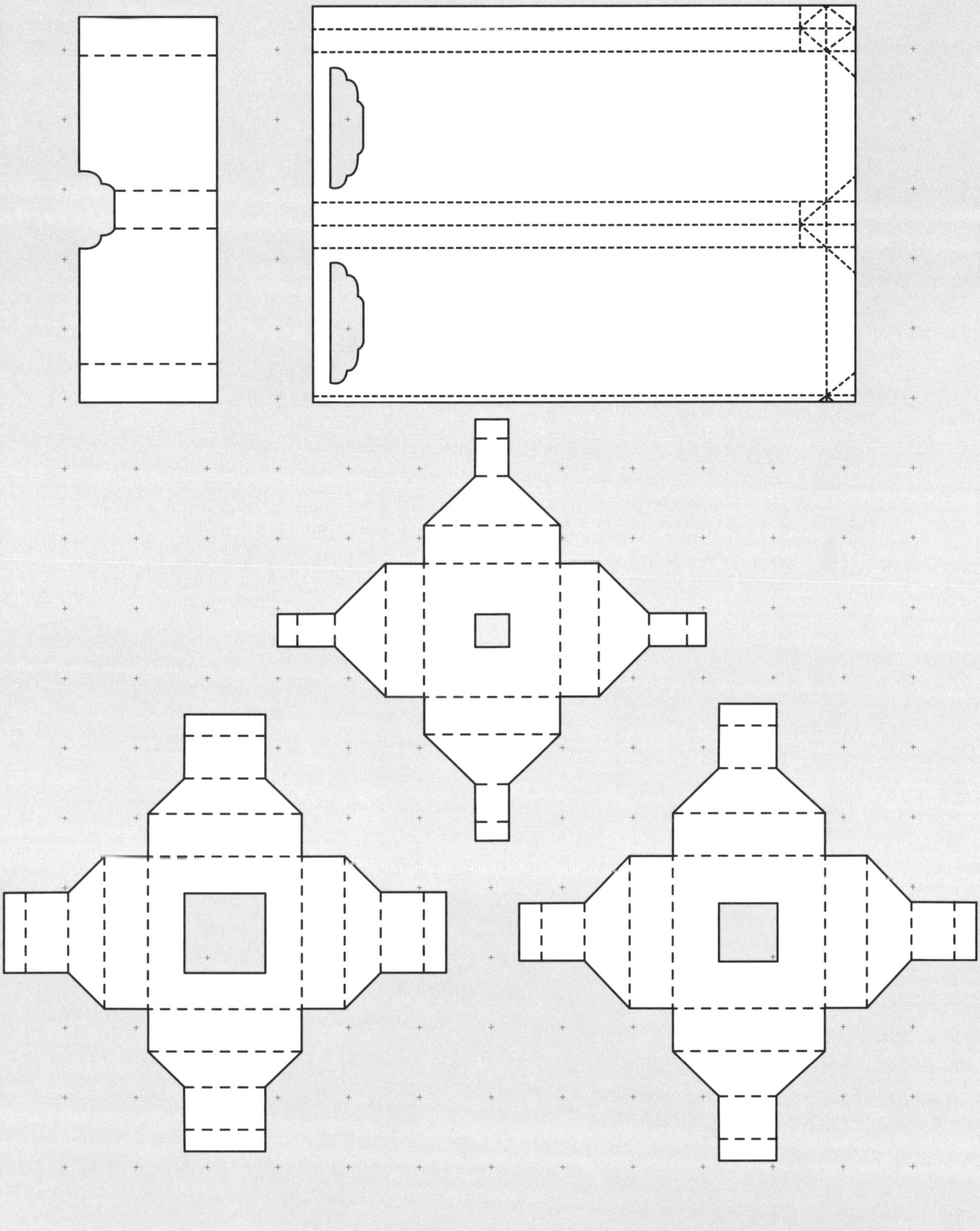

INDEX

ACKNOWLEDGEMENTS

We would like to thank all the designers and contributors who have been involved in the production of this book; their contributions have been indispensable to its creation. We would also like to express our gratitude to all the producers for their invaluable opinions and assistance throughout this project. And to the many others whose names are not credited but have made helpful suggestions, we thank you for your continuous support.

FUTURE COLLABORATIONS

If you wish to participate in Sendpoints' future projects and publications, please send your website or portfolio to editor02@sendpoints.cn.

Scan the QR Code to download all the templates.